"Of wings between the meadow and the moon"

Humbert Wolfe

Nine Chains to the Moon

R. Buckminster Fuller

Southern Illinois University Press

CARBONDALE AND EDWARDSVILLE

Feffer and Simons, Inc.

LONDON AND AMSTERDAM

To Alexandra and Allegra

"Your Strange Divinity Still Kept"

(FROM "To a Child" BY CHRISTOPHER MORLEY, 1922)

ARCT
URUS
BOOKS ®

COPYRIGHT © 1938,.1963, BY R. BUCKMINSTER FULLER.
Reprinted by special arrangement with
R. Buckminster Fuller.
ARCTURUS BOOKS EDITION MARCH 1963
SECOND PRINTING MAY 1966
THIRD PRINTING AUGUST 1967
This edition printed by offset lithography in the
United States of America
Library of Congress Catalog Card Number 63-10414

CONTENTS

Contents

AN OUTLINE

(For Pre-viewing and Re-viewing,—Book Begins at Page One)

Upon the premise that the sum-total of human desire to survive is dominant over the sum-total of the impulse to destroy, this book is designed. It does not seek to provide a formula to attainment. To do so would develop dogma and nullify the process of individual rationalization that is utterly essential for growth.

"Rationalization" is an act similar to walking through a half-frozen, marshy, unexplored country to mark out a trail that others may eventually follow. It involves not only the familiar one-two progression of shifting the weight and balance from one foot to the other, but an unknown quantity progression of selective testing to avoid treacherous ground before putting full weight upon the forward foot.

"Rationalization" is a time-word to replace "thinking," which is an ancient, mystically evolved word tentatively signifying an attempt to *force* the power of God into one's self. "Rationalization" connotes a constant, selective balancing of relative values, gained from experience, for the purpose of harmonious, inclusive *re*composition and subsequent extension.

It is central to my philosophy that everything in the universe is constantly in motion, atomically if not visibly, and that opposing forces throughout this kinetic picture are always in neat balance; furthermore, that everything invariably moves in the direction of least resistance.

The history of man's CREATIVE effort is the story of his struggle to control "direction" by the ELIMINATION of known RESISTANCES.

To the degree that the direction of least resistance is controlled by vacuumizing the advance and de-vacuumizing the wake, the course of society can be progressively better charted and eventually determinable with a high degree of certainty.

An Outline

This creative control, or streamlining of society, by the scientific-minded (the right-makes-mightist) is in direct contrast to attempts by scheming matter-over-mindists (the might-makes-rightist) to control society by *increasing*, instead of lessening, *resistance* to natural flows through such devices as laws, tariffs, prohibitions, armaments, and the cultivation of popular fear.

By controlling direction, it becomes possible, scientifically, to increase the probability that specific events will "happen."

Preparation of the material herein set forth dates from the very beginning of my experience. Up to a point in that experience, I lived by the common code of loyalty and good fellowship with all of its convincing and romantic "tradition." Then, through my own particular quota of *important* slaps in the face, it became apparent that in "tradition" lies fallacy, and that to be guided in conduct and thought by blind adherence to tenets of tradition is, as said in slang, bravely to "stick the neck out." I realized that experience is the vital factor, and that, since one can think and feel consciously only in terms of experience, one can be hurt only in terms of experience. When one is hurt, then somewhere in the linkage of his experience can be discovered the parting of the strands that led to the hurt. Therefore, it follows that strict adherence to rationalization, within the limits of self-experience, will provide corrections to performance obviating not only for one's self, but for others, the pitfalls that occasion self-hurt. By cultivating the ability to rationalize in the absolute, one acquires the power of so ordering experience that truths are clarified and susceptibility to self-hurt is diminished to the point of negligibility. Through rationalization anyone may evolve solutions for any situation that may arise, and by the attainment of this ability through experience one obtains his license to be of service to mankind.

Rationalization alone, however, is not sufficient. It is not an end in itself. It must be carried through to an objective state and materialize into a completely depersonalized instrument—a "pencil." (Who knows who made the first pencil? Certainly not Eberhard Faber or "Venus.") The "pencil" not only facilitates communication between men, by making thought specific and objective, but also enables men, coöperatively, to plan and realize the building of a house, oxygen tent, flatiron, or an x-ray cabinet, by virtue of the pencil's availability. The inventor, alive or dead, is extraneous and unimportant; it is the "pencil" that carries over. Abstract thought dies with the thinker, but the mechanism was building for a long time before the moment of recognized in-vention.

The substance of this book develops my conviction of these truths. In a final chapter, I have recorded certain thought-processes and results of abstract, intuitive thinking which would be obscure without reading the preceding sections. The reason for exposing myself to possible suspicion of "mysticism" is to show how important it is to transcribe the faint thought messages coming into our personal cosmos at the time of occurrence— sketchy and puzzling though they may be—because time, if well served, will turn them into monkey-wrenches and gas-torches.

The title, *Nine Chains to the Moon,* was chosen to encourage and stimulate the broadest attitude toward thought. Simultaneously, it emphasizes the littleness of our universe from the mind viewpoint. A statistical cartoon would show that if, in imagination, all of the people of the world were to stand upon one another's shoulders, they would make nine complete chains between the earth and the moon. If it is not so far to the moon, then it is not so far to the limits,—whatever, whenever or wherever they may be.

Limits are what we have feared. So much has been done to make us conscious of our infinite physical smallness, that the time has come to dare to include the complete universe in our rationalizing. It is no longer practical to gaze at the surfaces of "named" phenomena, within the range of vision in the smoking car of the 5.15, with no deeper analysis of their portent than is derivable from a superficial exchange of complexed opinion-notions with fellow commuters.

"After all," Jeans said, "it is man who asked the question." The question is survival, and the answer, which is unit, lies in

An Outline

the progressive sum-totaling of man's evolving knowledge. Individual survival is identifiable with the whole as—extension or extinction. There is no good old country doctor on Mars to revive those, who, through mental inertia, are streamlining into extinction.

I

Meet Mr. Murphy

Let us imagine an early fall evening in New York City. Rain and a high wind terminating the heat of an exceptionally warm Indian-summer day have brought on prematurely the blackness of night.

Into the gloomy downpour thousands of doors, architecturally designed for giants, have jettisoned half a million workers homeward bound. Subway entrances are jammed by inflowing masses in quest of swift transportation from local darkness to lighter suburbs. The stairways to the sheltered heights of the "elevated," linking, with steel rails, the Battery, Bronx, Astoria and Flushing with midtown Manhattan, are vibrant under the stomp of a multitude of mounting feet.

The pressure of traffic in the streets is terrific. Vast streams of upbound mechanical vehicles, interrupted by intersecting multiple crosstown flows, forge ahead, inch by inch—lines of cars, so closely compacted as to be in effect solid trains, miles in length, broken only by traffic lights and policemen's whistles, hundreds of thousands of dollars worth in every block.

The din of horns, the roar of the elevated trains, the spattering wind and rain, together with the brilliance of a myriad of automobile lights, neon signs and shop window glares (doubled in intensity by a galaxy of reflections on wet pavements and glistening automobile bodies) constitute a picture exquisitely confusing to the ear and eye. Heightened by the imaginative glamour of a swift, duskless nightfall, the scene would terrorize a simple savage and would have been utterly incomprehensible to ancestors who, only a few generations ago, laid the city's foundation unaware of portending electricity, steam and steel.

What a projection of "hell," this bedlam, this stirring inferno, for ancient man, yet so unquestionably accepted and so little understood by current city dwellers!

Nowhere visible a vestige of any other living organism than "man"; no trees, no horses, or other form of ancestrally familiar life, with the possible exception of a wet, scurrying cat. Not even a patch of raw mother earth. A completely by-man-fashioned environment, from the hard pavements serving dually as surface traffic lanes and as roofs for a honeycombed maze of arterial passages interweaving the depths below, to the roofs of brick, stone, steel and glass buildings. New York City! A one-piece dormitory, work, and play shop three hundred square miles in the horizontal plane and thirty to one thousand feet in thickness.

Suddenly the red brilliantines flash STOP. The traffic snake is cut. The foremost cars of a bridge-bound stream, their drivers' vision blurred by the wet confusion, stop abruptly within inches of a north and south bound traffic stream, surging forward again on the change to the green GO signal.

Mr. Murphy, worker, pushed his way through the traffic, paused an instant to buy a newspaper, and threaded his way sidewise between bumpers of halted cars to the opposite side of the street. Ducking into a plain man's open bar he called for a glass of beer, and one more, and then continued his few blocks' trek to an east-side subway.

Primed by the beer, Murphy elbowed his way good-naturedly through the crowd. At each corner he was caught in a mash of people, whose umbrellas held too high dripped onto his new $1.00 fall hat, or clutched too low caught at the sleeves of his suit. But he did not mind. Then, just before descending into a dank subway, he was jostled unpleasantly by several persons. He jerked backward quickly to escape being soiled by two cars, splashing crazily through a pool of water.

"You damned bastards!" Murphy exploded, using his neighbors as the arbitrary representatives of all automobile drivers. "Do you think you OWN the street?"

Poor Murphy!

He could not be blamed for relieving his feelings. The other pedestrians sympathized with him and the drivers of the cars, windows closed, did not hear him. If they had, they would merely have countered with blasphemy more eloquent than his own.

The transition in Murphy's mood from the pleasurable glow of his home-bound beer to a general condemnation of the world and all its mechanistic manifestations was not occasioned by the weather for, physically, the rain was a relief and Murphy was glad of it. His dangerous nerve snapping was the result of a multitude of over-riding factors not immediately obvious, amongst which may be listed the geographical disposition of shelters and economical factors, universe-wide in scope, controlling that disposition.

The solution of Murphy's inconvenience does not lie in meaningless words. It must be found in a control of circumstances far removed from questions of automobile driving ability. Traffic is not a willful demonstration of street usurpation. It is a composite of functioning transport media designed primarily for the transport of individuals from shelter to shelter.

Murphy dimly suspected that sufficient scientific thought exploration had not been done in the matter of shelter design and its attendant arterial hookups. He could not refrain from contrasting the utter inefficiency of the cockroach-breeding house, wherein his wife spent hours plodding, dustpan in hand, between cellar and attic, thirty feet vertically apart, and to reach which home took from his brief life-span two hours daily, and the magical efficiency of the radio by which, with merely a twist of a knob, he could instantly jump in actuality of the senses from wherever he might be in the flesh to a ringside seat in Chicago or to a ducal vantage in a Westminster coronation three thousand miles away.

If living were properly planned, Murphy vaguely and perplexedly conjectured, during the first few minutes of his subway ride, the status of man might be raised to a point where, instead of continuing longer as an impersonal, ineffectual, shuttling population-unit, he might become, at least, majority master of himself.

Reflection gave way to activity. Murphy had to fight to maintain a few inches on which to stand. On this particular night, due to the crowd and the warm steam of vaporizing human bodies packed into their transportation shelter like blood corpuscles in a noisily vibrating test tube, the struggle was particularly attention-consuming and very depressing.

When Murphy changed trains at City Hall station for the second half of his long journey home, he felt that he was no longer an individual. He was just anyone. Perhaps, even, no one.

Edging his way to a less congested portion of the car, he propped himself against a post, took his damp newspaper from his pocket, and tried to read. With two hundred blocks to ride, he speculated that he might arrive at the obituary section before it was time to alight.

Stomach Rhythms Not All Rhumbas

Contrast the confusing, soul-disturbing morning and evening treks of Murphy in a humpty-dumpty world, wasting precious lifetime because of the patent inadequacy of the architectural mentors of that world, with the following coolly deliberated incident in the scientific world.

On the basis of experimental proof that noise is one of the two stimuli which will bring out an overt fear reaction in babies, a number of students in a prominent American university coöperated with Dr. Donald A. Laird in the following experiment:

To determine the fear-reaction effect of noise stimuli upon gastric motility, a thick rubber balloon attached to a tube was swallowed by the students, after which it was inflated to a uniform pressure of 10 cm. of water. Contractions of the balloon in the stomach forced the contained air into a second balloon in a sealed flask, from which a tube led to a water column on which a piston attached to a counterpoised writing point was floated. Contractions of the stomach increased the air pressure in the balloon in the flask, altered it, and caused the water column to rise, thus lifting the writing point so that it might record the movement on a revolving marked drum.

Having swallowed the balloons, the students reclined quietly for twenty minutes and then were subjected to various degrees of sound.

It is well known that there exists a unique directional rhythm of the digestive tract, that is, unique as differentiated from the rhythm of respiration or of heart pulsation. In the course of this experiment, all of the students showed an immediate frequency change in gastric peristalsis when subjected to sounds even of low intensity. When the sounds were intense, for instance the sound of a pneumatic drill, the contractions were not only altered in character but were 50% slower than before the sounds were made.

People with headaches, digestive cramps, gastric overloading, *et cetera*, quite evidently cannot be either as receptive or effective in their internal or external world relationships as persons not so disturbed. Certain degrees and types of sound have, then, due to their retarding influence on the digestive process, a wide effect on the social relationships of man. Sound, therefore, is a primary social factor. Man progresses in spite of such frictional conditions, not because of them. Flowing in the direction of least resistance, the progression in the myriad of cases of over-sounding must be "down hill."

Noise is only one of many important human behavior conditioning mechanical factors known to exist, with the knowledge of that existence recorded and measured, which are as yet popularly unconsidered (beyond the area of the unscientifically phrased "very annoying"). These many known factors are but fractionally included in the obviously most important field of application,—controlled environment or shelter design romantically known as "architecture."

Murphy's physician had cautioned him against paving the way for a peptic ulcer by bolting his meals in restaurants that were noisy, overlighted, and fearfully upsetting. So Murphy, by buying a home in a suburb, substituted the noise of the subway for that of the restaurant. No rest for the weary!

Mrs. Murphy did not understand why Murph' suffered so much from noise. Julia was one of the lucky few who do not experience inconvenience from it. In fact, she rather liked the roaring rush into town by subway. She had found the rural silence very oppressive when she was first transplanted to Jamaica Gardens from noisy Herald Square. Murph's doctor told him, confidentially, that Julia was a ptupophilic, meaning fond of noise, and cautioned him that if she did not turn off the radio for at least a few minutes every day she would become ptupomanic.

"Toofy," Murph' called her, especially when he had to shout to be heard above "WOR."

When he tried to tell Julia penitently that he had lost his temper coming home, he found it impossible to compete with station announcers. Instead of turning off the radio Julia tried to shut up Murph'. But "the old man" had something on his mind.

"Even if those auto drivers had heard me," he persisted, "it would not have done any good." It is unlikely that either was a bastard, and whether 'God' could damn them is only mystically debatable,—was the gist of Murph's thought.

Julia merely smiled and suggested, "Timmy, why not eat your supper?"

"Damn supper!"

"I thought you were wishing you could control your temper?"

"How can I, with that thing incessantly grinding out meaningless words and croonings?" Murph' rose abruptly and went upstairs to the bathroom, where he dissolved some baking soda in water and drank it preparatory to retiring. He recalled disconsolately Edison's prediction that noise will grow ever greater and that the city man of future generations may be deaf.

The vast majority of the causes of abnormal human behavior, which modern psychologists and psychoanalysts, like yesterday's astrologists and alchemists attribute to "intangibles" in a *patois* used with mesmerizing and profitable skill, can be traced quite unromantically to mechanical maladjustments in the environment of the individual: bad plumbing of house or self-mechanism, bad sound or light control, unsatisfactory mechanics of sex equation. "Personality" talk to excuse uncontrolled behavior is vain, self-important nonsense. Unhappily the failure to recognize real causes and to utilize known remedies is preventing man's understanding of his fellow being and of the myriad of phenomena to which all men are continually exposed. Few, if any, crimes of misunderstanding, single or multiple, would exist if a small degree of latent understanding were allowed by environment to come "alive" and penetrate man's consciousness.

There are scientifically discernible potentials at hand for the solution of such crises as Mabel's fight with her boy friend, Mussolini and Hitler vs. Great Britain, or Julia's staying up while Murph' falls asleep.

If factors already ascertained were to be applied to living, it would become possible not only to prevent misunderstandings that separate members of the spoilt older generation, but to avoid—and this is far more important—breaking up the unity of the potentially unspoilt new generation of millions of children by preventing their being over-noised and under-nourished or starved in full view of bounteous surpluses which, instead of satisfying every need, have been and are being burned or plowed under. For what? "Recovery!" "Recovery" of inefficient ways of living and special privileges for individuals and groups.

There is a wider chasm between the understanding of the scientist and that which uncomprehending, groping Murphy would confess to be his understanding than there is distance between the earth and the farthest known star. Murphy's conscious "world" is perforce limited to his utterly unscientific shelter environment. He is forced to exist in shelters which mechanically prevent his adjustment to understanding, and it is fallacious to blame Murphy directly for his inability to see, hear, and understand.

Politicians and the privileged have realized that to keep Murphy environment-ignorant would be to control him. So long as Murphy could be so controlled, even though he might be "educated," their apple-cart concessions would not be overturned by science.

But science has no regard for "concessions," and ideas are pervasive. Murphy is on the verge of awakening to the fact that there is an "out," namely, the service of scientifically designed and industrially mass-produced shelters within the means of all. Such a service, however, cannot be had merely for the political asking. Neither political convention nor legislation ever brought a potato into being.

3

'S a House, Darling

W E HEAR much of designing from the "inside out" among those who constitute what remains of the architectural profession—that sometimes jolly, sometimes sanctimonious, occasionally chi-chi, and often pathetic organization of shelter tailors.

The pioneers who originally evolved the architectural "inside out" concept, now dogma to the profession, were led to it naturally through their own thought processes and deeds. They spared themselves no labor to go to the inside, and, once inside, were quick to realize the supreme efficacy of projecting from a central viewpoint.

After successful demonstrations by them of the inside out principle, their original trail blazing became the general formularized property of all whom the architectural guild included. Although ultimately the pioneers were acclaimed, according to the worth of their gift to various beneficiaries in terms of vanity or dollars, acknowledgment of the original quality of their creation was withheld until after the physical death of the designers. The lesser fry had need to prevent the foresighted few from cutting in on their "traditional" racket. So recognition was refused these deeply penetrating, hence visionary designers, while living, lest the schemes proposed by them be too popularly demanded before the untrained and unfitted "architects" had had time to re-educate themselves for the exploitation of the newer principles of design.

Obviously, to design a shelter from the inside out infers an outside with a key passage inward. However, if the architect does not think spontaneously in the terms of this primary philosophy, then to espouse it is merely to mumble a few words with the lack of objective understanding that characterizes most chanting

9

of academic *bon mots*. Worse! To act without this basic knowledge is to be a non-progressive, dogmatic dolt, a shuffler and dealer of the same old pack of 52 cards for *chance* winnings.

The thought process discovered by the pioneers, whose design eventually proved to be successful, was understood by them only upon *subsequent* reflection. When recognized, it proved to have been "from the inside out" thought. It was not professed in advance. Truly creative work cannot be professed. Only the academic may be touted. As applied to houses the pioneers' creative thought processes might have begun somewhat as follows:

"HOUSE—a phenomenon to which I am, upon first consideration, an outsider. What is a house? A block of brick, stone, wood, or steel, or a composite thereof? An object with various patterns of square openings called WIND-O-S applied to its surface? The alphabet-book illustration under "H" with an undeniable superficial child romance appeal? A major sensorial object of awakening life?"

"What IS that, mother?" asked little Tim, as Julia took him on a tour of inspection of the tiny garden of the new Murphy habitation.

"A rose, darling."

Biology, chemistry and physics can explain some of the characteristics of the mechanics and processes that constitute the composite, constantly changing living-machine, "rose," but neither Julia nor the scientist could presume to tell little Tim what a rose *is*.

"And what is that, mother?"

"A clothes line, darling." (Likely as not an aerial.)

"And this?"

"A hammock."

"What do you do in a hammock?"

"Rest or read."

"What is 'read,' mother?"

"Oh . . . what you do with a book."

"What's a book?"

'S a House, Darling

"Words, words!"—Symbols, in sound, to carry a diminutive degree of understanding into the limbo of goo-goo, broad designators of general categories of discussion.

If baby Tim were never again to be curious regarding the object designated by the sound "book" beyond tearing its nice-to-tear pages and dropping them from the hammock to the grass in primary, untutored, flutter-flutter-plop experiments in tensile strength, gravity, sound and air-resistance effects, he would never know that the audible word-symbol BOOK designates but an indirect means or an instrument to a certain vital objective, namely, the communication of ideas by its author to other minds in a referential form more permanent than if they were to be just orally expressed; a method of broadcast beyond the power of human speech. It would be almost preposterous (though provocative of deep consideration) for Mrs. Murphy to suggest to her child that Newton's "Optics" and "Bringing Up Father" are one and the same article, just BOOK.

From the hammock, Tim could see a mass that seemed to reach into the clouds.

"What is THAT, mother?"

" 's a house, darling. Where we live. All ours . . . at least it will be when Daddy finishes paying for it. . . ." A sigh concluded the answer, a sigh born of the faint suspicion that the "good buy" for which Julia and Murphy must skimp for years was not wholly modern.

Julia had not heard of "designed from the inside out," but she was beginning intuitively to sense that theirs was not that kind of house. The house tailors guild, through an enthusiastic house haberdasher, Mr. Jones, had high pressured the Murphys with the usual sample of the "own your own home" propaganda into contracting to pay for a house in Jamaica Gardens. Murph' had been "easy" to sell because he still believed that *any* house is better than no house, and was ready to admit that this one certainly was a distinct improvement over the suite of rooms in a second rate hotel in the vicinity of 34th Street and Sixth Avenue, the noisiest section of the city, that Murphy had been calling "home."

It would seem that the principle of "inside out" is not first to be applied to the tangible house. But the assumption that eventually it must be so applied is seized upon only too often by the sterile, philosophy-dodging dogmatist type of architect who, cleverly and smartly, jumps to conclusions and puts the end at the beginning. This pays him in "good times," when his neglect of principle is applauded and accepted by well-funded, stuffed shirts and skirts. Loathing to think, they are glad to patronize the professional academicians who, without recourse to boring thought problems, appropriate originality and submit pretty pictures of what is traditionally recognizable as good "front." It goes over both the patron's and his house tailor's head that the result is as shallow and inconsequential as any temporary motion picture set.

It is the usual course of such a professional house tailor to segregate and list the physical units that comprise the whole of the house. Next, having superficially rearranged these physical end-objects, he dogmatically and arbitrarily starts his drafting scheme at the geometric space center (bathroom or chimney) of the habit-postulated-surface of the volume of space ultimately to be controlled (by which the geometrical center was determined) with the sublime conviction that he is designing from the inside out. This procedure is *ipso facto* proof that the architect formulated his plan not only from an envisioned outside inward, further circumvented by a specific "lot line," but from a non-rationalized, habit-dictated "shell." His defense that the outside is "undetailed" at the start of the blue printing and takes form after the inside detailing has been accomplished is just sleight-of-hand trickery, fooling no one but the homeseeking, homesick Murphys.

The vast majority of Mrs. Murphys the world over are so horse-power tired from performing the function of a machine in their utterly inefficient homes as to have little horse-power left with which to concentrate mentally and, therefrom, to articulate rationally in reaction to the natural growth phenomena of the lives in their custody.

The conversationally frugal life of families is relatively unimportant if the only persons affected are adults who have reached a stage where a grunt of assent or dissent is eloquent for harmony. There is no objection to communication with few words, or extravagantly with many *per se*, except that man's intellect and words have evolved hand in hand at so high a price that speech, when resorted to without intellectual reflection, is wasteful, abortive, and paralyzing to the senses in the same way that an incessant radio "deafens" unwilling hearers.

The reaction of tired parents to the natural growth phenomena of the new lives in their custody is one of defense. It becomes expedient progressively to paralyze such inquisitive growth phenomena in order to effect a simplification of the parents', particularly of the mother's, survival problems. Convenient methods of doing this are:

1. Arbitrary negations imposed by physical strength: "lickings," or "lockings in" or "out."

2. The exploitation of the physical strength of new life: "You don't mind running down to the furnace?" or "To the corner for a pint, dear?"

3. The instillation of fear through the repetition of traditionally honored falsehoods, or by the invention of a lie, a moral, a code, or statute to suit the circumstance. (Fear is not innate. The fear reaction of the new born infant is brought about only by extraordinary noise or falling. If falling does not occur early, fear does not develop as dominant. It is fostered, however, by the exquisite stupidity and cruelty of singing, "Rockabye, baby—baby will fall, cradle and all," and for the child who has experienced falling this is by way of being an ultimate lullaby into lunacy.)

The consequences of carelessly, expeditiously and selfishly answering the young with would-be simplifications is the gradual unfitting of that new life for a naturally developed, comprehensive outlook upon, and non-complexed reaction to, the increasing demands of maturer processes. Thoughtless "simplifications" are paradoxically not only complexity builders but complexity amplifiers. Though born with vast energy and volition for including, analyzing, refining and composing, most people, by the time they reach maturity, have been so progressively exploited or depleted that often there remains nothing of their rich original volition. In its stead, there is listless surrender to quasi-security, inertia, laziness, and, occasionally, vindictiveness. All these results are directly attributable to the mechanical inefficiencies of environment control, which is 95% a shelter problem.

Some point out that the constant din of "housing" is like an over-dose of porridge—that it is a political device employed *ad nauseam*. If it seems that we are stressing "house" overmuch as constituting the "root of all evil" on the one hand, and on the other the area of panacaeic solution of social problems, we answer that very word "economics" springs etymologically from "ecology" meaning:—*the body of knowledge developed out of* the HOUSE. We stress not *housing* but the essentiality of *comprehensive research and design*.

Both Murphy's outbursts and Julia's fatigue are manifestations of man's growing pains in this most paradoxical period of his history, the paradox being the fact that although science is playing a dominant, behind-the-scenes role in all of the activities of man, mediaeval politics, morals, mysticism and usury are still visibly rampant on the stage. The situation in the human drama may be likened to a scene in the theatre. Backstage, smooth-running mechanisms and scientific light controls are collaborating with the actors who visibly are enacting a mediaeval drama. The great majority of the audience is intuitively aware of the silent backstage machinery, but, in the grip of imagination, prefers to accept the effects as magic.

Through all ages the crowd has relied upon magic. This has been particularly true in the determination of society's commonweal course. The populace has believed in the wizardry of political leaders, who, in turn, have been bossed by big-shot crowd exploiters behind the scenes. This mass reliance upon the politician is oddly contradictory to the average individual's almost fanatic desire for independence.

This desire for independence was temporarily satisfied in man's pathetically funny demonstration in the 20's of "me running it" for the first time.

Men surged out "of a Sunday" in their OWN automobiles to crawl at three miles an hour along limited arteries linking city to suburbia, happy because they were at last "the king himself resplendently *on tour*"—happy despite the slow pace, gas fumes, dust and horn-honkings. "*Get out of my way. . . . Who do you think you are?*" It was the great family joy-ride era, the beginning of the popular era of "ME-running-IT" as the result of the social incursion of machinery. The hazards inherent in the Murphys' habitual dependency on political leaders, or "somebody else" to make "first" demonstrations is now amplified in the industrial period, wherein ultimate coöperative activity must wait upon a host of correlated inventions, developments, organizations, and vast credit before popularly effective mechanisms can neutralize deleterious causes.

Until the majority of human beings individually perceive that the responsibility for the acquisition of a state of well being for others, and consequently for themselves, is first dependent on *individual rationalization* and, second, upon uncompromising *coöperative action*, in strict adherence to the former, they will not enter into that estate to which they are the specific beneficiaries by the will of every objectively-scientific human being in all history, some known, others (more often) unknown.

Involved in the foregoing is an attitude that makes the Earthian's problems as easy of scientific solution as are the problem plays of clowns for the children in a circus audience: for instance, the laugh-provoking plight of the clown menaced by a fire attempting to escape through a locked gate that has no fence on either side of it. If the *process of solution* of Earthian problems SEEMS arduous and enormous, it is so only from a size viewpoint, and man as MIND is as large as the universe.

The de-roboting of humanity by the transfer of labor-slavery from life processes to inanimate instruments represents human emancipation. Earliest recorded history reveals armies of human automatons toiling from birth until death, at the instigation of a human-plied whiplash, as elevators of stones for pyramids, patronized by death. That was the real humano-mechanistic era. Man must throw off his slave complex before he can fly.

It is not surprising that those who have grown up in luxury or even in simple well-being under the tradition of "good old superiorities," when experiencing the forces of cosmic equilibrium and the expansion of the universe (which willy-nilly must RAISE standards as upon a flood tide to a par with the mechanisms of their own earlier "exclusive" advantage) interpret the prognostications of leveling as implying an ebb-tide of their own estate, for their reactions are relative to ego.

To the most insensate soul, it must be evident that economic and industrial changes greater than any in history are at hand. The duration of the period of transition will be variable in direct proportion to the intelligence and support given to advancing industry. Prolongation of the transition will work great harm upon the welfare and mental equilibrium of the slothful-minded.

Shelter is by far the greatest single item among man's requirements in point of physical volume, weight, cost and longevity of tenure. Yet it is among the last to receive his *scientific* attention. The time-lag of the building industry—an industry in name but not yet in fact—is almost beyond belief. For instance, there was a span of 42 years between the invention of Portland cement and the time of application of re-enforced concrete to buildings. This is to be compared with a lag of less than seven years between the attainment of a new speed record in aeronautics and the routine repetition of this speed by commercial air lines. The home building field is still dominated by the activities of the interests in natural materials, who seek either stupidly or helplessly to force a preponderance of their material upon the market. The cement people seek to impose the all-cement house, the lumber people the all-wood house, and likewise with steel or gypsum, or asphalt or asbestos. There is no organized, centralized industry, having a testing, designing, sorting, assembling, distributing and advertising authority, with a definite responsibility to the public, by its advertised ideals of service, guarantee and resale value. All this happens because, through selfish conceit—unable to see ourselves as others see us, we have been laboring under the delusion in regard to housing, despite its having been disproven in all the lesser necessities, that material stylistic deformities and superfluous weight signify the character and individualism of its occupants. What would we think of a man walking the city streets in silks and lace neck ruffle today, or of a lady in a hoop skirt? Would we concede individualistic beauty to a girl with her nose in the middle of her back?

This "conscious withdrawal of efficiency," demonstrated in a willful adherence to mediaeval theories of design (the gaudy Beaux-Arts esthetics) and a profit-minded system of production, has made architecture the most backward of the technologies. Even the newest and most publicized skyscrapers are decades obsolete in terms of what science and industry have rendered attainable. "MODERN" architecture is but a return to basic-classic.

It has always been obvious that the dynamic life going on within a structure is more important than the static structure, but, like so much else that is apparent, this has been generally disregarded, with the result that shelter has been looked upon as an end in itself, and not as a means of life.

Once the problem of shelter service has been solved, the mechanical inefficiencies of environment-control will disappear. "The house will begin to live not by what it brings to the builder, but by what it gives to its occupants, and by what the latter, reciprocally, bestow upon it. It will become a triumph for the human mind through the human mind":* a place in which to live free from worry, free to explore, free to devise, include, refine, free to compose and synchronize.

* Theodore Larson, N. Y. C., 1931.

4

The Phantom Captain

WHAT is that, mother?"
"It's a man, darling."
"What's a man?"

Man?
A self-balancing, 28-jointed adapter-base biped; an electro-chemical reduction-plant, integral with segregated stowages of special energy extracts in storage batteries, for subsequent actuation of thousands of hydraulic and pneumatic pumps, with motors attached; 62,000 miles of capillaries; millions of warning signal, railroad and conveyor systems; crushers and cranes (of which the arms are magnificent 23-jointed affairs with self-surfacing and lubricating systems, and a universally distributed telephone system needing no service for 70 years if well managed); the whole, extraordinarily complex mechanism guided with exquisite precision from a turret in which are located telescopic and micro-scopic self-registering and recording range finders, a spectro-scope, *et cetera*, the turret control being closely allied with an air conditioning intake-and-exhaust, and a main fuel intake.
Within the few cubic inches housing the turret mechanisms, there is room, also, for two sound-wave and sound-direction-finder recording diaphragms, a filing and instant reference sys-tem, and an expertly devised analytical laboratory large enough not only to contain minute records of every last and continual event of up to 70 years' experience, or more, but to extend, by computation and abstract fabrication, this experience with rela-tive accuracy into all corners of the observed universe. There is, also, a forecasting and tactical plotting department for the reduc-

tion of future possibilities and probabilities to generally successful specific choice.

Finally, the whole structure is not only directly and simply mobile on land and in water, but, indirectly and by exquisite precision of complexity, mobile in air, and, even in the intangible, mathematically sensed electrical "world," by means of the extension of the primary integral mechanism to secondary mechanical compositions of its own devising, operable either by a direct mechanical hook-up with the device, or by indirect control through wired or wire-less electrical impulses.

"A man," indeed! Dismissed with the appellation Mr. "Jones"!

Common to all such "human" mechanisms—and without which they are imbecile contraptions—is their guidance by a phantom captain.

This phantom captain has neither weight nor sensorial tangibility, as has often been scientifically proven by careful weighing operations at the moment of abandonment of the ship by the phantom captain, i.e., at the instant of "death." He may be likened to the variant of polarity dominance in our bipolar electric world which, when balanced and unit, vanishes as abstract unity I or O. With the phantom captain's departure, the mechanism becomes inoperative and very quickly disintegrates into basic chemical elements.

This captain has not only an infinite self-identity characteristic but, also, an infinite understanding. He has, furthermore, infinite sympathy with all captains of mechanisms similar to his.

What is this UNDERSTANDING? It consists in an intuitive, non-graphable awareness of perfection, or of unity, or of eternity, or of infinity, or of truth. This awareness of perfection serves as a universal yardstick relative to which any sense experience may be measured, and by virtue of which CONSCIOUS SELECTION may be made.

("This is a better pair of shoes." How does one know? Because it the more closely approximates a "perfect" pair—the "perfect" pair that will *never* hurt, wear out, become dirty, or have weight. "Perfect," though impossible of demonstration, is nonetheless the criterion of selection. "Perfect" is not only a *direction*, but a *time direction*, "perfection" being *never* in "reality" attainable. There is herein to be discerned the meaning of *Never, Never Land*. Children dream truly.)

By the process of conscious selection relative to sense of perfect, the segregation of such phenomena as sounds has developed, followed by the selective recomposition of the segregated sounds into specific sound-continuities, or "words" (sound symbols) provocative of basic understanding in others, adequate for the *moment*. No matter how relatively imperfect the articulation, or the receiver-conception, there is nonetheless some characteristic of "uniformity," though not of "identity," of understanding between sender and receiver. For instance, the word "cow," ("black-white," "daisy" or "bossy" are inconsequential) conveys the concept of a mechanical process which is substantially understood as a composite "cow"—the milk factory. Each phantom captain for himself, however, associates "cow" with the most vividly impressive cow of his particular experience, the speakers a Jersey, the listeners a Guernsey.

This infinite communicating code, based on processes and continuities and not on static fixation identities, enables the phantom captain to signal, via the complicated visual, aural and oral, tactile and olfactory systems of his machine, to captains of other machines, who receive the message through complementary mechanical systems of reception. The success of the transmission depends upon the relative degree of communicated understanding, i.e., upon how "time"-rationalizing vs. statically-reflexing the receiving captain may be.

Curiously, each captain is so impressed by the command of such an elaborate mechanism and one so excellently attuned to operation that it readily yields to his un-self-conscious guidance of its processes and instruments, that he feels himself thrillingly and virtually a part of it. Only when the parts are abused is there awareness of a seemingly separate presence of parts; for instance, when the tongue has been bitten or burned its motions are painful whereas normally it wags merrily, carelessly and unnoted.

The Phantom Captain

Inevitably, the captain's habitual association of his infinite self with his subconsciously subservient mechanisms has inclined him to a dual "presumption": (1) that this mechanism is an ACTUAL (by extension) part of his phantom self, whereas it is purely an electro-chemical combination of inanimate energy molecules that are intrinsically the ship the phantom captain commands, and (2) an attitude of ownership: the mechanism of ordination for his will is "his" permanent "possession," whereas in reality it is only temporarily in his custody. This illusion of "possession" of the mechanism has been further extended, through accustomed relationship, to include "possession" of one's clothes, pencils, house in general, land, friends, wife and children, business, state, nation, world, and, finally, "God"—the last named quite naturally being "pictured" in the exclusively original form of his "own" egotistically important, special mechanistic and chemical process arrangement.

As the "possessor" of all of his extensions, the phantom captain automatically evolves a myriad of illusory necessities for which he assumes a vain, egotistical responsibility. This false-possession and always innocuous myth (which is consumptive of the complete lifetime, from four years onward, of the vast majority of people) stone-blinds the possessor to the simple, delightful truth-trends that are everywhere and at all times about us. For unspoilt children and happily debunked, emancipated grown-ups, these trends make life's courses as evident as a highway through a meadow. Ironically, the non-possession-blinded person's citation of evident trends has always been fearfully hailed as witchcraft, mysticism and quackery by the still mystified, self-be-quackeried majority.

The phantom captain is but mildly shaken in his preoccupation, or possession obsession, by the intermittent necessity of replacement of "his" parts, or by the dissection from, or application to, his mechanism by other phantom-captained mechanisms of such service parts as crude gold inlays inserted in "his" raw fuel crushers, additional lenses or color-filters for "his" range-finders, or an enema bag douching nozzle temporarily passed into "his" clogged canal. The inlay or the douche bag is, temporarily at least, as factually connected to self as a toe nail, tooth, hair, or eyeball.

This continual arrogation of "his" mechanisms is closely allied with the captain's habitual assumption that all objects are "seen" at locations outside the phantom captain's mechanism, whereas actually the captain "sees" them inside his turret through his peritelescopic range finders. A long history of mechanical reliability—attested by frequent accurate measurements of the deduced range of, and direction to, an object's external location with the ability to move a crane grappler into an assumed location so that contact with the discovered object is provided, and further attested by the receipt in the turret of affirmative telephone reports, from several of the myriad contact alarms in the crane grappler—seems to justify the captain's habit of thinking "I SEE IT OVER THERE."

The phantom captain's habitual notion not only that he is part of "his" mechanisms but that the mechanisms are himself, is extended still further. He frequently confuses the surface characteristics of other "observed" mechanisms, similar to those he controls, with the identities of the phantom captains controlling them. Forgetting the true, infinite *phantom* character of the other captains, he "logically" evolves two additional illusions: One of these is that the commanded mechanism of the other captain is all that there is to that other phantom captain; the other is that the *surface* is all there is to that mechanism. In other words, he assumes that the tangible surface of the "other" "person" *is* that person's phantom captain, and that this *surface alone* is "reality." (This is the "reality" of the "practical" minded or materialism-dominated personality.) So he customarily interprets the behavior characteristics of the whole of another's mechanism by surface clues only; there has actually developed a language in terms of surface reflexing.

To illustrate: If Mr. and Mrs. Murphy, out for a walk with baby Tim, were to see a plane flying overhead, they might readily exclaim to "darling," "See that aviator!" They might easily be wrong. Planes are being ably controlled by radio without a human pilot on board.

An illuminating rationalization indicates that *captains*—being phantom, abstract, infinite, and bound to other captains by a bond of understanding as proven by their recognition of each other's signals and the meaning thereof by reference to a common direction (toward "perfect")—*are not only all related, but are one and the same captain.* Mathematically, since characteristics of unity exist, they cannot be non-identical.

The phantom captain's *executive officer,* yclept "brain," is a mechanistic device similar to the metal "mike" of the Sperry gyroscope, whose gyroscopic directional-insistence, useful though it is while the captain is absent from the bridge is nonetheless provocative, if unwatched, of habit grooves of motion.

When the complexity of the metal "mike" currently used in aeroplanes and aboard ship in hands-off navigation is compared with that of the "mike" or "brain" of the human phantom-captained mechanism, it is as though one contrasted an Ingersoll watch and a battleship, in the matter of number of parts and precision of operation, except that the human "mike" is as small in relation to the metal "mike" as are the new complex seven-element, glass-lined metal radio tubes "small" in relation to their crude, large three-element forerunners.

The "mike" of the human ship may be "set" by the phantom captain to detect the slightest lack of balance, not only in every one of the ship's external relationships but in all of its interior synchronizing mechanisms. So many settings does "mike" carry, at most times, that he seems ALIVE, and he is so satisfactory to the captain that the latter flies the human ship "hands-off" much of the time. This possibility of hands-off flying encourages the phantom captain to regard the "mikes" of other phantom captains, also, as almost alive—that is, animate rather than animated.

Such a mistaken assumption of surface clues for reality must inevitably lead to a myriad of misunderstandings and erroneous conclusions, into "blind alleys" and "dead end" streets. This is just what happens when (rationalization of an illusion being *ipso facto* impossible and illusion being no further extensible, on the occasion of "death" or the abandonment of a mechanism) those "individuals" whose captains are still at their posts and who are still confusing themselves with the mechanism they are directing, ceremoniously "bury" the abandoned, now disintegrating mechanism under the impression that it is the captain whom they "honor." They might as well bury the can opener that "he" customarily used and which he regarded as "his." Indeed, it would honor the phantom captain more to bury his can opener, since it is a device rationally objectivized by him and is, therefore, more directly creditable to him than the involuntary custody and management of the unit mechanism he had under "his" control. The cans he opened might, also, be honored by burial in dirt.

There are two main types of phantom-captained mechanisms, differing only in their machinery for the reproduction of miniature replicas of themselves (a manufacturing process). The union of these complementary types, or "plants," allows the electro-chemical processing of raw materials into infinitely elaborate, replica structures and instrument ensembles.

There are, of course, innumerable subtypes of the male and female main types, varying widely in external color, size, smell and textural characteristics. In fact, no two are physically identical, although they are miraculously *uniform* from a mechanical, chemical, structural, and process characteristic viewpoint, even to the maintenance of an identical thermal characteristic which, when the machine is in proper running order, is 98.6° F. under most highly diversified exterior environment conditions.

When one of the phantom captains seeks a mechanism of the complementary type to join with his in the manufacture of an improved model replica of their mutual custody mechanisms, he misinterprets his un-self-conscious appraisal of the adequacy of the observed complement to his "own" half-plant as constituting suitable hook-up conditions in the terms of superficial or sensorial-surface-satisfactions. The result is often the peculiarly amusing selective sound-wave emission, through the major exit-entrance aperture of the turret, "BEAUTIFUL!"

Phantom captains have fallen into such a careless mythology of surface words and nicknames, to excuse slothfulness in telegraphing accurately the observed external phenomena to the turret laboratories, that, although Murphy's phantom captain meant by "beautiful" that he had noted in Julia a mechanism that was highly uniform, i.e., not deformed, and, therefore, so far as he was concerned one that was favorable for plant hook-up, he probably further elaborated inaccurately and meaninglessly, "Julia is the MOST BEAUTIFUL girl in the world!" (The writer does not mean to infer that he does not say "beautiful," and believes that he means it, over and over again.) Murphy also probably would say, "My Julia is a PEARL!" and send her a "rose," the latter being a broken-off portion of another highly intricate, phantom-captained mechanism, but of so relatively wide non-identity with the "Julia" mechanism as to allow of its becoming a "living" sacrifice on the altar of the Julia manufacturing-plant worship.

Had Murphy failed at first to convince Julia of favorable conditions for plant hook-up, through surface clues observable by her, he would not have ceased his campaign. No, he would have sought to impose on Julia an *illusion* of satisfactory surface clues, by altering his surface conditions—such as adding to the size of his turret with a new "fedora," or subtracting from its size by cutting off part of his hair—just as Julia, were the situation reversed, would have "dressed ship" in velvet "washed down" with attar of roses.

It has been but a step from false adornment and artificial surface extensions of the human body, in the matter of clothing, to shelter; and from shelter to the myriad of tools and instruments that were rationally evolved at an earlier time by the phantom captain in the extension of his own mechanism. The tools were born of the necessity to perform a specific function either with greater precision or with greater leverage than could be effected by the integral mechanism of the primary machine,—a tooth-pick, for instance, is better than a fingernail for tooth-picking and is more expeditiously replaceable.

The Murphys are not content, as their "wealth" (mechanical extensions) increases, with simple tooth-picks. Unless completely bereft of "hook-up" potentials, they will probably go in for gold tooth-picks, even gold filagreed tooth-picks, "individualistic" tooth-picks; embroidered roofs and arches; tattooed everythings.

So pleased are human beings by the artifices with which they constantly attain *self*-satisfaction, *despite* bad hook-up conditions, that they experience a constant urge to evolve codes of morals, ethics and laws for the purpose of making permanent the conditions of self-satisfaction that they have attained by artificiality. Out of these morals, ethics, artifices and vanities have been evolved so many "mike" sayings or brainistic words, that, although they are utterly meaningless from the viewpoint of the true phantom captain, they constitute 99% of today's broadcast, printed and person-to-person communication.

The artificial illusion extensions provided by the momentum of the gyroscopic "mike" display a wide range in various races variously located. For instance, when Doctor Jung, able student of psychology, made an extensive visit to Africa for the purpose of carrying on basic psychologic studies, he discovered that the primitive people there demonstrated a most interesting seemingly factual illusion extension from their simple experience memory storage. What had been regarded as purely ghost or demon fabrications, inherited through mythical tradition, proved to be none other than vivid memory concepts. When a leader or a parent died, the people had such simple, clear, visual memory pictures of the deceased that they were able satisfactorily to objectivize him as though still in bodily presence. In other words, they simply reversed our particular civilization's assumption that we SEE objects at a point EXTERNAL to our self-mechanism, although, in fact, the seeing is done, not even in the eye but in the brain or reception end of the nervous system that records the exterior light reflections.

Jung found, also, that African primitives, in common with

others throughout the world, have such a simple cosmic problem that they have only two categories of numbers, *viz.*, "*one*" or "*many*." Because they "SEE" either "one" or "many," they have evolved fabulous legendary stories. They recognize that one stranger may be readily matched in physical combat, whereas two or more may be overpowering. So two or three or more strangers are "seen" as hordes, the fear instinct warning the beholder of the risk of being overcome. Combining this "seeing" of either "one" or "many" with the extension of a SEEN factual memory form of a father or leader calls forth the illusion of the close proximity of multitudes of fathers, leaders, demons, *et cetera*.

There is, also, a tracery of the simple number sense limitation in certain old cultures. In Chinese, for example, one carriage is a carriage, many carriages are "noise." The Chinese symbol of "tree" is one tree; "two trees" equals "woods," and "three trees" constitute a "forest"—one, few, many.

Jung had the strange experience of noticing that, while he was endeavoring to understand primitive illusions, his own particular modern civilization's illusion broke down to such an extent that he, too, began to "see" partially in terms of the primitive illusion and partially in his own earlier illusion, with the result that he seemed to himself almost to be crazy, for there was no reliability in any illusion.

In connection with the phantom captain's illusion that the mechanisms of his survival are an intrinsic part of his abstract self, it is to be noted that every physical extension has been a matter of survival adequacy in the phantom captain's command of specific animal and vegetable species. It might almost be said that a new "type" of human animal has developed in the United States and that this type is by way of being an advance demonstration of a world-wide type, inasmuch as the evidences are all in terms of scientific world trends. When a sufficient number of members of a species has become characterized by relatively identical extensions, these extensions may properly be called part and parcel of the "being"-entity of that species.

If we will admit that a section of Julia's hair is just as much Julia's hair after it is cut off as it was when on her head—and it certainly is as much Julia as is the name "Julia," which is a most arbitrary appendage—we must admit, also, that if Julia's cut-off hair were woven into a fabric and worn on her head in the form of a hat, everything in the ensemble would still be "Julia." This would apply equally to any other hat that Julia might don or to the pigment which, for improved hook-up allure, she might apply to her lips and cheeks. Everything that Julia uses in her sometimes by-seeming selection, and again by-inadvertence choice, is "Julia."

The phantom captain of the butterfly has a great variety of mechanical externals for survival, but the apparently different stages of moth-caterpillar-chrysalis-butterfly in no way alter the identity of the phantom captain, which persists as unity throughout. Similarly, at sea, the various ships that Captain "Smith" commands are known to his contemporary skippers simply as "Smith." As Smith's ship, the Mary, appears on the horizon they exclaim, "Here comes Smith!" Smith may change commands but the other skippers will continue to say, "Here comes Smith!" whenever they recognize the externals of the ship he happens currently to be commanding.

In the United States passenger automobiles number approximately one per family, and the head of the family is usually the driver thereof. So accelerated are the time-space characteristics of the auto in comparison to the time-space covering ability of the man on legs that every reflex characteristic of the phantom captain of the driver is amplified in direct proportion to the time-space differential between the car's and the unmounted driver's tactical maneuvering ability. People who are not recognized as nervous or physically unbalanced while walking and talking are often seen to be distinctly so in their operation of an automobile. The traffic manners and ethics of people while driving reveal their character as a whole far more readily than would their cultivated mannerisms and behavior while walking.

Holding the full significance of this thought in mind, one can suddenly comprehend, while driving along a heavy traffic artery, that the automobiles seen are extensions of their drivers, just as are the "drivers' " hats, coats, shoes and faces; it is the progression of boxes within boxes of childhood play. Accepting this rationalization of man's unity extending into his automobile, it may be said that the average young working American man now weighs better than a ton, since the average automobile weighs 2800 lbs., and that the composite American extensible into his group mechanisms (aeroplane, railroad train, the *Normandie*, and Boulder Dam) is larger by millions of times than any historical animate organism. It is quite possible that Lewis Carroll was writing the poetry of this concept in *Alice Through the Looking Glass*.

There is another interesting phase of the phantom captain phenomenon. There is to be distinguished in the current era—as differentiated from the early crafts period of individual survival without the aid of mechanical extensions—a set of mechanisms, such as the power dynamo in the city, mutually commanded by phantom captains. When either Julia or Murph' pushes a certain button, the act serves to bring about a mechanical extension of the visual ability of both, although "seeing," let us remember, occurs within the turret and not externally to the mechanism of the phantom captain. This introduces an extraordinary rationalization, namely: Industrial mechanisms so gargantuan as to be without warrant as an extension of any one person are justifiable as extensions of multitudes of persons, proving to mathematical satisfaction that all people, of a species characterized by participation in the use of such mutual extension mechanisms, are one and the same person at the time of such utilization.

This conception of the phantom captain leads to a viewpoint quite the opposite of the "mechanistic" bogey so fearfully heralded and decried in recent years because of an apprehension that the man-created machine will overpower man somewhat as would a Frankenstein monster.

The thrilling inference of the phantom captaincy conception is that it not only precludes the possibility of the operation of extended machinery without the volition of inner man, but that the unit mechanisms are doing for man what politics has consistently failed to accomplish.

Industrial man, being unit, can only be effective in the direction of his own best survival interest.

5

What Is a House?

A HOUSE, darling,"—indeed.

The accompanying sketch is symbolic of the ordinary depth of penetration into the phenomenon "house."

"Come now," says the average reader. "I am not as dumb and old-fashioned as that. Why only last Sunday I was immensely interested in pictures of a Moto-home. Surely that is scientific?"

Answer—NO.

Compare "Jones" and the Moto-home as to complexity of requirement and as to efficiency of fulfillment of that requirement on a spacial, weight, mobility, adaptability, longevity or maintainance basis. Consider further that the abortive Moto-home is not even crudely valid, inasmuch as it is completely beyond the price range of the populace for which it was designed. The price of a Moto-home is approximately $14,000, or three times what 75% of the population can pay.

No, Mr. Average Reader, you are wrong. You don't know what a house is. The house in your mind is but a composite image of confusion, ineffectuality, and romance, of the exploitation of every weakness of "Jones" and "Murphy." There is no scientific sincerity apparent on the part of the producers of the Moto-home. It was devised as an outlet for their particular products of exploitation (electric toasters, wall paper, vacuum cleaners, *et cetera*). They carefully saw to it, not malevolently but because their "modern accessories" are dependent thereon, that the design of the Moto-home was subject to every land arterial tie-up and to political and finance bogging.

The Moto-home was successful as an advertising display and as a bauble for the bauble-affording 2%. It was, moreover, most pitifully a *teaser* to hundreds of thousands of home needers and longforers. There it ended, and baby may now draw the Moto-home thus:

The peak-top and the chimney are omitted, but the same old Wind-O-s are present (despite the fact that it has "air-conditioning"). There are books on plumbing (to be read while using the plumbing), asbestos or cement (instead of wood walls) covered with washable celluloid-collar paper, and several electric gadgets. There is no furniture, other than displayed in it by the department store from which it is hoped Murphy will buy, after being saddled with the Moto-home. In other words, the Moto-home relative to a cotswold cottage replica is analogous to the transition from Mother Goose's shoe to Uncle Don's flaked-cereal "premium" paper house.

Returning to the inside-out designer who was so boldly prosaic and scientific as to ask, "What is this phenomenon, house?" we find that before designing a house from the inside-out, he probably asked himself the further question, "What *do* I know about a house?"

"It is evident," he reasoned, "that to see what a house MAY look like, if it is not to be a confused symbol of superstition, compromise, perversion, exploitation, and even of social degeneracy and sloth, but a dwelling that will be truly articulate of satisfaction of requirements, it is essential that a sincere attempt be made to take stock of all known forces, current facilities, and trends."

In the language of various "human" groups residing on the isotherm of central population (the latitude of an average mean low temperature of 32° F.) there is a remarkable similarity in the "sound" that designates a house.

It is "hus" in Anglo-Saxon, old Saxon, old French, mid-low, old-high and mid-high German, and in the Norse and Gothic tongues. (In Gothic it is sometimes used in combination with Gud—Gud-house.) In old English, it is "hus," "hous," or "howes"; in Danish and Swedish "hus," in Dutch "huis," and in German "haus." It is etymologically connected with hut—hide—hoard—hood and hat, and among its various synonyms are residence, dwelling, abode, lodging, booth (bothy) and shelter. Its multitudinous special meanings include:

Whorehouse
Warehouse
Special chamber (smokehouse, toolhouse, etc.)
Household (meaning the family)
House of Rothschild (meaning a family of ancestors)
Legislative body
Audience of a play

Commercial firm
In astrology, 12th part of heaven.

The Anglo-Saxon origin of the synonym "shelter" would be: SHELL<scyld (shield) TER<trum (firm): That which covers or shields from exposure or danger; a place of safety, refuge or retreat.

"Since I am particularly interested in the shelter-dwelling-house," continues the inside-outer, "which of its multitudinous requirements may I set down on paper as universal, that is, not only for the Murphys of New York but for Murphys everywhere, from Africa to Alaska, the tropics and the Arctic, as well as in the temperate zones?" *See opposite page* →

There is no traditional, mechanical or esthetic solution *implicit* in any of the foregoing requirements, which are universal to 2⅓ billion Earthians, since they have no specific continental, linguistic, racial, spacial or calendar-time limitations. Air transport passengers have digestive functions identical with those of householders. There is not implied in the solution of the requirements a replica of a 600 B.C. *cloaca maxima* with such appendages as a Tammany sewer commissioner, improvement and maintainance taxes, and a mortgageable land-wedded arterial tie-up.

In his column of December 1, 1937, Westbrook Pegler reported a hypothetical citizen's testimony before a Housing Commission which clarifies what we mean by "mortgageable land-wedded arterial tie-up" or political-finance bogged housing:

Q. You claim authority on housing? Why? .
A. Well, I built a house, I own a house and I live in a house.
Q. You built a house yourself?
A. No, I paid for building it.
Q. You think a government housing program would run into trouble?
A. Well, judging by my own case, yes.
Q. State your experience.

A. Well, there was the sewer. The real estate promoter promised to put in a sewer, but he went into bankruptcy without putting it in. He had several corporations. Every time he bought another lot he

(*Continued on page 36*)

UNIVERSAL REQUIREMENTS OF A DWELLING MACHINE

1. **OPPOSITION TO EXTERNAL DESTRUCTIVE FORCES,**
   via spacial control against:

Earthquake	Flood	Gale	Gases
Fire	Pestilence	Tornado	Marauders

   Selfishness (Politics, Business, Materialism)

2. **OPPOSITION TO INTERNAL DESTRUCTIVE FORCES,**
   via spacial control for:
   - A. Nerve Shock Proofing:
     - 1. Visual 2. Aural 3. Tactile 4. Olfactoral
   - B. Fatigue Proofing (Human Robotism, Drudgery)
   - C. Repression Proofing (Don't-proofing, Removal of Fear of Mechanical Inadequacy Developed by Accidents or Arbitrary Cellular Limits of Activity, i.e., Negative Partitioning)

3. **PROVISION FOR *UNSELFCONSCIOUS PERFORMANCE OF INEVITABLE MECHANICAL ROUTINE* OF THE DWELLING AND ITS OCCUPANTS:**
   - A. FUELING of House or Occupants (Eating—Metabolism).
   - B. REALIGNMENT of House or Occupants (Sleeping—Muscular, Nerve and Cellular Realignment).
   - C. REFUSING of House or Occupants (Internal, i.e., Intestinal, etc.; External, i.e., Bathing or Pore Cleansing; Mental, i.e., Elimination by Empirical Dynamics; Circulatory, i.e., Atmospheric Control.

4. **PROVISION OF ADEQUATE MECHANICAL MEANS FOR ALL DEVELOPMENT REQUIREMENTS OF GROWTH PHENOMENA** allowing the Facile, No-time-loss, Scientifically Efficient and Unselfconscious development of:
   - A. SELECTIVE AWARENESS OF UNIVERSAL PROGRESSIONS, i.e.:
     Vital data on:
     - 1. History—News—Forecasts (Library, Radio, Television)
     - 2. Current Supply and Demand Conditions
     - 3. Current Dynamic Conditions—Weather—Earthquakes—Latest Scientific Research Findings.
   - B. ADEQUATE MECHANICS OF ARTICULATION (Prosaic or Harmonic) through Recording by Typewriter, Drawing Board, Conversation, i.e., Communication, Direct or Indirect, Aural, Visual, or Tactile. (This also includes the necessity of Transportation and bespeaks any and all Means of Objectification or Crystallization of Universal Progress.)
   - C. PROCREATION.
   - D. RECREATION.

would form another corporation, and the corporation that sold us our lot went bankrupt. So the sanitary inspector wouldn't let us dig a cesspool and the corporation couldn't build the sewer. So they had a receiver, and after a long time, with our house standing idle, they got things straightened out, but the receiver and his lawyers had taken all the money. So finally the town built the sewer and taxed us for it.

Same way about the sidewalks and pavement. We paid for them in the purchase of the lot, but, after the little corporation went bankrupt, we had to pay for them again, in taxes. (The real estate man still had plenty of money, personally, but the corporation was broke.)

Q. Was there something about a furnace?

A. Yes, sir. The contractor made a deal with a furnace contractor and he installed an old furnace, just painted over, instead of a new one, as the contract specified. It wouldn't heat, the pipe froze, the furnace blew up and we had to move to a boarding house while they fixed it. I had to redecorate the boarding house walls where the children drew pictures with their crayons, all because of that furnace.

Then, when they went to fix the frozen pipes, they discovered that the builder didn't leave that little trap door so you could get at the pipes to fix them. So we had to get a carpenter to tear out the wall and a plasterer to make it over. Meantime, this new plumber discovered that the original plumber had used wax instead of solder on a big joint 'way back under the bathroom floor. That was leaking, too. He could see it with his flashlight, but couldn't get at it, so we had to wreck the floor and rebuild it.

The furnace contractor didn't have any backing, so couldn't replace the furnace with a good one. And then the junk man who sold him the second-hand furnace came and got it, claiming he had not been paid for it. That didn't leave me any furnace at all. And then the furnace workmen sued the furnace contractor for their wages and slapped a mechanic's lien on my whole house. They said I had no right to let the junk man take the furnace off the place so they couldn't attach it.

Q. Any other liens?

A. I guess you could call them liens. Some lumber company that sold the builder the shingles served a paper on me because he didn't pay them, although I paid him. Then some workmen who worked for the builder on another job served another lien on me, claiming I had to pay them a balance of $400 which I owed the builder because he owed them some wages. I said I wasn't intending to pay him the

What Is a House?

$400 because of all the expense he had put me to. But he claims he is broke, too, so where do I get off suing him?

Well, he had to rebuild the roof because it leaked, and some walls where the water destroyed the plaster, and now some union stands in front of my house yelling "SCAB!" because some of the workmen weren't union. But I didn't hire them. The contractor wouldn't let me. Anyway, that would have canceled his responsibility.

Q. So you think the government might have a serious difficulty building 3,000,000 houses?

A. Difficulty? It would be a war!

To add another "slant" in this picture from the design and method viewpoint, I quote from an article I wrote in 1927, after five years' experience in the building business, during which I succeeded in aiding the erection of some 150 homes large and small out of more than 10,000 seriously discussed and partially attempted.

"If, today a man, wishing to acquire an automobile, were to visit one of five thousand automobile designers in New York City, equivalent to New York's five thousand architects, and were to commence his retention of the designer by the limitation that he wanted the automobile to resemble outwardly a Venetian gondola, a jinricksha of the Tang Dynasty, a French fiacre, or a Coronation Coach of Great Britain, pictures of which he had obligingly brought with him, all final embellishment, of course, to be left to the election of his wife; and he and the 'designer' were together to pick and choose (from automobile accessory catalogues, advertisements, and 'shows') motors, fly wheels, fenders, frame parts offered in concrete, brass, sugar cane fibre, walnut, et cetera, and succeeded in designing an automobile somewhat after the style of some other fellow; and they were then to have the design bid upon by five local garages in Queens Village, picking one of the bidders for his ability, or price; and the successful bidder, chosen, let us say, because of his having built grandfather's velocipede, were to insist on the use of some other wheels than those specified; and the local bank, in loaning the money to the prospective 'owner' to help him finance, had some practical man look over the plans so that, guessing at the cost, he might base a loan thereon, incidentally insisting on the replacement of several parts and methods by others in which the bank was 'interested'; and then the insurance company were to condemn a number of the units used because they had not been paid for their 'official approval' and compel the substitution of other units; and fifty material and accessory manufacturers' salesmen were informed by a reporting agency, whose business it was to ferret out this poor man's private plans, that he was going to 'build' a car, and were to begin hounding him with specious promises; and, finally, if the local town council had to approve of the design and materials and give a permit for the automobile's construction, sending around assertive inspectors, while it was being erected, it is certain that few of those desiring automobiles would have the temerity to go through with the ardors of acquiring them on such a 'craft' and 'graft' basis. Should they have the hardihood, the automobile would finally cost in the neighborhood of $50,000, and be highly unsatisfactory, being full of 'bugs,' and completely without service when finished.

"This is exactly the condition in the home building field. Is it any wonder people crowd the city apartment? In the building of such an automobile, not one but many ill trained mechanics from different oddly named 'trades' would have to be employed, 'carpenters' to apply the carburetor and 'masons' to assemble the chassis frame, though many times there would be but room for one man to work. The contractor, who would also be building other cars in Far Rockaway, Roslyn, *et cetera*, would stop in for an hour a day to look over the work, outside of which the job would receive no organization of method. There would probably be strikes by the plumbers or electricians who would insist on most of the improvements in design being left out due to their having no 'jurisdiction' permitting them. To cap all, the car would take from six months to a year to build, inasmuch as mechanics in the building trades average 30 steps per net useful contact today as opposed to ½ step in highly developed modern factory conditions, which fact, coupled with the consideration of high discomfiture of building trades' exposed working conditions, and the fact that it is found by insurance companies to be second only to coal mining in point of fatal accident, indicates the extraordinary change of status that will occur in new housing industry, when mechanics will perform effective shelter service, economically rewarding such labor on an efficacy basis, indicative of wages many times higher than the present scale."

It is a law of evolution and design that designs, whether by man or by "nature," are reproduced in direct proportion to their mechanical adequacy of satisfaction of universal requirements, whether it be a book, a rose, a pencil or a baby.

The 1936 "Moto-home," by this law, was not subject to mass production due to its inadequacy. Whether the government or private enterprise ever becomes successful in producing or reproducing 3,000,000 homes or 50,000,000 will be dependent upon the adequacy of the design, not only of the prototype end product house but of the prototype industrial service. It must be a *"natural."* If it is, no one will be able to stop its mass production and world-wide distribution by either the government or private enterprise.

There is not implicit in this statement of the law of reproduction an attainment of *immediate* "perfection" in rendition of the prototype. Any present level of knowledge, standards, technique and available known elemental sources will tend to confine the physical characteristics of design-solution within that special era. Nevertheless, the development of public enlightenment and industrial management awareness is bringing with it recognition of the fact that any economic survival plan for industry must include not only accredited primary survival of shelter, but the expansion of shelter design to the point of maximum efficiency. Shelter of the human life process involves, in its most comprehensive meaning, consideration of all forces acting to retard or destroy it. It represents the measure of man's intuitive and conscious mastery of equilibrium.

A new dwelling service industry must inevitably develop, even to the point of commanding all other industries.

HOUSES, like other instruments, have not only to be SCIEN-

TIFICALLY DESIGNED but MUST BE PRODUCED, otherwise designers are going to be justly condemned for bringing about academic esthetic race suicide through a battle of words.

Final chapters in this book will discuss such production objectively. If successful performance is sincerely longed for, we must research broadly, then consolidate.

Obviously, with the achievement of adequate housing, existing theories of land economics must undergo a profound change, and as the new dwelling service industry correlates and engulfs other industries architecture itself will become enlarged in scope and definition.

The function of the architect will be to RAISE the level of universal existence to the progressively HIGHEST standard of survival and growth. This will manifest the EVOLUTIONARY COURSE of human growth as opposed to the revolutionary, lazy, stop-short method of levelling high standards of existence down to the lowest common denominator to satisfy an inferiority complex and excuse the political imposition of a devastating "class" wedge upon the masses.

The function of the architect-engineer will be the irrevocable integration into society of an universally accredited primary survival. This will be done through the adequate disposition of a constantly improving, available "best" shelter, clothing and sustenance, in a world which can already—through the effort of one man out of every five working but one day a month—produce and distribute the goods and services necessary to all.

Resourcefulness and industriousness, in the conscientious perusal of the myriad of available technological data for the integration involved, will triumph. Buck-passing of technical responsibility and hopeful guessing, progressively self-invalidating, will cease to be profitable.

The proper activity of the architect-engineer is purposeful. "It is not to devise a better society so as to arrive at a finer architecture; it is to provide a better architecture in order to arrive at a more desirable society."* The combined function of architect,

* Theodore Larson.

industrialist and synchronizing architect-engineer, since WHAT to do is known, is, first, to determine not causes but purposes, and, then, acting within this knowledge, to evolve an adequate shelter design that will make possible the rational and spiritual self-realization toward which man has ever so longingly striven.

In this connection, Dr. Alexis Carrel holds that "The quality of life is more important than life itself," and asks, "Is not this more important to man than the goods consumed by him?"

The answer is that if the quality of goods and shelter is improved, the quality of life automatically will improve.

Carrel further asks, "Are health and comfort of any value if we become mentally and spiritually worthless?"

To this we reply, "The phantom captain will abandon ship and find a better one if the old one springs leaks and the machinery breaks down to the point of uneconomical repair."

What is Carrel's yardstick of worth? Both the mental and energy components of life are abstract. He confuses the articulation means, i.e., the mechanical body, with the cause. Aid man by eliminating drudgery and breakdowns in what he HAS to do, and make available to him, even to the point of unconscious awareness, complete tools of articulation for his every growth requirement, and the meaning in mind will flower forth with redolence. Intelligence is not quantitative.

Intelligence says, "Conscious inefficiency and non-adaptability to purpose, or change, are SUICIDAL."

Therefore, as a stimulant for the mind-over-matterists to whom the privilege of furthering human emergence through shelter service will accrue, the adoption of the following resolution is recommended:

WHEREAS industry, which is science instrumented and coördinated coöperation, is more efficient than have been the arts and crafts tailoring methods in the mass production of universal requirement extensions and supplies, and

WHEREAS the scientific element of industry recognizes that we must do the most with the least, which, in view of change through the growth of knowledge, imposes not only "doing" but a specific "in-time-doing" if the search for the most with the least is not to delay an equation of use performance, and

WHEREAS, efficiency makes it mandatory that we USE forces, not FIGHT them, now, therefore,

BE IT RESOLVED, that in any plan of human emergence through shelter service the following three points become integral and necessary preliminaries:

1. The segregation and correlation of currently gleanable "attained conditions" of human survival, dramatically emphasizing the relative importance of the various "conditions" to a progressively growthful survival;

2. The summation of currently available knowledge, techniques, and instruments, as well as of the sources and extent of power for production and operation of all the means of satisfying vital requirements; and

3. The determination of mankind's present status by an estimate of the general animate and inanimate trend momenta (evolutionary kinetics) for, and general animate and inanimate obstacles (evolutionary inertia) against the forthright, intelligent solution of the condition first mentioned by the means enumerated.

The proposed inventory, to be efficient, must be all-comprehensive of man's estate, that is of his UNIVERSAL *status quo*.

Once the accounting is made, with calm deliberation, an improved future may be envisioned and rationally brought about; known defects can be remedied; and areas of advance achievement can be limitlessly extended.

The goal is the emergence of humanity.

The means is industrial. Not re-form, but to form.

Evolution tends toward the accelerated development of new form, embodying one or many of the basic elements, but in ever new streamlined alignment.

In architecture "form" is a noun; in industry, "form" is a verb. Industry is concerned with DOING, whereas architecture has been engrossed with making replicas of end results of what people have industrially demonstrated in the past. "Noun," in our phonetic etymology, means "now-one," i.e., the most recent chaos of thought reduced to an answer. The "now-one" or "noun" must, in due course through selection by the intellect, become two or more observed characteristics of the one, *there being no absolute identity*. Nouns, from a language viewpoint, are tenable *only* as "names" for facts recently determined. The noun is, therefore, more subject to constant revision than is any other part of speech. No longer is it "stone." No longer is it "steel." Industry is dealing in hundreds of different steels, physically more dissimilar than the Chinese and the Swiss.

The goal is not "housing," but the universal extension of the phantom captain's ship into new areas of environment control, possibly to continuity of survival without the necessity of intermittent "abandoning ship."

6

Teleology

A NAME for the process of OBSERVING consciously, or absorbing subconsciously, from the OUTSIDE INWARD so that one may do from the inside outward is TELEOLOGY. When finally solving from the inside out, the teleologic perspective will be universal, and the equation of performance will be:

Degree of satisfaction encompassment = degree of factor inclusion.

Let us symbolize teleology as $\bowtie$, like a bow tie. This is a neat and specific equation mark, combining the symbol of symmetrical expansion (the "$\times$," multiplication, or "times" mark) with the equation mark (=). It is currently more fitting as an equation symbol than the old equation mark because we now know that parallel lines, or conditions, are impossible. Moreover, quasi-parallel lines, never coming in contact, are procreatively sterile. The "=" is, then, inaccurate as a sign to link integrators and product:

$$(2 \times 3 = 6 \text{ theoretical})$$
$$(2 \times 3 \bowtie 6 \text{ factual})$$

Our teleologic symbol $\bowtie$ represents, by its loose-ended "$\times$" inclusion and by the conjunction of its ends, a finite radial limit of the *segment of inclusion* and the *segment of conclusion*, like an hour glass on its side. It is offered, then, as the logical successor of the familiar equation symbol for use in any consideration of the now apparently expanding universe.

A Teleologic Demonstration

I see an apple.
The light of the sun is reflected from the surface of an apple,

44

after the occurrence of the spectroscopic action of light segregation through the medium of crystals on the surface of the apple.

Not all of the energy ray tones are reflected, however. Those that are useful to the apple are absorbed by it, while the remainder, i.e., the non-useful, or non-digestible, or, more specifically, non-chemically combinable ray tones are reflected from the surface of the apple through the air to and through the lens of the human eye, where they are analyzed by the retina and telephotographed to the brain of the beholder.

Incidentally the light that the apple gives off is a negative, that is, the opposite of the light complementary to the growth phenomenon "apple." It is not one of the chemical apple's actual constituents. This is something like the phenomenon of the camera film negative except that the latter is more honest than the eye's for the eye reverses light and shadow instead of properly appraising them as does the camera. In printing, the black and white of the film have to be reversed in order to represent the illusion of the apple as the eye sees it. Many apples are probably blue, having taken blue from the spectrum, but the eye, taking up the rejected red, "sees" the apple as red.

Whether or not the eye sees a negative or a positive of the apple, light absorption and reflection are mechanical considerations because neither life nor mind activity is involved until the essence of the *picture* has been articulated in the "brain" and has been automatically referred to the memory filing department (the system of which is even more complicated than the worldwide Bertillon system of finger-print identification) for comparison with all of the apple experiences of the "see-er." The new picture of "apple" is laid out on the table for comparison with the whole reference file by the executive officer, "brain," who never sees the phantom captain although under his permanent orders to lay out the file in the captain's outer study. Then "brain" retires through the front door, closes it behind him, and the phantom captain enters from his inner sanctum to peruse the exhibit.

If interested at all—generally he is not—the captain considers the progression of apple phenomena, as indicated by the pictures in the file, and decides that the latest addition is a better or worse apple, i.e., it is an apple that would, or would not, be useful as fuel for his ship, in the cleansing process of his machinery, as a missile, or as bait. Having decided "yes" or "no," he leaves a message for "brain" beside the exposed file and retires.

"Brain" re-enters, scans the message, returns the file including the latest apple picture back to the memory chamber, and executes any order the captain may have left.

If the execution of that order calls for a signaling operation through the sound detonating mechanism, the executive officer proceeds to pump a little air into the air storage chambers by the hydraulic inflation and deflation of the flexible tubular members of the wall structure of the pump bladder. When a high fluid pressure is exerted in the tubes, the air chamber expands in the form of a globular Japanese lantern with spiny, spiral, horizontal arches. As soon as the liquid pressure is released, the air chamber is forced to contract by the spring leaf diaphragm against which it was expanded.

"Brain," thus able to inflate and deflate the air storage, first sculpturally arranges the passage to the orifice of the raw fuel receiving hatch and shapes the orifice as well as the wall structures of the tubes leading from the orifice to the air chambers; then, by an adjustable mutable tongue cone, which proportionately occupies the orifice and has a tip which is free to vibrate gently, "brain" causes a continuity pattern of sound control to issue forth with high variation frequency. The segmental units of sound are known as words, which might be—in the present illustration—arranged by the executive officer as a series of seven air syllabic emissions: *"I'd love to eat that ap-ple!"*

This process, which has required some time for its description due to its complexity and necessarily detailed efficiency, actually consumes but a fraction of a second in its operation.

It has been described to make clear this essential point of teleology: The phenomenon of the original inclusion was a light analysis consideration. The analysis of light was transmitted through a complete telegraphing system to headquarters where an abstraction of its effect occurred. After this, an abstract order was issued by the phantom captain to "brain" which subsequently articulated itself in a sound wave phenomenon with a special directionary implication which the apple, in itself, did not possess. In short, a light phenomenon was converted into a sound phenomenon.

The process could more easily have been described in terms of lips, mouth, bronchi, lungs, breasts, *et cetera*, but the layman has been so confounded by tradition as, inseparably, to correlate the names of physio-biological parts with ethics, morals and sex frustrations that, to evoke a true perspective upon the wonder of the phantom captain and his ship, it seemed best to use purely inanimate mechanical terms. Even on inspecting so scientifically and intelligently evolved a demonstration as a glass woman, man is hampered in his appreciation of the revealed mechanical and chemical miracle.

Now, the phantom captain may have found, in his memory file of "apple," a record of how badly apples had affected his ship's mechanism some years past, which might have prompted a command *not* to eat the apple. But before issuing the command he might have drifted into reflecting on his childhood maladies, which were often representative of bad reciprocity of the ship's mechanical parts, and then have realized that, for a number of recent years, he had had no mechanical disynchronizations. This realization might have occasioned rejoicement in the pleasurable nature of his captaincy of late. Feeling quite radiant, as a result of this reflection, he probably would have wished to share his radiance with another, wherefore he would have left for his executive officer, "brain," this message for Mabel,—"Let's go out and get drunk."

Such a command could scarcely be *directly* apparent as having been provoked by an apple's reflected sunlight. This would be an *indirect* effect of the apple. It is a better illustration of teleology than was the first example which arrived directly at the conclusion, "I'd love to eat that apple." In the second example, a sensorial reflection inclusion, passing through the abstract center of the captain's study (it was the captain's personal debate) demonstrated itself subsequently in an articulation quite indistinguishably correlative to the item of detonation or the original causal phenomenon, i.e., the energy of a star, the sun, bouncing off an apple. Nevertheless, the *principle of teleology* implies that *the adequacy and effect of conclusion are directly proportional to the degree of ramification and penetration of the original inclusion.* In other words, the energy applied to the end effect and satisfaction of the reflex would be directly proportional to the care and energy invested in looking at the apple.

The words "telegraph" and "telephone" have quite naturally been derived from teleology. The process they represent mechanically abstracts the original, with the minds of operators interpolating at abstract stages to produce an ultimately sensorial result. ("Telefacture" may well supplant "manufacture.")

To illustrate the process in "telegraph," let us suppose an original phenomenon such as the death of Uncle John.

A telegram is sent to a florist by someone, the message being transmitted as a dot-and-dash interruption on an electrical circuit. The dot-and-dash symbols are converted at the receiving end of the wire into ink symbols, codified with the dot-and-dash system, on a piece of yellow paper. This piece of paper is transmitted to a florist who sends flowers to #37 Bond Street,—flowers but that morning growing in a field only to be suddenly severed from their roots, covered with waxed paper, packed in a cardboard box, and later delivered, at #37 Bond Street, into a receptacle of water standing next to a black box in which has been deposited a discarded human machine. The telegram sender, rueful of death, caused further death to be a paying business, an odd result from the original cause.

The means of provoking the effect by the cause was not merely a mechanico-electrical process; more important were the phantom captains who performed the function of "interpolation" at the various receiving instruments by transforming the dots and dashes not only into ink symbols but into further botanical death.

The essence of this phenomenon is that the interpolating function is one that no machine will ever perform. The art of teleologic design is, then, one of delicacy of attunement in the interpolation of every seemingly casual event of life into nonhaphazard objective instruments,—whether written words, medical prescriptions or pencils, the function of the instrument being, in turn, the harmonic abetment of the trends intuitively to be detected by the teleologist through the keyhole of his "own" phantom captain's study. Teleology will have more and more significance as the teleologist carries on the vast task of exploring and including all factors making up man's universal *status quo*.

The consumption and digestion of facts and statistics is somewhat like eating and chewing hay and thistles. There is nourishment in them in their raw state, to be sure, but a cow is needed to convert them into milk. Likewise the average human mind needs an intermediary—a teleologist—to convert vital factors into digestibles for his objective use.

To the student of teleologic design, particularly as applied to shelter service, we offer a "cowing" of the vital factors of man's estate at this moment of ken. Only by awareness of this estate can the teleologist interpolate therefrom an adequate industrial design of world encompassing shelter service, which will be so utilitarianly adequate and harmonic as to insure man's irrepressible appetence for such shelter service's industrial reproduction.

At the outset, certain new words must be introduced, among which are *vitalistics* to replace the dead word *statistics*, and *mobilata* to supersede *data*. These substitutions are necessary in order to incorporate a TIME element and to make allowance for the constant adjustment of figures into the meanings of words. Statistics are static, Time-less, the blinding dust of death. Vitalistics and mobilata, on the other hand, are appropriately used in connection with a cosmic inventory because scientific events and corrections may cause an one hundred per cent. amplification or refinement in our cosmic inventory even before the manuscript reciting the items can be printed.

7

We Call It "Earth"

Of ONE planet, the earth, in one little star system (the sun's) in one relatively small galaxy, we know a little: its superficial geography, measurements, conditions and processes.

Of the nine planets in our solar system, the earth is the third nearest the sun, being 92 million miles distant from it. Mercury is nearest, with a minimum distance from the sun of 28 million miles, and Pluto is the farthest, being distant 3 billion 800 million miles. The ratio of distance from the sun to axial revolutions, or days, *per annum* is approximately of inverse proportion for all planets. Mercury has 88 days in a year, the earth 365, and Pluto 90,500.

We know that the earth is the densest body of the sun group, including the sun itself. If we were to call the density of the earth 1, Venus would be .88, the moon .60, and the sun .26.

The diameter of the earth is twice that of the smallest planet, Mercury, but is only one tenth that of Jupiter, the largest planet, the diameter of which, in turn, is but one tenth that of the sun. (The sun itself is a relatively small star, a new one having been discovered and measured in '37-'38 so large as almost to equal that of the whole solar system.)

Three fourths of the earth's surface is covered with a layer of moisture that is relatively thin (9/100 of 1%), its greatest depth being only 35,410 feet in the Mindinao Deep between the Philippine Islands and Japan, as compared to the earth's 8000 mile (42,000,000 ft.) diameter.

The remaining quarter of the surface of the earth consists of dry land concentrated within a relatively small sector. Indeed, one may so revolve a globular replica of the earth that 85% of all dry land is visible from one perspective point. When so revolved, there appears a "land hemisphere" in which the north pole is approximately one eighth of the way down from the top center. The center of the "land hemisphere" is the Spanish Riviera. In this "land hemisphere" two main continental bodies are apparent. One comprises all of Africa, Europe and Asia, penetrated by a small canal (the Mediterranean and the Red Sea); the

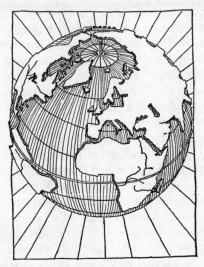

An SSA graph of universal architecture's prime "town limits" for an industrially emancipated human community.

other consists of the Americas and Greenland. These two great bodies are joined at their upper limits by Alaska and northern Siberia, with the Aleutian Islands re-enforcing the juncture. Bering Strait is scarcely discernible.

The Equator appears as a draped line girdling the globe one quarter of the distance between the bottom and the top of this view of the earth. It transits the center of Africa and what can be seen of South America. Above the line designating the Equator lies 85% of all the earth's dry land.

The "town plan" of an architect intent on devising an universal shelter service design is a fairly concentrated affair so far as the earth is concerned. This is emphasized by a study of population concentrations upon the earth's surface. Of the 2 1/3 billion people currently on this earth-globe, only 13 million, or approximately ½ of 1%, are in the non-visible area of our "town plan." No teleologic designer, in view of the current world integration, can profess concern with building only within the "town plan" of Podunk when the materials, structures and tools he uses are so obviously derived from the entire surface of the earth. It is a different story from an early New England settler doing the best he could with the materials at hand quarrying for himself a bit of granite for shelter construction. That was *architecture*, for he did the most with the least out of the available materials and tools. We cannot claim that we are doing the most with the least without carefully referring to our cosmic inventory and ascertaining what is now most suitable and available.

Although the earth's land and water surface is protected by a blanket of atmospheric gas, which is frictionally cohesive to the earth in its fast rotation, the differential of speed of the earth's revolutions to that of the air and water produces a constant rotational current, in both its air and partial water covering, in a general direction of west to east. Scientifically, this is explainable as a slight rotational lag of the earth ball within its surface films of more mutably drawn liquid and gaseous elements,—drawn tidally by the electrical pull of the moon and possibly of the sun.

Were it not for the dry land projections into the gaseous and liquid films, these apparent currents would probably be true west to east currents. However, the continental projections, which, like three fingers, extend down from the north pole, set up turbulent back eddies in both the liquid and gaseous films around their southern extremities. Thus, warm equatorial waters are catch-basined into S-shaped depressions between the two main continental bodies, where they swirl about in such manner as to cause great vagaries in temperature in relation to the earth's theoretical parallels of latitude. These thermal conditions have a direct bearing on the areas favorable to human survival because the water content of the human is approximately 9 to 1, and water freezes at 32° F.

The west-east currents of the gaseous film are further interrupted by great mountain ranges on the windward slopes of both main continental bodies. Molten snow and ice, flowing down the windward side of these ranges, have caused small alluvial plains to form like a shelf along their windward base. This windward lip is so slight as in no way to alter a general cross-sectional contour of the continent, similar to a cross-section of an aeroplane wing foil, as the continent tapers from its western mountainous edge to its eastward leeward flat-lands.

Whether or not there is significance in the coincidental streamline form of the continents (possibly so formed by air and oceans of yore passing over them from west to east), the fact remains that these westerly continental lead-edges cause a peculiar disturbance in their wake, to the east and over the hinterland. This still further affects the isotherm of average temperature, areas of moisture precipitation, and man-growth abetment conditions that must be heeded by the teleologic shelter designer.

The isotherm, or abstract temperature belt or zone, of an annual average variation of 48° F. and 32° F. mean low and 72° mean high, swirls from Alaska down the coast to Vancouver, B. C., thence to lower Kansas, after which it rises gradually to Lake Erie, Boston, Newfoundland, South Greenland, and midnorthern Russia. Then it veers back to and down through the Scandinavian Peninsula, centrally through Europe to the Black Sea, and, finally, passing through the Caspian Sea, Turkey, Persia, northern India and central China, rises again to traverse Japan and follow the coast of Siberia back to the southern tip of Alaska. *The significance of this isotherm is that it coincides with the central line of concentration of man population.*

One and one half billion or 70% of the total 2 1/3 billion world population resides along this 48° range of temperature isotherm. This zone has an average rainfall of 40 inches annually and an average constant wind speed of 15 m.p.h. We are certainly get-

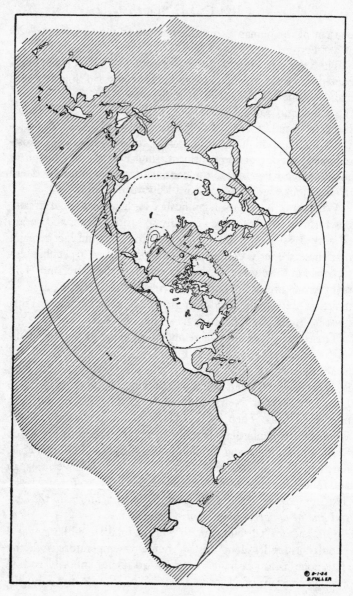

ting down to specific conditions for the teleologic dwelling designer.

We now submit a new world map more suitable for our teleologist than the "land hemisphere" previously sketched. It centers on the North Pole and in it the whole dry land of the earth may be seen to be ONE CONTINENT instead of two as shown in the first sketch. There is one continent similar to a 3-bladed propeller with the hub at the North Pole. The winding dotted line is that of our population isotherm.

It will be noted from the following table that, if man were to be deployed over the whole surface of dry land, there would be but 40 persons to a square mile. At this rate, there would quite evidently be ample room on earth for man for a long time to come, this density being but one tenth that of the British Isles, or Rhode Island.

TABLE 1

Continent	Sq. Mile (Millions)	Population (Millions)	Population (per Sq. Mile)
North America...	8.50	180.0	21
South America.....	6.8	81.5	12
Europe............	3.7	550.0	149
Asia..............	17.0	1,155.0	67
Africa............	11.5	150.0	13
All Other Land	10.0	197.0	—
Total..........	57.5	2,313.5	40 (average)

Actually, however, population is highly concentrated in certain portions of the land area and sparsely existent in others. For instance, in Java the concentration is 804 to the square mile.

TABLE 2

Comparative Special Population Densities

Country	Sq. Mile (Millions)	Population (Millions)	Population (per Sq. Mile)
Japan...........	.148	64.0	432
Australia........	3.000	6.6	2
British Isles......	.120	49.0	409
Java............	.051	41.0	804

Of the dry land but approximately one half is arable and the population, were man theoretically deployed over all the pleasantly livable and arable land, would total 80 persons per square mile.

Reducing these figures further to comprehensible areas, on the basis of 80 inhabitants to the square mile of livable land, there would be 16 pleasant acres of land for each and every man, woman and child. However, the family unit is currently five and so, if mankind were completely deployed in family units over the "livable" dry land area, there would be 80 acres per family, or an area so large that, unless the family shelters were on hilltops, man need not be aware of the existence of others beyond the members of his immediate family group.

Man has evolved two unit measures of a mile: "statute" and "nautical."

The statute mile represents the earth's surface equivalent in feet to a longitudinal minute at the latitude of Greenwich, England,—Greenwich being, also, the starting point for the longitudinal reckoning of standard sun time. This statute or "legal" English mile was arbitrarily arrived at by England, and, with the zero longitude, was imposed by her on the world by means of her commercially dominant position as Queen of the Seas during the sailing era. It has been perpetuated by habit and the "necessity" of property title continuity. It must be irritating for the Japanese sailor-man always to find himself, as it were, in Row Z of the audience.

This lawyer's or "statute" mile was a "flop" at sea. The mathematical navigator had to have something much more actual and reliable to go to sea on. So he evolved the nautical mile, which is 6,080.20 feet in length and is equal to one sixtieth of a degree of a great circle of a sphere whose surface is equal in area to the area of the surface of the earth. This serves as an identical unit of measure on any great circle with but negligible error.

The nautical mile, which is 1.152 "statute" miles, was more scientifically determined, and is, therefore, more universally utilizable.

We Call It "Earth"

Although it may seem to be a digression at this point, it is nevertheless vitally significant to the comprehension of our book to state that a RATE of speed of *one nautical mile per hour* is known, at sea, as one *knot*. The name derives from the knots in the chip log line thrown over the stern of the old sailing ship whose run-out count, by means of a sand glass, determined the vessel's speed. It is improper, accordingly, to say "one knot per hour," which is like saying "one mile an hour per hour." The sailor says we are "making five knots at the present moment," or "we have covered ten nautical miles." We have no such speed or rate word relative to land miles, for land thinking has been relatively static and there has been no necessity for such a mobility word. On land, one measures in miles *or* hours. This has occasioned much mental confusion, in parlor talk about relativity, over the really very evident, from a rate viewpoint, integration of time and space. Among the first people on land to offer a rate word were the electrical engineers who evolved the DYNE (of the dynamo, dynamite, and dynamic family).

DYNE is a measure of force which, acting on a gram for 1 second, imparts to it a velocity of 1 centimeter per second. Result = 1 erg = 118 feet an hour. 1 dyne = the additional force exerted by a clock 30 ft. in diameter to carry a fly weighing 1/453 lb. on the tip of its "minute" hand for one second. The exact additional *work* done by the clock to carry the fly completely around its circumference on the tip of the big hand would be an ERG hour. Three billionths of 1¢ is the hydraulic power cost of this erg-hour fly transportation. This is typical of the currently fine degree of appraisal of work costs, through these *rate* integrations.

The layman knows little about this except that he must pay for his electric light at some obscure rate, but the power sellers were quick to use it in their exploitation of this scientific phenomenon.

The earth's circumference at the equator is 24,903 nautical miles, and its total surface is approximately 197 million square miles, of which 57½ million are dry land. As there are 33 million

57

square feet to a square nautical mile, or 189 billion cubic feet to a cubic mile, the earth has a volume of 260 billion cubic miles, and weighs 6½ thousand billion billion tons.

How does man stack up in size with all these volumes, weights and measures?

If all the earth's 2 1/3 billion people were to stand on one another's heads, they would form a chain 2,423,000 statute miles long, or nine complete chains to the moon; that is, they would reach to the moon and back four and one-half times. It would require only 50 such chains to reach the sun. Man is, therefore, empowered to a sense of *personal* contact with all astronomical bodies of the universe in addition to his earth.

Were all the members of the human family to gather together in one spot with a density equivalent to that of people jammed in a New York subway car aisle, they would cover an area of 139 square miles, which is approximately that of the Virgin Islands or Bermuda. Compare this with the 31,820 square miles of Lake Superior, the 121,000 square miles of the British Isles, and the 472,000 square miles of Hudson Bay!

The whole of our present human family—only one-ninth of which would be required, standing on one another's shoulders, to reach to the not-so-far-away moon, could readily be housed overnight on the little speck of earth known as New York City, if the floor space of all the buildings were utilized for the purpose, although, of course, they could not be serviced with the city's present facilities.

There are 10 billion cubic feet of people on earth (1/19 of a cubic mile). They weigh 115 million tons and would fill 111 Empire State Buildings. Yet if put under a gigantic hydraulic wine press, so that all the water and gas might be squeezed out of them, they could be compressed into one Empire State Building.

There are approximately 50 Panama Canals to a cubic mile and there are 317 MILLION cubic miles of ocean. The "nine chains to the moon" would make but a small splash in those 317 million cubic miles of water, which, however, the moon lifts tidally twice daily from a few inches to fifty feet. This earth-moon force, compared with the minute muscle power of the human army, indicates well the vast excess of man's POTENTIAL mind power over his brawn potential, for he already CONTEMPLATES harnessing at least a portion of this vast earth-moon gravitational force.

The 115 million tons of people on the earth have an annual turnover, by birth, growth and death, of approximately 2 1/3 million tons, with a net one million tons increase. This weight increase of human flesh and bones is equal to 14 S/S *Normandies* (the total weight of man being equal to 1400 *Normandies* or 287 Empire State Buildings). Although new human units weigh-in at only 25,000 tons, they are increased by the conversion of energy from the sun and other stars (directly or indirectly, but from no other source) to twenty times their original weighing-in weight by the time they reach maturity.

The source of power for the operation of all man's instruments, inanimate as well as animate, is sun and other star energy, direct or indirect, primarily through latent storage depots of multitudinous forms. All people are nurtured and energized by the ultraviolet and gamma rays, as well as by most powerfully penetrating, highly energized cosmic rays. The latter are responsible, apparently, for all electrical polarity changes in integral-with-life mechanisms upon the earth's surface, these polarity changes or ionizations, in turn, sponsoring the birth of all new species in plants, known as "sports." The laws of chance, change and animate evolution are here involved.

Scientific shelter design, therefore, is linked to the stars far more directly than to the earth. STAR-GAZING? Admittedly. But it is essential to accentuate the real source of energy and change in contrast to the emphasis that has always been placed on keeping man "down to earth." The teleologic dwelling designer MUST visualize his little shelters upon the minutely thin dust surface of the earth-ball, dust which is a composite of inert rock erosion, star dust, and vegetable compost, all direct star (sun) energy resultants.

Man, living in shelters scattered over the earth's dust film and energized and nurtured by the stars, has evolved, through self-research and the comprehension of the dynamics of his own mechanism, the phantom captain's extension mechanisms. Through the leverage gained by his INANIMATE INSTRUMENT EXTENSIONS OF SELF, he has attained an extended mechanical ability far in excess of his own integral mechanical and energy content ability.

Utilizing sun-energized "fire" to work his metals and exercising intelligent selection and dynamic experience, man has harnessed inanimate power (of sun-star origin) to operate his extended depersonalized mechanisms. Thus he has "set" his environment under increasing control by the ceaseless operation of his depersonalized inanimate-powered mechanisms and, concomitantly, has broken down the original limitations of time and space (days, nights and seasons). We repeat: All of this has been done through radiant energy from the stars.

By means of his harnessed inanimate servant, power, and his extended mechanisms, man has now explored, measured, and "set" under control much of his earth's crust and his once-"outside" universe, entirely *despite* the inertia of vanities, superstitions, exploitation, humpty dumpty moralities, laws and destructive selfishness. He has flown in his imagination-conceived, intelligence-wrought, de-selfed mechanisms at 72,000 feet above the earth's surface, almost three times the height of the earth's highest mountain, and sixty times higher than the Empire State Building. Yet this is an insignificant feat compared with flights and heights to be attained in the NOT FAR AHEAD "NOW," in new intelligence-to-be-wrought mechanisms of flight.

Most extraordinary of all man's extension activities—and far superior to his extension physically into his physical universe by physical means—is his mental extension, on the basis of observations of the dynamic progressions involved in his tangible mechanisms, inferring progression continuity beyond the tangible bands, into an AWARENESS OF and EXPERIENCE IN the ABSTRACT. I do not mean the abstract of humpty dumpty, academic philosophizing or mysticism, but the mathematically rationalizable abstraction of electrical phenomena representing the 66 octaves or bands of radiation which he has discovered despite their non-sensorial nature. Not only has he explored much of the realm of RADIATION, but he is using it and ACTUALLY THINKING IN IT. The phantom captain's extension into participation in events of exterior mechanism occurrence has provided an "actual" sense in the realm of radio in our younger men.

In this sense-extension into radiation lies the promise of man's eventually understanding all the secrets of life-in-time, which, down through the ages, have evoked an intuitive, mystical and superstitious awe. Miracles, once irrational, will be continually rationalized and set under service to man by man.

8

"E = Mc²" = Mrs. Murphy's Horse Power

Is it possible to arrive at an "a-b-c" visualization of the relationship of radiation to every day life? If we can do this, then the rationalizations of Einstein will have a bread-and-butter significance for all Murphys.

Let us try.

The unit of quantitative radiation measure is the PHOTON, which has mass momentum and energy like any particle when in motion, but when in collision has perfect elasticity, that is, there is no rebound loss (or energy loss) as a result of the collision.

The mass of a photon is inversely proportional to its wave length. If the number of photons in red light is doubled, the result is not an intenser red light but a violet light, with half the wave length of the red light. There are 10,000,000,000,000,000,-000,000,000,000,000 (that is, ten thousand quadrillion quadrillion) photons to an ounce of light. Photons retail at approximately 1½ billion dollars per lb. This price is to be compared with the current relatively paltry price of $418 per pound for gold (London market). No wonder the finance capitalist acquiesced to broad governmental abandonment of the gold standard of monetary evaluation. Finance capital makes "standard" for media of intercourse the element of most concentrate value, broadly available. Finance capital strategically moved into the "energy (or power) standard" some time ago and therein lies the essence of the fight today between democratic governments and finance for the control of "power" or "utilities."

Prices, of course, vary in direct proportion to monopoly. The monopolies for the marketing of scientifically harnessed products are, however, threatened on every hand by science itself. Should finance capital corner all of the hydraulic power sources, there are a thousand other "outs" for man. For instance, as

"$E = Mc^2$" = Mrs. Murphy's Horse Power

Crowther states in *The Great Design*, "The power poured out by the rays of the tropical sun upon a tennis court would suffice to run a 200 h.p. engine if we had the skill to collect and utilize it." Evolution has shown that whenever the need arises the art develops.

It is an interesting thought that gold hitherto unfunctionally (mechanically or structurally) used except in minor ways such as for tooth fillings, and which is now being governmentally hoarded in man-made mines of pure concentrate, may in the not distant future become a most highly functional element of *wireless power distribution*. Gold has the highest light (or any form of radiation) *reflective ability* of any element. Short wave radio beams can be reflected. Radio is radiant broadcasting of power or energy. Radio, reflected in concentrated beams, instead of being diffused to the universe may be received as power just as the sun's rays may be reflectively focused as hot spot power. Steam power engines have already been run on sun reflection by aluminum which has less reflective ability than gold. The United States may readily find in due course that it has unwittingly collected the specific means of complete overthrow of the power monopolies by its withdrawal of gold from circulation and that its ownership of this element will be the functional key to Democracy's wireless distribution of power.

The visible band of light waves ranges from radiations in the octave of eye-visible light from 1/50,000 to 1/100,000 of an inch. Invisible Roentgen-rays measure 1/1,000,000 of an inch, and there are more than two million times a million cosmic-ray waves to an inch. The width of heat waves may be as great as 1/100 of an inch and are perceptible to some eyes; the shortest radio "short-wave" is almost nine feet wide. Radio "long-waves" measure out to widths of a mile.

The speed of *light* is approximately 187,000 miles per second, the *fastest motion known*. Light travels 16 billion 86 million miles a day, or 5,871 billion 536 million miles in a year, the latter Time-space *distance* being known as a "light year." Light from the sun reaches the earth in 8½ minutes. Spiral nebulae have been observed as far off as 150 million "light years," i.e., approximately

900 billion billion (900,000,000,000,000,000,000,000) miles. Since first we made this notation of farthest star distance in July, 1935, a star three times farther out has been sighted and measured by Shapley. This was before the world's greatest giant lenses had even had time to cool. With the discoveries inevitably soon to be made, one can safely predict that our sum-total of knowledge will jump forward incredibly, if past far-flung achievements, growing out of astronomically attained knowledge, are taken as criteria.

"Radiation," says Crowther, "is characterized by its unique speed; *all* radiation travels in free space with the same high velocity, i.e., 187,200 miles a second, a velocity, if Einstein is to be believed, not attained or attainable by anything else." If this is so, the *speed of light is "TOP"* and is an actual unit measure of "perfect" speed, and, as such, is the practical yardstick of truth for the phantom captain's signaling operations.

A formula evolved by Einstein is today the most able means of astronomical eleocentral calculation. The data deriving from these calculations are used daily by electrical engineers, chemists and others in providing man's necessities. The data gleaned from a spectrum analysis of the stars are utilized in every day metallurgy and are contacted by Murphy, for example, in the metallurgical product, the automobile shift lever.

Says Einstein: "$E = Mc^2$," or

$$\text{"Energy equals mass times the speed of} \begin{cases} \text{light ray} \\ \text{x-ray} \\ \text{gamma ray} \\ \text{cosmic ray} \\ \text{infra-red} \\ \quad \text{ray} \\ etc. \end{cases} \text{squared,"}$$

or

"Energy $=$ mass $\times$ the volumetric speed of radiation, i.e., 33,369,000,000 volume miles per second."

"$E = Mc^2$" = Mrs. Murphy's Horse Power

This radiant energy SPEED is not only "TOP" speed relative to an infinity of individual speeds, but it is the only TRUE speed or TIME RATE. It is the speed of unfettered energy radiant, which we are sensorially aware of as "light." All other apparent speeds are but friction-retardments of perfect speed, seemingly lost energy being latently articulated, or stored, in frictional effects. All lesser rates of speed attained by the man-mechanism or by his extension mechanisms are relative to this "perfect" speed, which is PURE LIGHT-IN-TIME, infinitely radiant.

On one side of Einstein's formula, the universe is represented by a single symbol—a unit symbol—of infinity itself, i.e., energy complete ("E"), the unity sensorially unattainable, intuitively heralded, and certified to man only through mathematics. On the other side, is posited energy segregated as two symbols, representing the sensorial bi-polar limits of our "beginning-and-ending," "birth-and-death," "black-or-white," "male-or-female," "short-or-tall" world concept of thought and experience. These bi-polar limits are (1) *apparently* motionless mass (M), and (2) speed of radiation, squared (c^2). Speed is "squared" because, since it represents the *rate* of radiation expansion relative to radial space distance from the center in all potential diametric directions, it must be radiant at the square of the speed rate of any one measured radial speed.

To summarize this explanation of Einstein's equation, it is rather amusing to reproduce its expression telegraphically (for $10) by the writer in New York to Isamu Noguchi, the sculptor, in Mexico City, on receipt of the latter's startling wired request: "Please wire me rush Einstein's formula and explanation thereof."

EINSTEIN'S FORMULA DETERMINATION INDIVIDUAL SPECIFICS RELATIVITY READS "ENERGY EQUALS MASS TIMES THE SPEED OF LIGHT SQUARED" SPEED OF LIGHT IDENTICAL SPEED ALL RADIATION COSMIC GAMMA X ULTRA VIOLET INFRA RED RAYS ETC. ONE HUNDRED EIGHTY SEVEN THOUSAND MILES PER SECOND WHICH SQUARED IS TOP OR PERFECT SPEED

GIVING SCIENCE A FINITE VALUE FOR BASIC FACTOR
IN MOTION UNIVERSE. SPEED OF RADIANT ENERGY
BEING DIRECTIONAL OUTWARD ALL DIRECTIONS EX-
PANDING WAVE SURFACE DIAMETRIC POLAR SPEED
AWAY FROM SELF IS TWICE SPEED IN ONE DIRECTION
AND SPEED OF VOLUME INCREASE IS SQUARE OF SPEED
IN ONE DIRECTION APPROXIMATELY THIRTY FIVE
BILLION VOLUMETRIC MILES PER SECOND. FORMULA IS
WRITTEN LETTER E FOLLOWED BY EQUATION MARK
FOLLOWED BY LETTER M FOLLOWED BY LETTER C
FOLLOWED CLOSELY BY ELEVATED SMALL FIGURE
TWO SYMBOL OF SQUARING. ONLY VARIABLE IN
FORMULA IS SPECIFIC MASS. SPEED IS UNIT OF RATE
WHICH IS AN INTEGRATED RATIO OF BOTH TIME AND
SPACE AND NO GREATER RATE OF SPEED THAN THAT
PROVIDED BY ITS CAUSE WHICH IS PURE ENERGY
LATENT OR RADIANT IS ATTAINABLE. THE FORMULA
THEREFORE PROVIDES A UNIT AND A RATE OF PER-
FECTION TO WHICH THE RELATIVE IMPERFECTION OR
INEFFICIENCY OF ENERGY RELEASE IN RADIANT OR
CONFINED DIRECTION OF ALL TEMPORAL SPACE PHE-
NOMENA MAY BE COMPARED BY ACTUAL CALCULA-
TION. SIGNIFICANCE: SPECIFIC QUALITY OF ANIMATES
IS CONTROL WILLFUL OR OTHERWISE OF RATE AND
DIRECTION ENERGY RELEASE AND APPLICATION NOT
ONLY TO SELF MECHANISM BUT OF FROM-SELF-
MACHINE DIVIDED MECHANISMS. RELATIVITY OF ALL
ANIMATES AND INANIMATES IS POTENTIAL OF ESTAB-
LISHMENT THROUGH EINSTEIN FORMULA.

The bi-polar symbols on the right side of the equation represent complementary phenomena, in different octaves. Mass (matter expressed in terms of density and specific gravity) is radiant,
but at so relatively slow a rate that it impinges within a band
recognizable by man's sensorial mechanism. As isolated by the
Einstein formula, mass represents frictional imperfection, cohesively gravitational through friction produced "static" electricity,
apparent in retarded speed "form." Actually, mass is the only
variable inasmuch as unit energy and its unit speed represent an
identical unity.

Einstein's formula, explaining as it does imperfection and interference in terms of diffused but non-lost energy, provides a specific means for the scientific measurements and rationalization of all life phenomena. This formula quite interestingly represents, as a mathematical explanation of LIFE, what the Christian religion attempted intuitively and philosophically to express in name-words: GOD (the father in heaven) = SON and HOLY GHOST (on earth).

What has this formula to do with Mrs. Murphy? Precisely what energy has to do with her,—EVERYTHING. No energy— no Mrs. Murphy, either as the mother, or as Mrs. Murphy the prime mover. It is going to do for her what the "Holy Ghost" and prayer could never do.

Tell me, Mrs. Murphy, why you parrot the propaganda phrases about "Gov't spending," and "Who is going to pay for it?" and "It can't go on," and "We're saddling it upon the next generation," when all energy and growth and wealth emanate from the stars and energy is pouring down upon us? Energy = potential wealth. Energy is actual wealth if its rate of conversion through work is rapid enough to stem natural chaos and leave a residue of arbitrarily spendable time. Wealth does not come from the bank. It is not gold. Man's moral necessity to "work" is highly valid and ∴ his essential religion.

Nine million U. S. families, or 30% of the population (considered by some as cause for despair, by others as at least a sign of man's portending emancipation) either have no income or are on relief, displaced by an hundred-fold-man-productive efficiency of machines driven by an aggregate 46 million h.p. motor, in turn energized by a 49 million h.p. inanimate hydraulic "water wheel" generating plant, supplemented by plants fueled with coal, gas, oil, *et cetera*, providing an additional approximately equal amount of horse power.

The electric power furnished by hydraulic power stations is almost completely inanimate as to source, but coal and other fuel power cannot be so considered inasmuch as coal mining is done at the vital expense of the miner. The miner is the human family's most abject slave today, his slavery being necessitated by the inefficient use of available hydro-electric power, and the distance limitations between the hydraulic power source and the use requirements. The gap between, however, is daily being lessened.

Were it not for this inefficient use and the distance limitations, hydraulic power could currently displace three-fourths of the man-power of the whole population. It is to be remembered, also, that additional inanimate hydro-electric horse power is constantly being harnessed to keep pace with the construction of thousands of tons of production mechanisms of even higher manifoldings.

The capacity of presently installed electricity production plants in the United States is 37 million kilowatts. If run at their maximum capacity, they would produce 888 billion kilowatt hours per annum. However, only an average of 100 billions are being produced annually, or 12% of the total capacity. This represents an operation of 2½ hours per day per dynamo, utilized approximately as follows:

> 12%—domestic
> 7%—commercial
> 2%—municipal
> 6%—rails
> 73%—industrial

It is admitted that the running of plants 24 hours a day would be inadvisable, if not impossible. First, it allows of no breakdown. Secondly, more than one third of the total dynamos or engines are designed with an emergency load safety factor and are directly connected with manufacturing plants which normally operate at less than peak load. In fact, since the operation of dynamos is directly proportional to the production hours of the plant per annum, this is the main factor in the reduction from 100% to a 10.5% current output of kilowatt hours.

Another reason for the present small ratio of production is our as yet limited ability to distribute centrally produced power efficiently to distances reaching all potential users.

With EFFICIENT use and with new adequate methods of power transportation, the 123 billion kilowatt hours per annum producible by water power alone in the U. S. will be sufficient to care for all the industrial, rail and municipal requirements of the U. S. Mechanisms are already in use and improved units are in process of design to power individually all decentralized dwellings and plants outside the scope of already wired suburbia. The latter will continue to be supplied from a central station since most of the domestic consumption occurs at night, balancing the output of the central station whose industrial peak occurs during the day.

A fascinating insight into the *per capita* benefit that will accrue, when water power is efficiently utilized and capably distributed to serve man, is to be had by comparing the horse-power output by man, unaided by electrical power, and the additional power that he can command through his inanimate slave, electricity.

HORSE POWER is a term devised to represent mechanical power super-to-man and is not the actual energy-conversion work-ability of a horse. One horse power is equivalent to 33,000 foot-pounds-per-minute. A foot-pound-per-minute signifies the energy or "work" required to lift one pound one foot vertically in the space of one minute. One horse power represents the energy ("work") required to lift one pound to a height of 33,000 feet in one minute.

A man weighing 175 pounds with a 25-pound load (a total 200-pound load including himself) would have to climb vertically 165 feet in one minute in order to develop one horse power of energy. Since 165 feet is approximately equivalent to a 16-story building, obviously a man cannot develop one horse power. An agile, energetic 100-pound boy with no extra load can run upstairs three stories, or 30 feet, in one minute, thus developing, for that moment, 1/10 of 1 horse power. He is not, however, consistently able longer to maintain this speed of climbing.

Numerous attempts have been made to estimate the horse power that an average American worker can generate on an all-year-average basis, in the course of which various interesting and useful facts have been ascertained. It is well known, for instance, that a miner can sustain an actual average of continuous picking at rock-face of six hours a day, five days a week. It is known, also, that a well trained army of young men, carrying a 70-pound pack, can march 25 miles a day, although 20 miles is a high average for the general army's daily march. However, it is next to impossible to calculate just how many inches of elevation the average soldier accomplishes, step by step, as he vaults forward on his legs (walking being minute pole-vaulting). Hence, in order to arrive at a conclusion regarding man's sustainable horse power ability, we must find some method of estimating his load carrying ability in an upward direction.

Since man cannot walk up a vertical wall, let us imagine that he is climbing the highest negotiable grade, i.e., one on which his feet will not slip backward and which he can negotiate without having recourse to climbing with both legs and arms, a slower method of leverage than with legs alone. The energy expended by a man climbing a ladder might be calculated, but there is no ladder tall enough for an all day climb. A satisfactory test is that of hill climbing with a pack.

Whether energy expenditure be measured by direct vertical load lifting, or by lifting of the load with a geared or pulley-block mechanism, the resultant figure is equivalently proportional to the energy expended except that, in the latter method, there is a slight loss of energy due to energy consumption by friction between the reciprocal parts of the pulley mechanism. The use of geared mechanism reduces the specific amount of energy expended during a moment of time, but greater time or distance of motion is required at the energy application end of the mechanism. Therefore, climbing a negotiable grade represents the gear ratio most efficiently adaptable to our "work" or energy conversion problem.

The importance of arriving at a man's "work" or energy conversion rate is that the determination of the means of accomplishing work with the least energy and time loss is the primary need of the day, and is, therefore, the goal of all scientist-artists, and the criterion of efficiency amplification is unimplemented man.

It is estimated that the average American worker, a composite of man, woman, and helping youth, averaging 150 lbs. in weight, can, throughout the year, negotiate daily a 50 lb. pack 3000 feet up a walkable mountain slope from sea level, allowing six hours to the average day, five days to the week, and two weeks yearly for illness or vacation.

This means that the average American engaged in work of any kind, at home or afield, can consistently develop a total of .172 horse power per "work" diem. This would be called, scientifically, .172 horse-power hours a day. In a year, the 90 million American potential workers in the home, field or factory, could each develop 43 horse-power-hours-per-annum and 1290 horse power hours in their average of 30 years of work ability. Converting horse power figures to kilowatts and kilowatt hours, for the purpose of comparing man with his inanimate power slave, electricity, we have:

$$748.5 \text{ watts} = 1 \text{ horse power}$$
$$\text{or}$$
$$1 \text{ kilowatt} = 1 \ 1/3 \text{ horse power.}$$

We find that man can develop .13 k.w. hour a day for an average day of 4.3 sustained, full straining, working hours in a year of 365 days. This .13 k.w. hour per diem represents directly the rate of energy conversion by the man machine from food, air, water and sun. This *average* toiling "man" develops 47.5 k.w. hours of work in a 365-day year, or 1423 k.w. hours of work in his life, accepting 30 years as the average work-life period.

The average American family comprises slightly more than four persons, i.e., father, mother, and two children. Let us assume—for the purpose of scientific computation—that the two children together, helping, can perform one unit of computable sustained work. Multiplying the 47.5 k.w. hours of one man by three, we arrive at a family energy ability of 142.5 k.w. hours of work per annum in the U. S.

Compare this potential output with what man consumes from outside sources. This same family consumes 638 k.w. hours of electricity per year for illumination, refrigeration, cooking, radio playing, ironing, vacuum cleaning, *et cetera*, all brought into the home to serve mankind. This is his energy consumption from electricity and does not include the energy developed and utilized in his automobile or group transportation or by his furnace, *et cetera*. Actually, the family consumes very much more electrical energy, not alone because of the power utilized in industry to manufacture consumable goods, use instruments and services for man, but, also, the power expended behind that power to make the instruments and provide the services. The power utilized in the category of "tools-to-make-tools" is vastly greater than that consumed in the category of industrial end-product production. The domestic consumption of power is only 12% of the total power produced, 88% being utilized by "industrial activities," "services," and in the "tools-to-make-tools" category.

Compare the 4 1/7 billion k.w. hours of work per annum which all the 29 million families in the U. S. can produce at top if none are bogged down by sickness, discouragement, worry, *et cetera*, with the 92 billion k.w. hours now being produced by stationary dynamos, one half of which represent water-power energy conversion and one half primarily coal energy conversion (which combined could produce over 800 billion k.w. hours if run 24 hours daily). It becomes apparent that 11 inanimate power slaves and 11 fuel power slaves are currently serving each individual. In order to produce fuel for power, a man would have to be taken from the family so that the comparison is not fair. So let us confine ourselves to potential hydro-electric power.

If all available water power were fully harnessed and utilized, there would be conservatively 123 billion k.w.h. annual output, and man would have 29 inanimate slaves at his command, or 87 inanimate slaves per family of three working people. Remember this is in his home, only, and does not include the 85 inanimate horses standing ready outdoors to pull his chariot, *et cetera*.

Man is highly demanding of his inanimate slaves and expects them to work continuously day and night, not just 4 1/3 hours a day. This is not inhumane, as inanimate slaves are truly inanimate, having no feeling. Man will, therefore, when water power is fully harnessed, be able to divide his 29 inanimate slaves into shifts of 5.2 inanislaves for 4 1/3 hours each per diem, so that he will have 24 hours continuous service from them. 90,000,000 potential U. S. workers would each have continually at hand to support them in their work, 5.2 inanislaves on duty 24 hours a day, and every household would have 15.5 inanislaves continuously on the job all day. They would be slaves requiring no feeding, clothing or sheltering, who could work at sustained speed with the utmost precision since their work is articulated through inanimate mechanisms being made ever more precise.

This is as if the total U. S. animate population had a 2,610,-000,000 inanimate population working for it domestically,—the latter a greater number than the world's current population of 2,300,000,000, of which the U. S. represents but 7%. It is, then, as if through science the people of the U. S. are enjoying by conquest of the mind an ease of living equivalent to their having conquered by the sword and enslaved the whole animate world to serve them. Obviously, the new way is better: world empire without human cost and with a clear conscience.

The three main factors by which man may determine ultimate WORK satisfaction are:

$$\text{Available} \begin{cases} \text{ENERGY} \\ \text{TIME} \\ \text{PRECISION of} \\ \quad \text{a. Measure} \\ \quad \text{b. Articulation.} \end{cases}$$

The foregoing considerations of U. S. man's current energy conversion ability (his ability to convert energy into work), not alone by his direct personal machine but in 29 times that degree by his mechanistic extensions of himself, are emphasized as the most extraordinary characteristics of man as differentiated from any other "living" organism. This unique extension characteristic of man has been demonstrated to the extent of his being able to think-and-use mechanisms in media, only 6% of which he is sensorially aware, which leads us to an interesting consideration of what the "dollar bill" for which he now "works" represents.

73

I maintain it to be, on last analysis, Mr. Einstein's "E." All man has basically as wealth are his: (1) Energy Conversion Ability, (2) Time, and (3) Precision.

A dollar bill in time to come will be recognized as a time-captured and saved unit of energy by man. Mr. Einstein, therefore, has provided Mrs. Murphy with a universal standard of effort interpolation in the nature of which she is invulnerable to exploitation.

9

Dollarability

Money was devised primarily as an abstract means by which man might convert his specific-work (energy conversion) into the acquisition of those products of the work of others necessary to his completeness of growth.

The more industrialized man has become in harnessing his environment for mutual inter-service, protection, routine and growth, the more specialized—that is, the more scientifically coöperative—he has also become.

The main difference between the agrarian world, with its dominant animate slavery, and the industrial world, which is characterized by the inanimate servitude of abstract power, is that, in the former man could—and did—essentially consume and support himself out of the direct products of his work, whereas today's industrial worker could not possibly survive by the consumption of the glass bulb turned out by the machine he tends, or of an electric winding.

In the agrarian era of local intercourse, man could barter his surplus product directly with the local producer of other necessities. Money, as an abstract interpolation medium, was unnecessary. Such money as was then in circulation functioned as a means of product conversion in the export, by the landlord, of the surplus products of his serfs. In foreign lands these were converted into tangible forms of intrinsic wealth for the landlord's account.

In the current industrial era, the "dollar" is an utter necessity for the worker in the interpolation of his specialized work into essential goods and services; not, however, the metallic dollar, which is a relic from the buccaneering age when exporting landlords had little knowledge of the value of goods to be received in exchange for their produce. They were trading, as have, also, frontiersmen, even up to now, with unknown people and toward whom they had not by experience established credit. In the course of early trading, a metallic money was developed as a concentrate medium of exchange and a *belief* grew up as to its potentially direct value, which in due course was improperly termed "credit." Money, metallically, was relatively the safest medium of temporary value maintenance, being almost non-corrosive and non-substitutable due to its rarity. Moreover, because of its high concentration it was easily stowable and defendable.

This metallic characteristic of money is no longer a primarily essential part of the internal U. S. dollar. Not only is the industrial worker of America willing to interpolate his work stint into a paper dollar—an intrinsically worthless medium—but actually prefers it to a metallic dollar, since he credits every worker in the United States with an understanding of, and belief in, the integrity of coöperation that obviates a metallic specie in favor of the far more efficiently transportable "greenback." He goes even further. He writes his own dollars in the form of checks, signifying integrity in a still higher degree.

In the course of his employment by an industrial establishment, the American worker often receives a check for his services which says, in effect, that he has industrially done his stint on the basis of so many hours of precise energy conversion, the value of his length of service being at least theoretically amplified in direct proportion to the technical nicety of his precision-ability in the process of energy conversion.

This check, which represents an account of his work, is usually deposited in an accounting-storage for subsequent conversion into whatever services and goods he needs within the limits of this storage. Very often the check is immediately exchanged by the "bank" for dollar bills, for efficient reasons, a few of which we shall relate.

If a worker's accounted total of work is small and his requirements minimal, the individual value of the goods and services of which he is in immediate need is low, the true value being *bas-*

Dollarability

ically determined by the quantum of converted energy involved in the product of service, despite popular misconceptions of value due to a "royalty"-to-"royalty" or "profit" superimposition.

Coins of small denomination represent a particularly useful work conversion medium for the individual in the interpolation of work into low value goods and services since cash sales minimize "overhead." Such coins, however, seldom represent the real intrinsic, or open market, value of the metal out of which they are stamped; for instance, a dollar in pennies may be worth only about 15¢ as copper metal. Coins of small denomination are denominationally valid only by *popular credit*. As fractional units of paper dollars (by man's habit of thinking) they are so quickly and therefore so efficiently handled that their use eliminates the costly accounting necessarily involved in the acquisition of minor goods and services through the medium of a paper check.

It costs the accounting agent ("bank") approximately 5¢ to handle a check. This charge is now in process of being shifted directly to the accountee in various systems such as the "master checking account." In these plans a balance need not be kept by the depositor, who simply pays 5¢ for every check or sum of cash deposited to, and 5¢ for every check drawn against his account. Should this practice become general the banking system's necessity of making hidden-from-the-populace profit for existence would be eliminated.

Accounting is quite as definitely an energy conversion process as is any other physical work, involving our three "satisfaction" factors: Energy available, Time, and Precision. It may be accomplished efficiently in relation to large operations and highly complicated energy conversion problems, where there is an uniform sequence of events permitting the use of mechanical calculators, but it cannot be efficiently utilized in highly variable, small transactions in which the whimsy and opinions of men are involved.

Whim is most specifically involved at the present moment in the matter of WHERE and WHEN and into WHAT man is going to convert small portions of his time-energy credits, particularly in the field of low value products and services, for the acquisition of which empirical fractional metallic equivalents are efficiently essential. For instance, in the 5¢ and 10¢ store where, seeing a lamp shade or writing pad for only 10¢ which he "might" want he "whimsicalizes" his small credit of 10¢ for one or the other,—or for another beer.

The fact that exploitation of this naïve, whimsical intercoursing and trans-acting of man, granted a job, or a "relief" sense of any security still exists in "credit-storage-establishments," does not minimize the importance of the factual trend *from* metallic specie *to* abstracted credit certificates—progressive ephemeralization of the expanding universe.

This exploitation confusion is due to the physical (though otherwise non-identical) relationship between metallic money—efficiently still necessary to "small changing"—and the distinctly different international trading requirements for actual metal not only in ounces and pounds but often in tons of gold and silver bullion to be stored in continental banks as collateral in the international export-import trade.

Such export collateral is still necessitated by dissimilarity of languages, especially money languages (remembering that our definition of language involves sympathetic understanding), and the numerical and symbological variance of the accounting systems of various nations, just as in earliest trading days. The difference between Roman and Arabic numerals provided "cause" for profitable misunderstanding. None of the nations whose monetary policies are locally dominated by self-interested metallic bullion holders has, as yet, signified its willingness to standardize, or, as they call it, "stabilize" in relation to any other nation. Why? Because they do not as yet have to, by virtue of any laws of physics, except those of ballistics, and there are fortunes to be made overnight in the guessing game fluctuations developed by world-wide important "chance" events. Among such factors are obviously the vagaries of season, storms,—a million "Chinks" drowned by a flood—which make international stabilization almost impossible. Nationalism itself is the big "fly in the ointment."

Dollarability

There is still current a scarcity of rare metals with which to cover the volume of international export and import trade. This scarcity can be increased in any locality by shipment of the metals from any one country to another by those who own the dominant "units." Wherefore the international money game is one of chess playing, bullion being the pawn. The great variable occurs through an admixture of interlocking directorates who have their hands in all four pockets, both sides and back and front, money and commerce, manufacture and transport. When one of these players finds that he has goods to sell and the buyer has too little bullion to handle the trade, the former is in the market to buy bullion. When both have made a profit through the transaction the bullion which they induced into the trade, provided either has no further goods immediately for sale, is put on the market, the collateralizer becoming a seller.

International metallic money traders are the direct descendants of the parasitic underwriters of the buccaneering might-makes-right fighting world of old. It is quite likely that none of its current representatives will succumb to stabilization without an actual fighting showdown. Searching analysis reveals that the current militaristic world activity is specifically fanned by, and indirectly originated by an intramural "big shot" fight over metallic money's stabilization dominance among the advocates of divergent policies in the matter of exploitation of man's needs by virtue of the legalized status of their intermediary.

The international metallic money group early usurped, through their feudal dominance of workers, the credit storage mechanisms (banks) of the workers. They are now fighting to retain their hold on these because there is an intrinsic-wealth turnover value in the utilization, for their own gain, of the workers' credit while it remains stored with them. Bankers use people's credit when entrusted to them with no more moral equity than a storage warehouse proprietor has to use for himself the automobiles and furniture of people stored with him.

The metallic money bankers have, by dint of the *obscurity* requisite to the pursuance of their legalized and tradition-"honored" racket, blinded the populace to a true interpretation of the meaning and all-mighty power of their dollar or work unit equivalents. Given the opportunity to understand the truth, the populace will no longer be willing to have their banks run as they are at present, but will infinitely prefer that the government run them; i.e., they will run them themselves, emancipated entirely from management by metallic money racketeers who, as "compensation" for their services, assign to themselves a credit "take-out" of some 10% of all that the workers produce. In full consideration of these facts, the workers may *insist* on government management of their credit storage and credit interpolation with a fixed overhead charge through affixed stamps.

When government handling of personal credit accounts is incepted (it has already been willy-nillied into taking over the bulk of major utility, R.R., and realty credit handling) an efficient means for the elimination of "small change" transactions will unquestionably and inevitably have to be evolved, certainly at least for the conversion of an individual's work into goods and services of immediate true necessity.

Irrespective of the myriad of trade names for specific food products that have won preferment through poetic and dramatic advertising, every man, woman and child can—and should—consume a specific average amount of standard foods per annum.

It would be an highly efficient move on the part of the government, as the representative of a specific number of people for whom goods and services in satisfaction of every essential need are now produced, and are continuously more abundantly producible, to accredit *basic* rations on Bureau of Standards classifications. This would obviate the multitudinous accounting intricacies of the present method, with a high supercharge for legal enforcement involved in the rightful acquisition by the people of essential goods and services produced by the one for the other. It would eliminate, also, the daily three trips to the grocer's, if he is near, and the once-a-week trip if he is far away. This elimination could be accomplished by the bold stroke of automatically accrediting each and every human being with the acquisition-ability of those essentials of survival and growth which have attained "plenitudinous" status—grade "B" milk, for instance—just as the government has already accredited primary education with a bookkeeping system reduced to simple arithmetic. There is no problem in education of necessity to account for the high "take" of the student who is a glutton for knowledge against the child who eschews it. Similarly, the food balance would be maintained because no stomach is so big that it could upset the credit system.

Lest such an accounting efficiency provoke stagnation and retrogression, the government need only reserve the right of decision of placement of monthly, or other progressive time-unit contracts, with the industrial groups competing for the provision of staples. The basis of arriving at such decisions would be that of competitive bidding for the furnishing of the required goods and services, relative to an itemization of standards scientifically determined.

It would be even more preferable if the individuals of the populace, having been accredited at their central bank, be allowed to place their own contracts monthly at the local A. & P. or Reeves, *et cetera*, thus indicating an authentic vote as to the quality of service provided by the suppliers, whom the government will accredit centrally at their bank on the basis of *per capita* contract placement.

This credit of the people, by the people, and for the people, through the medium of government (themselves) could be inaugurated and maintained without changing the present industrial and banking systems. It would be necessary only to eliminate the monetary *entrepreneurs* from these inevitable basic functions.

It is not suggested that this method of accounting simplification should supersede the present procedure of credit-storing by individuals of EXCESS credits EARNED by them from their industrial service by reason of ingenuity and super-to-minimum-stint activity.

This is not a new plan. The government already acts similarly in the matter of awarding monthly contracts for the furnishing of goods and services to government establishments, such as the Army, Navy, Panama Canal, *et cetera*. It does not do this, however, as a blanket United States contract. The awards are made locally by the supply officers at the Brooklyn Navy Yard, Boston, Pearl Harbor, and elsewhere, which allows for adjustment to local conditions and meritorious branch service. This system has not been confined simply to governmental contracting. It has been demonstrated in partial effect and to a high degree of efficiency in the great coöperatives of England and the Scandinavian countries, where the accounting efficiency, however, has been fouled by the fact that it is not an all-people's accounting, which would eliminate the actual mark-up of the individual item of every bill of goods currently adding 2¢ to every loaf of bread.

This system is not to be confused with the "bread lines" of the purely communistic meal ticket because, as advocated, this plan would apply in the first place only to basic food stuffs and not to the caviare of the scarcity category, and, secondly, it would promote competition among the purveyors. That there is a great surge toward such a system is demonstrated not only in the ever normal granary types of solution of mal-distributed products, but also in the several thousand coöperatives that have mushroomed up in the U. S. and which have been attempting to organize consumers, but which will never be highly effectual as compared to the efficiency involved in the foregoing governmental, all people's, energy-credit interpolating procedure.

At present the value of super-to-stint service is appraised haphazardly by operating managers who are in a dilemma or "on the mat" between *enterpreneuring*-for-unearned-increment directors, on the one hand, the workers on another, and, kicking them in the pants from behind, the engineers and scientists indicating increased efficiencies of operation to be obtained by the continual change of process, instrument, management and distribution.

These "on the mat" industrial operating managers are controlled, through fear of job loss, by the "directors" of profit extraction and are dealt with, by the latter, also on an OPINION basis. "Directors" are continually of the OPINION that greater profits should be produced, and no improvements instituted. This attitude makes it generally impossible for managers to listen to the scientific rationalization of ingenious and willing-to-work, super-to-minimum-stint people. It is impossible for them to listen to and rationalize (ratio-analyze) the efficiencies urged upon them in the name of science or equity of worker-credit.

The fact remains, however, that improvements of service and product ARE reducible to a *specific energy conversion* terminology. Furthermore, it is not only possible but highly efficient and facile to determine, in advance, the precise energy and time-saving involved in any improvement of industrial operation. This is already being done, in a degree, by industry in the flow sheets of its research departments.

Were managers relieved of the necessity of justifying their decisions to the OPINION of directors, they could calculate scientifically, in terms of precise time and energy saving, the specific value of the ideas evolved by any person, whether or not the latter is fortified by an academic diploma.

In this connection, the therblig studies of the Link Belt Company are important. A therblig is the lowest common denominator of human mechanical motion, the therbligs are now actually in use for basic "cost" determination in many scientifically managed industrial establishments.

A mechanical study was made of the human structure (somewhat as in our phantom captain analysis). So many "cranes," *et cetera*, were catalogued, together with the limiting swings and balance of the cranes, for checking up, turning, addressing work to external machines for forming, polishing, *et cetera*. Slow motion camera studies showed whether the total energy available was being efficiently articulated or whether the "crane" under consideration was describing an inefficient arc further complicated by interspersed unnecessary muscular contractions and expansions.

It was thus possible to determine what the simplest crane *motion* could be and how much energy it would require. Consequently it was possible to demonstrate the efficient motion to the worker in such a manner that any worker, after two days of learning, irrespective of educational advantage (provided he was not deformed), could perform the operation within the specific energy and time equation indicated by the advanced theoretical analysis. It was found that, after two days' experience, there was virtually no variation between the performance by a worker who had been skilled in one of various arts and the man of no tutoring or skill, when reduced to this "simplest" operation. The flow of work was then composed of these completely segregated simplest motions.

This system, which was developed for simplification, for the safety of the worker, and to provide every physical worker with an EQUAL ADVANTAGE to any other, involved the employment, if properly followed, of a vast number of workers, due to the multiple segregation. It has never been widely applied, however, as it was "too theoretical" for profit directed management. It did not constitute a "speed up" of the individual, but was a natural, rhythmic and safe motion that did not deplete the worker's energy storage or mental balance.

A further purpose of the therblig studies was the idea that such a system, if carried out in full, would make it possible to inter-account work activity, not only between departments of an industry but between whole industries, with the same accuracy that costs can be determined where inanimate electric power and machines alone are concerned. The cost could be determined with the accuracy with which power production itself is now determined: to the millionth of a cent. Such a system would automatically provide a yardstick of basic energy conversion for every worker and every product cost throughout the world, and furthermore would completely segregate his *super-to-stint* activity which emanates individually from his abstract or initiative and rationalizing activity.

These therblig studies are of true scientific determination and are in no way to be confused with the Bedaux or "B" (B-damned) system or any other of the speed-up or piece-work schemes that have been promoted for the specific purpose of higher profit.

Dollarability

The therblig unit is a basic motion unit beyond which no speed-up can be made. It is something like Einstein's "c^2," i.e., TOP *efficient* speed. Therefore no speed-up system could be imposed upon the therblig *studies*. The latter bring us to the determination of a basic physical work unit, involving no invention or mental resourcefulness. These units make up into a yardstick or basic rate in the terms of which the worker's TRUE dollar is interpolated: "A dollar an hour" for basic energy conversion into work without recourse to initiative, which anyone can perform if scientifically instrumented and instructed.

No legislative peg of minimum wages and maximum hours, even on an annual pay basis, can be of any value to the worker until his dollar is standardized upon this unit physical energy conversion rate, instead of upon a basic metal unit, which unit in turn is subject to scarcity manipulation and to monopoly. Individual "work" belongs to all men, is in the plenitudinous category, and cannot be taken from them except by a political system that countenances slavery in one form or another. The democratic theory is the only political theory thus far advanced that does not, on the one hand, countenance "slavery" and yet, on the other, is complementary to "industry."

Once this basic rate of conversion-of-energy to products is established, then super-to-stint activity of the individual with initiative can come into account to be reckoned and rewarded very specifically as mechanical inventions that may be demonstrated to convert energy by inanimate mechanics into work in a more efficient manner than already demonstrated in the particular field involved.

Compensation for such activities as acting or playwriting, seemingly foreign to the production of essentials, will always be determined on the basis of pure demand and supply, or by acclaim.

When the basic pure physical energy activity, as above related, is compared with the supplying of man's basic survival essentials, a balance sheet can easily be taken off which will certify the opportunity of work to all healthy people. It is sheer guess to estimate what the basic annual stint requirements to pay off annual basic supply would be, but it may be reasonably hazarded to be in the nature of a month's service *per annum*.

This area of man's occupation in production and consumption IS socializable, but only by straight engineering and science. All other activities of man are super-to-stint, to be rewarded, either by mechanical analysis or by popular acclaim. If you happen to be Mrs. Gotrocks, and think you have plenty of dollars to avoid basic stint, okay. This is not a social system involving tearing the top down. If you have enough dollars to last the rest of your life, fine! This system does, however, allow the nomination of a dollar on which all people of the world can be self-supporting—a basic rate to which all other service is not only relative, but relative-plus.

Now, what is our true dollar?

We have already determined that a worker can develop .13 k.w.h. a day. What is the electrical production industry's charge for a k.w.h.? It has been charging all that the traffic will bear. But the k.w.h. costs the electrical industry delivered within a 150 mile radius of the dynamo approximately $.006, when produced from fuels, and approximately $.003, when produced hydraulically.

In view of the fact that the 30 watts per hour maximum life-average energy-conversion-to-work by man from sun and stars, direct and indirect, is worth, on the basis of 1938 U. S. hydraulic power cost ($.003 per k.w.h.) but $.000906 per hour, and his day's work $.00039, year's work $.1425, and his total lifetime's work $4.30, it is obvious that an hourly wage rate must be established, which, in addition to man's energy output, will compensate him for self and mechanical extension control ability, responsibility of parenthood, and for his legacy of literacy, knowledge in general, and civilized attitude toward voluntary coöperation.

If we adhere to today's intuitively integrated "dollar" value as a unit, in order to evolute instead of revolute, we find, after calculating the total cost of man's arriving at the age of mature service and of maintaining himself thereafter during his 30 years of social usefulness, that, in order to "break even" man must receive a $1 an hour BASE-WAGE. How do we arrive at this?

We will make an appraisal of all work and time-energy conversion cost involved in spontaneous family continuity based not only on work done for others for money, which is all that is now legally accounted in U. S. "income," but upon home duties, farm activities, voluntary direct prosocial activity, and self preparation for greater service.

It now costs U. S. society approximately $10,000 to nurture and educate the average child until the age of 18. This not only includes his education, but all other costs, direct or indirect, as, for example, food, clothing, shelter, as well as the paving of the streets the child walks to and from school upon and the policing and lighting of the same. On reaching maturity the average U. S. human will, at present writing, have 30 years' expectancy in which to refund society for this investment in him. Each average individual, therefore, must amortize himself at $333 per annum. (Succeed by intelligent design in increasing "expectancy" and the rate will decrease proportionately.)

The amortization for two parents is currently	$666.00 per annum
Cost of maturing 2 children, at the "now" rate of $10,000 each for 18 years (This figure might be greatly reduced with increased efficiency of end result by television education)	1110.00 " "
Maintenance of the parents, including shelter, food, clothing, industrial and government services in general, at $1500 each (decency standard)	3000.00 " "
	$4776.00

87

The average American family consists of the parents and two children. In accounting the work of the family, the mother's labor in the home must be included, as equal to the father working either at home or for someone else, in the pertinent aspects of energy, ingenuity, time, and precision involved, as must also that of the children as helpers during non-educational and play periods, the work of the two latter being assumed to be the equivalent of one adult. This makes a total of three adult equivalents. The average energy-work of an adult per day in a life-time's span, as we have previously determined, is 4.3 hours a day, 365 days to the year, a total of 1570 hours each per annum. Three adults would represent 4710 hours of work a year. If we will acknowledge that man's TRUE CAPITAL is his TIME and that his true dollarability is an objectivized hour of that time and not a chip of metal in somebody else's pocket or in a Kentucky mountain vault, then a true hour accounting of average intelligent effort, farm, factory, or fireside, would adequately balance "costs" as now determined by our abstracted fear-longing-and-credit poised dollars which total up to $4710 minimum annual family output.

If Murph or his wife work "out" on a 40 hour-week basis, they can accomplish their 1570 hour social-stint in 39 weeks and take a 3 months annual vacation; if they work on a 30 hour-week basis 52 weeks will be consumed, ergo no vacation. If they use their "bean" a bit one or two months a year of "out work" might get them "by."

There are many $50,000 a year executives in the U. S. If they were paid at the hydraulic power rate, they would have to develop an efficient energy-management-ability of 16,500,000 k.w.h. per annum, or the equivalent of a 2000 k.w. hydro-electric turbo-generator, running 24 hours a day for a year, or a 20,000 k.w. generator on the basis of the present running time of power equipment. Our $50,000 executive, *granted he is worth this,* is the equivalent, as an energy-articulation-motor, of the 4 combined 1000 horse power motors of the Boeing

Dollarability

"Flying Fortress" when turning-up at full roaring speed, hypothetically engaged in a non-stop flight of 110 trips around the world at the equator within one year. "Some" executive! Yet Mr. Ford is probably demonstrating 10 times this power management ability ('Tho, allowing it to compound, he has never "cashed in").

Compare this power interpretation with our overall-accounted $4710 a year by-guess-by-God-and-by-love work of the average family, or with the $1569 of the man of the family if he is hiring out at the rate of $1 an hour for "pickanshovel, passthebuck labor." At that rate of pay, as an energy articulating mechanism, he is at least equivalent to an 80 h.p. Ford motor running 24 hours a day for a year; while as a moron-prime-mover he *or the executive* would be but the equivalent of a ½ candle power flash light bulb glimming for a year.

10 million unemployed American workers considered only as tread-mill power producers, Roman galley slaves, or pyramid stone-elevators, sum totally as a team of 10 million, are but the mechanical power equivalent of a 67 h.p. or "little Ford" motor running 24 hours a day for a year. En masse, as pure might, the 10 million are worth less than one man at our base rate of a dollar-hour—to such a dominant equation has *right* progressed over *might*. We have indeed developed a long way from slave days in actual mechanical, energy, and brain fact, and it is either to be:—man's hour yardsticks the dollar; or the metallic dollar will have to be deflated 99.999% to have tactical meaning. Gamblers who have set their traps for the "great inflation" might well apprentice in stenography while waiting.

The *overage* momentarily in favor of that relay of executives who really earn $50,000 a year, represents compensation for the latter's investment in self-training, time speculation, and the mastery of knowledge which brought them to the point of proven and accredited compositional ability of the activities of man with his mammoth mutual mechanical extensions and inanimate power harnessings to a total equivalent of 16½ million k.w.h. per annum harmonic group articulation.

In view of the $4.30 life-time energy conversion value of men as moron-prime-movers, we understand clearly why evolution spontaneously banished animate slavery throughout the British Empire, the U. S. and elsewhere within the immediate 10 years which simultaneously broadcast the invention of the dynamo and production steel.

Many are the "economics" professors who have told us with a grin or a smirk that CAPITAL IS, after all, TIME, but now we, involuntarily born into time, perceive, through mechanical attainment, that conversely TIME IS CAPITAL, to be articulated by us individually after our own progressive evaluations, at least cost to society on minimum-standard relief, or as often and as broadly amplified as we self-conrtolledly and all-inclusively may comprehend the phenomenon.

In an improved system of industry, freed from non-scientific director control the inventor responsible for work-saving equivalents—not only for one but indirectly for all, since industry is so highly integrated that the slightest ripple of improvement reaches the farthest shore—would be accredited on the basis of his precise energy-time-saving contribution. If he saved 1/3 of a million k.w. *per annum* (this would be "some" invention) he would be accredited with $1,000. This would be payable, however, only as the time-saving accrues, thus allowing for adjustment of the invention's contiguous aptitudes. The invention *per se* might theoretically save time, but it must be logically synchronized with contiguous inventions and conditions before the inventor can be accredited in accurate terms. If the credit were $1000, the inventor would be free to convert this sum into goods and services super to those of prime necessity, with which he would already have been automatically accredited.

In such manner, wealth—which should be pure credit for prosocial ability super-to-minimum-stint—would become the specific utility of the articulator, not at the cost of any human but through super-specific benefit to all humans. In this scientific economy, wealth would not have the characteristics of feudal intrinsic wealth. That kind of wealth was based on a you-or-me

survival philosophy, and, being material, was theoretically be-
queathable in perpetuity through an extension of the principle
of the "divine right of kings," as finite property for the privilege
of the heirs of the original feudal profiteer. But its values were
physical and anything physical "wears out" relative to TIME.
Time does not "wear out" so long as there is life. Time is directly available to all. Controlled time is our true wealth.

The degree to which we control and are masters of our time
and have harnessed our environment to our will and weal, by our
time *use*, determines our numerically specific relative wealth as
individuals, or as a social unit comprised of individuals of any
number.

No one in our proposed economy of scientific service and efficiency could justifiably resent vast amplifications of individual
credit as directly proportional to pro-social service entailing in
no way deprivation of others' time-control wealth, but, contrariwise, signifying the provision of greater time-control means
for others. The amplification of individual credit for thoughtful-
service would obtain during and only for the life of the individual. Such credit is specifically individual and abstract, though
readily able to render puny by comparison the fortunes of today,
or of any time in the past.

If a man were so scientifically able as to evolve a practical
thought that would eliminate cancer forever from the human
mechanism, surely none would resent his interpolation of his
popularly accrued credit for such thoughtful and beneficial service in the acquisition of the most able boat to sail the seven seas,
or of an aeroplane to fly to Mars. Indeed, the individual evolving
so able a thought might possibly be expected, through enlarged
perspective and contemplation, in his aeroplane flying to Mars,
or in his boat on the Indian Ocean, or in his private laboratory
at the North Pole if that were his preference, to evolve further
vastly efficient pro-social thought. If a thousand guests on his
yacht would accelerate such thought, then let him have a thousand guests if they are spontaneously willing. It is certain that his
yacht would not be run by coal-slinging slaves.

How would the saving to humanity be accounted?

In terms of government-collected figures, which, in the present hypothetical instance, would compare the aggregate previous number of cancer victims and numerical value energy depletion caused by the disease with the subsequent dwindling average loss. Although assumed averages would have to be used at first, these would continually be corrected by census findings, the system becoming progressively more equitable with increasing uniform, universal knowledge. A vast amount of data already exists in the actuarial departments of the great quasi-coöperative insurance corporations upon which the original postulates of every saving by cancer or analogous cures may be determined.

Today in the accounting branches of an industrial establishment, the simplest over-all annual accounting system is employed. No moneys are exchanged—not even dollar bills. This is true not only intramurally in a single industry, but obtains between many corporate entities in industry.

In the economy herein proposed it would be unnecessary for Mr. Murphy to *deposit* his work-representative checks. The work performed by him could be automatically and more simply industrially inter-accounted and, consequently, far more efficiently.

Workers would not be able to overdraw their accounts, for the check-up on the accrued excess of credit of the super-to-minimum stint of any individual would be but a matter of seconds' determination. The one desiring goods and services, super to automatically accredited essentials, need only signify his desire at some point of distribution contact, where facilities would exist to determine, possibly by telegraphic exchange to a central bureau, the dollarability of the acquirer in proportion to the energy conversion value of the product or service desired.

There would be no place, in such an economy, for an opinionated appraisal of the purchaser by any *salesman*, that unfortunate being of today. This would obviate current risks on either side of a transaction, growing out of opinionated personality perquisites of the purchaser or equally opinionated "claims" for the product. The elimination of opinion would be succeeded by true scientific appraisal and credit of both product and purchaser. No more "bad account" merchants,—no more process servers.

With such an improved system would come the welcome elimination of an infinity of traditional stupidities regarding dress and all the fallaleries of "keeping up with the Jones's" essential to opinionated credit "build-up." Gone would be the temptation to stretch the opinionated and, therefore, unknown quantity credit of individuals either by themselves or by others. No "overdrawn" accounts, indeed.

At present Mr. Murphy's opinion that he has given freely and well of his thought and acts to society has to be articulated by "finger-in-the-fire" or trial-and-error wanderings.

Despite his inability, under our current scarcity-and-profit economy, to convert his "gifts" from himself to society into dollars that *he* considers commensurate with his service, this failure does not preclude his continuing to believe that he does contribute goods and services beyond the dollars he receives. He assumes that he has that much credit, and often seeks to interpolate it into goods and services for his own consumption. If he over-accredits himself by his opinion, he finds himself in "hot water" even though his erroneous appraisal was sincerely attempted.

This self-opinion accrediting leads, in the aggregate, to threats and claims beyond all calculation and provokes continuous woeful court proceedings, and wide nervous debility, all of which would vanish in a system of truly scientific credit.

The "dollar" is already practically employed as a measure of energy conversion despite this fact's obscurity at the hands of the profit-manipulation system. This impending time-energy based economy is precisely the eruptive force against which "manipulation" is today aggressively articulating.

How is this known?

If it were not so, the financier would not still be fighting for "recovery" and would not be resistant to every step toward socialization of the obvious plenitudes. Neither would he be fighting his "partners-in-crime" for a division of what is left of the spoils of the old racket. Such a conflict would no longer be necessary because the financier and the "boys" would, under the new economy, be getting "plenty" out of the people in full measure of their worth. Albeit many astonishing salaries might be drastically reduced if service were scientifically appraised.

The "attractiveness" of war to Finance would diminish. There would be no war in China or in Spain. Wars are an "out" and "out" manifestation of the resistance of the old profit system to the rise of worker well being and the world-wide demand by the workers to be heard effectively in politics.

The old profit system has too little imagination to foresee universal wealth and comfort implicit in the trends which the "new" deal has allowed to become popularly visible. Equally unimaginative must the workers also be who scare off the profit system operators from any possibility of envisionment of the mutually delightful commonwealth now looming up, by their suppression-born subversiveness which infers pulling down the top and the revolutionary guillotine for all financial aristocracy. To such a perverted frame of mind have many active so-called "Communists" arrived that, indeed, they would refuse an open gate to the promised land and would only enter through a bombed breech in the wall. Fortunately, the over-all chronology of industrial scientific history indicates that, despite the extreme hostility of these extreme out-camps, the commonwealth of "you AND me" is willy nilly approaching. The speed of the approach is thrilling.

Technocracy? No. Technocracy failed because it made no allowance for passion, fashion, chance, change, intuition, the mysticism of harmony, and, most important of all, for—"*it happens*."

Technocracy called for an autocracy of engineers to fulfill its scheme. Political movements that call for an autocracy of a special viewpoint are ever doomed to failure as the trend indicates segregation of issues and a recomposed balance of all-time forces. SPECULATION and INITIATIVE in the acceleration of CHANGE, are ALL-TIME FORCES, and are as essential in a scheme of realism as suffrage and the socialization of essentials and plenitudes.

Superstition is another important all-time force, but it was derisively dismissed by the technocrats as mystic pish posh, allowing man to fall into the piteous pathologic condition that they sneeringly considered engulfs so many men. Many world-wide superstitions, however, are scientifically rationalizable and sustainable as of high importance.

The superstition that singing too early in the morning is a forerunner of tears in the evening is universally current in primitives and among supposedly highly developed, socially cultured people. This superstition is actually—in view of the wave phenomenon and unit of energy output clearly measured and charted in emotional attitudes—an indication of man's ultimate anticipation of the necessary balancing of lows and highs. In it, therefore, is a distinctly scientific proclivity. Yet emotion, so essential to selective growth and survival, was denied by technocracy as a social factor.

As power systems become integrated and the network pool becomes more balanced by invention in the matter of greater distance transmission we shall eventually come to a point where there is attained a balanced power pool available at equal cost at any point in the land. Then man, eschewing any "brain work" and working only as a "prime power," will be able to earn but $4.30 in a life time, on the basis, as stated above, of present hydropower cost. Not until this continentally pooled power condition has arrived, however, will the system of integration of man's energy conversion rate on a basis of *time* dollarability be possible.

Until that time, granted raw materials for conversion to end product and the fabricating machinery for that conversion, the dollar rate of the worker as a simple animated energy conversion medium for activation of the fabricating machinery will be directly proportional in amount to the ratio of the distance-cost increase of the inanimate, potentially competitive, power source from the specific factory under consideration.

A worker's time-energy-dollar credit is not representative

merely of his maximum limit of personal physical servitude, i.e., .13 k.w. hours a day. It also represents a compound of .13 k.w. hours' serviceability to others, and the precise application of this serviceability (with understanding and credit of its original significance) to the management of his 21 inanimate, electrical slaves, the work of which is articulated with varying efficiency by means of man's self-extension.

These machines have amplified the ability of the inanimate electrical slaves somewhere near a thousandfold above the original caveman's precision and leverage ability. The progression is geometrical. The choice of machines and the place consideration—that is, where man will have them work-serve him—are thought-occupation-necessities of each and every individual, as a result of which one is able to arrive at a preferential "contact" for maximum relative efficiency of individual specific service to the whole of the human family.

This last consideration immediately brings to the fore the vital role of EDUCATION and complete unbe-tampered news dissemination as a primary means for society's egress from exploitation to active self-captaincy. It emphasizes the importance of maintaining a teleologic attitude when acquiring an education for one's self and when educating others.

An example of teleologic rationalization has been given in the presentation of this new concept of a scientific economy. It began with a consideration of the starry universe and ended with an analysis of the time-energy conversion dollarability of the individual.

Einstein's equation "$E = Mc^2$" may now be teleologically translated to Energy $\bowtie$ Man $\times$ Intellect, the latter being true rate maker of energy conversion. Thus Einstein has served us, by providing, through his simple statement of the meaning of the physical universe, a formula for developing uncompromisable and untaintable dollarability.

10

Primary Motivations of Man: Fear and Longing

In an article analyzing the relationship between religion and science, Einstein said: "Everything that men do or think concerns the satisfaction of the needs they feel or the escape from pain. This must be kept in mind when we seek to understand spiritual or intellectual movements and the way in which they develop. Feeling and longing are the motive forces of all human striving and productivity—however nobly these latter may display themselves to us."*

Einstein went on to reduce these two motivating forces to two defining words. He chose FEAR and LONGING because he needed a biological or polar terminology. They are, however, arbitrary terms.

To clarify somewhat the selection of these words by Einstein, we define FEAR as CONTRACTION and EXCLUSION, with a consequent compressively squeezed out potential of knowledge.

LONGING, conversely, is EXPANSION and INCLUSION, with a consequent vacuum pulled absorption of potential knowledge.

KNOWLEDGE means checked and double-checked UNDERSTANDING.

Inasmuch as we can think consciously only in terms of experience—despite a willing subscription to "inclusion"—UNDERSTANDING comes periodically to an impasse through lack of experience. At such an IMPASSE, a temporary condition other than fear or longing is provoked. This is the condition of LONELINESS.

* *Religion and Science*, Professor Albert Einstein, N. Y. Times Sunday Magazine, Nov. 9, 1930.

An inability, despite willingness, to understand, yet part of a motion (the pure motion of the expanding universe), forced to grow, this non-experienced expansion representing a state provoked neither by longing nor fear, is L-ONE-liness.

There are two kinds of L-ONE-liness, namely, that experienced in the macrocosm, and that experienced in the microcosm. All scientist-artist-explorers experience L-ONE-liness at one time or another.

The scientist-artist, in either the microcosm or macrocosm, is, however, a dynamically balanced, primarily longing-dominated being.

In contradistinction to the scientist-artist, there are beings in whom fear or longing is dominant, but who are dynamically unbalanced (crazy) and who attain the loneliness of relatively permanent isolation through mechanical deformity or maladjustment. Reluctant to understand, yet impelled progressively outward, they are, if fear-dominated, popularly called "maniacs"; if longing-dominating, "balmy."

In his analysis of the feelings and needs that have brought mankind to religious thought and to faith in the widest sense, Einstein continues: "A moment's consideration shows that the most varied emotions stand at the cradle of religious thought and experience.

"In primitive peoples, it is, first of all, fear that awakens religious ideas—fear of hunger, of wild animals, of illness and of death. Since the understanding of causal conditions is usually limited on this level of existence, the human soul forges a being, more or less like itself, on whose will and activities depend the experiences which it fears. One hopes to win the favor of this being by deeds and sacrifices, which, according to the tradition of the race, are supposed to appease the being or to make him well disposed to man. I call this the religion of fear.

"This religion is considerably stabilized—though not caused—by the formation of a priestly caste which claims to mediate between the people and the being they fear and so attains a position of power. Often a leader or despot, or a privileged class whose power is maintained in other ways, will combine the function of the priesthood with its own temporal rule for the sake of greater security; or an alliance may exist between the interests of the political power and the priestly caste.

"Fathers and mothers, as well as leaders of great human communities, are fallible and mortal. The longing for guidance, for love and succor, provides the stimulus for the growth of a social or moral conception of God. This is the God of providence, who protects, decides, rewards and punishes. This is the God who, according to man's widening horizon, loves and provides for the life of the race, or of mankind, or who even loves life itself. He is the comforter in unhappiness and in unsatisfied longing, the protector of the souls of the dead. This is the social or moral idea of God.

"It is easy to follow in the sacred writings of the Jewish people the development of the religion of fear into the moral religion, which is carried further in the New Testament. The religions of all the civilized peoples, especially those of the Orient, are principally moral religions. An important advance in the life of a people is the transformation of the religion of fear into the moral religion. But one must avoid the prejudice that regards the religions of primitive peoples as pure fear religions and those of the civilized races as pure moral religions. All are mixed forms, though the moral element predominates in the higher levels of social life.

"Only exceptionally gifted individuals or especially noble communities rise *essentially* above this level; in these there is found a third level or religious experience, even if it is seldom found in a pure form. I will call it the cosmic religious sense. This is hard to make clear to those who do not experience it, since it does not involve an anthropomorphic idea of God; the individual feels the vanity of human desires and aims, and the nobility and marvelous order which are revealed in nature and in the world of thought. He feels the individual destiny as an imprisonment and seeks to experience the totality of existence as a unity full of significance. Indications of this cosmic religious sense can be found even on

99

earlier levels of development—for example, in the Psalms of David and in the prophets. The cosmic element is much stronger in Buddhism, as, in particular, Schopenhauer's magnificent essays have shown us.

"The religious geniuses of all times have been distinguished by this cosmic religious sense, which recognizes neither dogmas nor God made in man's image. Consequently there cannot be a church whose chief doctrines are based on the cosmic religious experience. It comes about, therefore, that we find precisely among the heretics of all ages men who were inspired by this highest religious experience; often they appeared to their contemporaries as atheists, but sometimes also as saints. Viewed from this angle, men like Democritus, Francis of Assisi and Spinoza are near to one another.

"How can this cosmic religious experience be communicated from man to man, if it cannot lead to a definite conception of God or to a theology? It seems to me that the most important function of art and of science is to arouse and keep alive this feeling in those who are receptive.

"Thus we reach an interpretation of the relation of science to religion which is very different from the customary view. From the study of history, one is inclined to regard religion and science as irreconcilable antagonists, and this for a reason that is very easily seen. For anyone who is pervaded with the sense of causal law in all that happens, who accepts in real earnest the assumption of causality, the idea of a Being who interferes with the sequence of events in the world is absolutely impossible. Neither the religion of fear nor the social-moral religion can have any hold on him. A God who rewards and punishes is for him unthinkable, because man acts in accordance with an inner and outer necessity, and would, in the eyes of God, be as little responsible as an inanimate object is for the movements which it makes.

"Science, in consequence, has been accused of undermining morals—but wrongly. The ethical behavior of man is better based on sympathy, education and social relationships, and requires no support from religion. Man's plight would, indeed, be sad if he had to be kept in order through fear of punishment and hope of rewards after death.

"It is, therefore, quite natural that the churches have always fought against science and have persecuted its supporters. But, on the other hand, I assert that the cosmic religious experience is the strongest and the noblest driving force behind scientific research. No one who does not appreciate the terrific exertions, and, above all, the devotion without which pioneer creations in scientific thought cannot come into being, can judge the strength of the feeling out of which alone such work, turned away as it is from immediate practical life, can grow. What a deep faith in the rationality of the structure of the world and what a longing to understand even a small glimpse of the reason revealed in the world there must have been in Kepler and Newton to enable them to unravel the mechanism of the heavens in long years of lonely work!

"Any one who knows scientific research only in its practical application may easily come to a wrong interpretation of the state of mind of the men who, surrounded by skeptical contemporaries, have shown the way to kindred spirits scattered over all countries in all centuries. Only those who have dedicated their lives to similar ends can have a living conception of the inspiration which gave these men the power to remain loyal to their purpose in spite of countless failures. It is the cosmic religious sense which grants this power.

"A contemporary has rightly said that the only deeply religious people of our largely materialistic age are the earnest men of research."

11

Genius and Talent

Assuming Einstein's postulate of fear and longing as the prime motivators to be correct, let us analyze the implication further, and utilize fear and longing as yardsticks in a general tracery of the history of creative design and the latter's effect on economics and social movements.

While neither fear nor longing is experienced in pure form, nevertheless one or the other is always dominant for every specific moment. A person may be at one instant 90% dominated by longing and 10% by fear, at the next *vice versa*, and tomorrow 50-50. When, however, that person's life span has terminated, he may be analyzed sum-totally as having demonstrated for instance a 60% fear motivation and 40% longing. So, in terms of indicated sum-total of a personality, one may say that a person is dominantly to date a fear or a longing type. The genius and the talented person are specific members of the longing dominated group, although manifesting greatly diversified performance characteristics.

The GENIUS, as discovered by genetics, is characterized by a combination of highly divergent physical life cells that are representative of widely cross-bred parent chains. These cells engage in a ceaseless polar tug-of-war for dominance of the specific human offspring and the result is a dual or multiple personality manifestation. Each progressively revealed momentarily prevailing personality is a summary of the dominants of the whole hereditary line.

Dual or multiple personality provides, then, two or more viewpoints,—equivalent to the two eyes of a range finder, an instrument which mechanically widens the distance between the two human eyes; or to the multiple eyes of the Fairchild aerial camera.

Thus genius has the ability to "fix" events by the convergent angle of two or more sight "lines," not only in time (or space) past, but, also, in time (or space) ahead, from the central perspective of self-NOW. Resultantly it becomes possible for genius first to analyze teleologically such "fixed" phenomena, and then to objectify them in a precise time-energy composition. Genius's dual or multiple personalities may be said to be representative of a breadth of viewpoint, more-than-average, highly worldly, and having an exquisite sense of Timeliness.

Conversely, in the talented individual there is relatively no tug-of-war for dominance on the part of the life cells, for talent has been found to be born of two parents of almost similar life cell characteristics. This talent in human beings is similar to a specific trait on which, and for which, breeders of horses or dogs continually concentrate and inbreed; for instance, "speed" in the horse, a special head in the dog, which requires parenthood as closely identical as possible. The product, "colt," may be said to have a *talent* for speed. The word "talent" as applied to persons is derived from *talentum*, the name for a coin of varying value, or a measure of money. Its application to persons was intended to indicate, in a rate sense, persons of a special measure, not persons of a generally inclusive, average rate ability of performance.

In contrast to genius, talent has not the two or more viewpoints of genius, but has a "single track" visualization. The absence of a time-and-space measuring ability limits the sight to a single non-worldly view,—non-"worldly" because, as we pointed out in our interpretation of Einstein's formula, *the conscious "world" is in fact energy radiantly manifest at relative rates of retarded speed*, rate being the inseparable relationship of time and space.

The harmonious concord inherent in this characteristic of the solitary, talented personality, in contradistinction to the dual or multiple personality of genius, enables the talented individual calmly to preoccupy himself with the exquisite refinement of, or better rendition of, the compositions of genius, in all special articulation fields.

There is no implication, in this discussion of talent and genius, of a greater importance for either proclivity.

The function of genius is to provide new instruments and the process-means for the progressive growth of man; talent's function is the precise and harmonious popularization of the otherwise popularly undetectable, and, therefore, otherwise non-useful products of genius. What is often mistermed as "plagiarism" is more precisely "talent." "Plagiarism" is an ethical off-shoot label of the false property illusion described in our phantom captain chapter.

The genius, in this postulate, may, however, be said to be initially responsible for all objective changes in world growth. A study of the interior and exterior functioning of genius would shed much light on paradoxes of history, and on current trends. But how may the processes of rationalization and objectification of genius be graphed?

The criterion of selective judgment in TIME, or TANGI-BLE LIFE, is an inarticulate though truly present awareness of perfection. How may we graphically portray this perfection, this "truth," which as Margaret Fuller said is "the nursing mother of genius"? How may we graph genius's abstraction of perfection?

To demonstrate what we mean by "truth," when we use it as a gauge against which to measure the relative perfection of the selected articulations of genius, let us examine the postulate that the shortest distance between two points is a straight line.

Scientifically, a pencil-graphed point is microscopically evident only as an erosion-deposited dump-heap of lead upon paper. But lead is electrically radiant matter. Therefore, a graphed "point" is undemonstrable in any static graph. Nonetheless, a teleologist may *employ* this postulate for communicating with other teleologists in the endeavor to develop mutual understanding. It should not, however, be used carelessly in communicating with non-teleologists, which would pauperize it into a mere means of dogmatic formularizing, inevitably short-circuiting rationalization growth.

Says genius—the artist-scientist-inventor-explorer (in-vention being the bringing into sensorial realization of that which already exists in the abstractly contacted universe of reason and radiation)—"I am ready to admit that I can make neither a perfect point nor a perfect straight line composed presumably of a series of tangent points. However, an inability to make a perfect straight line is no reason why I should not now articulate the straightest line within my power, and, later, through experience-born improvements, a straighter, and yet a straighter line. If I do not TRY to do so, I shall not even have a starting-point means for my desired activity. This activity is to translate that truth of which I AM AWARE into articulation trends and specific progressive mechanisms for the survival-and-growth-use of others. I can at least express what my relativity or time-fix awareness enables me to see in the physical world about me."

So genius proceeds to draw a relatively straight line.

Inspecting it carefully, he detects its errors or curves, then draws another, straighter line, and repeats the process again and again, using more and more precise tools, and operating under microscopic observance. Despite the fact that the line becomes ever straighter and finer, errors of curvature are always detectable by an increasingly high-powered microscope so long as a graphic depositing means is used. Obviously, at the very instant an absolutely straight line might be attained, it would physically cease to exist, and become what it originally was: non-physically-demonstrable because conceived in the mind, which, alone, can conceive perfection. Moreover, it was made up of a series of points which are abstract convention centers of the radii of the radiant matter, lead, which genius by scientific privilege employed for graph progression purposes.

A graph progression is the only way in which a static spacial demonstration can be made of that which is, in truth, time-and-motion. The abstract straight line indicated by inference in the progression may, however, be quite precisely demonstrated as the "line of sight" between the surveyor's telescope and the "rod." In short, the progression of the articulation of truth by genius is one of progression toward ephemerality.

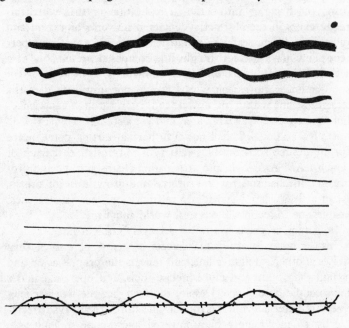

Truth or perfection is abstract only, just as Einstein's factor of truth in his $E = Mc^2$ formula is an abstract, that is, speed or rate. Though detectable only through interception this abstract, "speed" is nevertheless a *perfect reality*. Stand in the path of an onrushing auto and deny this truth!

"Now," continues genius, "granted that the mind perceives the abstract straight line of truth, how can I formulate this for the Murphys? How may the lines—without digression from truth—be made sensorial and consequently useful to them? Useful in a bread-and-butter sense for abetting their daily growth? The Murphys cannot see abstract straight lines, and are not spontaneously interested in anything abstract."

Genius may, for instance, articulate the line with light-refracting materials,—let us say with red or blue crayon—without digressing from the demonstration of truth. Furthermore, the colored line may be divided into harmonic intervals, or it may be made to smell thus and so, or it may be endowed with textural characteristics discernible directly by frictional touch (contact), or, indirectly, by vibratory radiation reception.

"But," reflects genius, "this method of demonstration might not appeal to *all* people. There are two major classes of human beings in the world, the fear type and the longing type, or the might-makes-right and the right-makes-might types. The longing type likes to be pleased or reasoned into doing things; the fear type must be damned or irritated into action. Can the line of truth be deployed to appeal to or be understood by both?

"My first demonstration with color or by synchronization or by textural treatment is of appeal particularly to the longing type. If the straight line is considered structurally as a rod of wood then, when tensed at its terminals, it will be seen to tend to pull 'true'; when compressed at its terminals, it tends to bend. I can employ the pulled or tensed line to appeal to the longing or right-makes-might type, and I can use the compressed or bent line to appeal to the might-makes-right minded or fear-dominated person. I am not saying that relaxed tension will not also appeal to the longing type."

Since genius's function is to make sensorial use contact with the Murphys, he is entitled to tense or compress the line of truth as required. The tensed line may be called the major mode, the bent line the minor mode.

In flexion as in tension, the line of truth may be exposed by means of color, smell, tactile or aural appeal, in continuity or alternately. The tensed, bent or slacked line is still the same "truth" representative so long as genius, always aware of the abstract straight line, remains responsible for the specific tension or bending.

Here, then, we have not only a scientific means of graphing truth but, also, a theory of art which we define as the harmonic objectification, or harmonic synchronization, or syncopated articulation of truth within the "satisfaction" ken of the Murphys.

"The further art advances the closer it approaches science," said Leonardo da Vinci, painter, sculptor, architect, engineer, and inventor of the wheelbarrow, and other useful instruments from the speaking tube to a mechanically gyp-proof whorehouse, "and the further science advances the closer it approaches art."

12

Patrons of Art: Death and Life

GRANTED that the foregoing teleological theorem of the cause and process of genius articulation is acceptable for understanding what Einstein meant by man's "doings" being motivated by either fear or longing; *granted* that genius is responsible for the progressive inventions by man; and *granted* that the genius, like all others, has to eat (economics), it becomes of interest, in a study of the vital *motifs* and trends underlying man's history, to trace the patronage of the artist throughout the historical ages of our particular civilization. In other words, who actually accredited genius with the bread, butter, shelter, and clothing, without which he could not have existed, and, consequently, could not have provided man with the means of progressively conquering his environment?

The first great patron of art, in its earliest days, was DEATH. The King or Pharaoh, for whom life expectancy was short (20 years) and who belonged in the fear-dominated group, patronized the artist and artistan out of fear of death. He patronized the artist in order that he might be enshrined after-death and provided with the appurtenances necessary for "after-death" life. Precious stones, gold and other objects, seemingly eternal from a practical service viewpoint, were garnered and entombed for the eternally long period of "after-death." In short, there was a complete animate enslavement to a single absolute, inanimate monarch,—DEATH.

Subsequently, when the static populace center of the Pharaohs was invaded by roving monarchs and their hordes, the situation changed. The roving monarchs, in consequence of having constantly to adjust themselves to the conditions of an ever-changing habitat, were competent, intelligent fighters, and, being mobile, were easily victorious over the static Pharaohs and their huddling subjects.

The new monarchs were concerned—by proclivity and of necessity—with LIVING problems. Said they to genius, as his new patron, "Aggrandize *me* in your art. Show how great are *my* LIVING deeds!"

Thus LIFE—though not yet popular-life—supplanted Death in becoming the patron of the artist.

Next came the prophet and philosopher era—Isaiah, Jeremiah, Socrates, Archimedes, Jesus Christ, Mahomet, and others—mind-over-matterists whose rationalization wrought greater "miracles" than had the influence of the matter-over-mindist or "bully" type of leader. Some were personal mind-over-matterists or dramatists: the prophets; others were abstract and impersonal: the scientific philosophers.

Common to both mind-over-matter types, personal or impersonal, was the assumption of the attitude that progression by intellectual selective-compositional *growth* is superior to progression by material erosion, cleavage, survival, albeit *progression* by one or the other means is *inevitable*.

Progress we must, progression being expansion toward ephemeralization, though the way is dual. It is precisely in this matter of arbitrary choice of the "high road or low road" to the same destination that the only demonstration of "free will" is discoverable. The early philosophers chose the "growth" way instead of the course of sheer "survival," for in "growth" man does a majority of the selecting.

Wheat was selectively segregated from chaff by these philosophers, but they did not burn the chaff as had the bully-leaders; some was held over for further selective compositional use,—a "place for everything" in the "we run it" scheme. These were the early scientists. Democritus (400 B.C.), the widely traveled, "laughing philosopher," evolved the atomic theory.

"Nothing is created out of the non-existent," he said, "or is destroyed into the non-existent."

As a group, they were early efficiency men, theoretical technologists, which made it possible for them to segregate abstract forces from substance experience. They mentally segregated the sail from the wind instead of continuing, paganly, to ascribe the phenomenon of "sailing" to the mysterious action of a non-rationalized God existent in the sail.

The expansion of rational segregation eventually led, by necessity, to the development of an abstract mathematics capable of expressing "progression," which might also be teleologically re-applied to fields of expression other than that of the original progression observed. The results seemed little less than miraculous.

When, within recent memory, Watt observed the expansive energy of steam in a kettle on the stove, instead of allowing this mist of the devil to go to the devil, he rationalized the phenomenon so effectively that all factors were included with scientific adequacy wherefore he succeeded logically in harnessing the steam to propel an engine. If one realizes the advanced stages of mathematical computation which Watt had necessity of employing at the central point between observation and articulation, and the long areaway traversed by the prophet and philosopher, which mathematics at that stage represented, one pauses appalled before the distance covered by mind-over-matterists from those B.C. days down to our modern period, ushered in by Watt. One marvels even more at the contributions of the Greek philosophers, in view of their isolation as shown on the charts included in this book,—an isolation marked by a 2000-year gap prior to their occurrence, and a 1000-year gap subsequently thereto.

The prosaic, impersonal, scientist-philosophers held a philosophic attitude identical with that of Jesus Christ and the other prophets, but parted company with the latter in the manner of articulation of mind-over-mattering.

Christ's articulation was confined to the limits of Aryan-Hindu Yogiism, in which mind had developed to such a complete control of the individual body as to be able to make it impervious to elemental exposure and which could levitate, transport, kill, or keep it in a state of suspended animation. But all these Yogi abilities had a mutual limitation. They remained a *personalized* art. The power gained by one could be practiced upon but not transferred to others. It is true that a technique for the acquisition of the power could be recited, but its adaptation was a matter of individual ability; "going the long road," as they called it. The attainment of this ability required years of exercise in mental self-control through physical relaxation and mental concentration to the point of exquisite utilization of energy.

Since Yogi is a personalized art, the art dies with the person. The abstract power involved remains as real and true, always, but it cannot be made utilizable in increasing continuity for the world in general. Christ and his counterparts realized this and were unique in their refusal to apply this power to self ends. It was this personal limitation of the Yogi art which led the *prosaic* philosophers to search further. They sought a means of limitless articulation.

The Pythagorean type of philosopher, evolving observations of potential laws of radiation, and the Democritus type, evolving observations of potential atomic laws, jointly evolved a geometry for their own objective mental guidance. To certify this rationalization, they further deduced trigonometry, an objectified measuring means in which the certain relationships of the angles of triangles formed by abstract straight lines became understandable and utilizable.

This art was a step beyond demonstrating truth by means of an abstract flexed or tensed straight line. It realized that angles are the *abstract* "*space*" between radial lines, and that the latter are "representative" only. The abstract angle can be numerically dissected without possibility of error in terms of parts of a finite whole, the circle, whereas the terminals of a "straight" line are but arbitrary parts of an infinite whole.

Thence evolved a mathematics based on the proportion of reciprocal forces, complements, and functions of a mobile, non-static, TIME-world. Thus the scientist-philosopher-artist, by the teleologic mechanism of mathematics which contains in its infinite ramifications all the secrets personally contacted by the knowledge of Yogi, made possible continuity of the expression of truth beyond the "great wall" of the body and of personal death. TIME became a continuous scientific factor and was no longer an interruption-of-life-by-death theme. This new specific teleologic continuity gave to man not only a means of dominance over matter of first contact (inherent in Yogi) but a technique of dominance that could be transmitted to others. So long as the phantom captain retains philosophy and mathematics he will have a progression means of selective life; the presence or absence of personal equations is unimportant.

The two types of mind-over-matterists—the Christ Yogi and the scientist-philosopher—soon won popular credit away from the monarchial bully.

The appeal of the dramatic Yogi was first and foremost to the pagan-minded populace. He steadfastly maintained that there was no formula for mind-over-mattering and quite consistently refused to *write* down "rules." Christ, when pressed for a "rule," said only ONE word, a *dynamic* word,—LOVE. Today this may be scientifically defined as the non-retarded, RADIATION OF PURE ENERGY, harmonically digestible and scientifically utilizable by all the Murphys through the selective and recompositional functioning of intellect. He did not give the "rule" in two words, for that would have been formula. The source of his designating word was identical to that which was symbologically developed by the Egyptians in their supreme sun-god, "Ra," from which we get the "ra" in ra-diation, ra-dio, and ra-dex or root, and ra-dius, the direct line from the center outward. The artist-invented "halo" of Christ is simultaneously symbolic of the corona of the sun and the form root of the cypher "O."

After the "death" of Christ, the disciples dogmatized "Love" down into the language of humpty-dumpty; into illusion rules of ethics, symbolism, ritual, and formula; as, for instance, "Love thy neighbor as thyself," and, conversely, "Thou shalt not covet thy neighbor's wife." These disciples, in ignorance and good conscience or over-conscience racketeered a free shelter for their activities, through exploitation of popular credit of experienced proximity to Christ, and started a property estate tradition that was to acquire undreamed of matter-over-mind power and to constitute the greatest known hindrance to the mind-over-matter growth of original causation. Thus the fallacy of personal equation religion was destined to demonstrate itself.

Likewise, the "intellectuals"—the dilettante fans of the scientist-philosophers—started an academic dogma racket that still makes mathematics (geometry, calculus, *et cetera*) an obscure and to-be-eschewed complication of the schooling ritual. Mathematics in its present frozen state is murderous, as a rule, to an understanding of the simple true thought that first evolved it. Just as the religious racketeers chiseled chapels and monasteries, so have the professional intellectuals "acquired" academies and "endowments."

Despite the racketing-down by professor and priest, however, each has indirectly provided a boon for mankind.

In every hamlet and in every kingdom there were shrines or churches, the equivalent to the populace of those days of our motion picture theatre, town hall and market place all rolled into one. In the church there was one spot known as the sanctuary into which any victim of a temporal ruler's disfavor could run and be immune from temporal wrath so long as there.

The king, being fear-motivated, dared not penetrate this area lest he provoke the wrath of his irrationally accredited pagan bully gods, of whose "frat" this new god, worshiped by the people, *might* be a "regular" member. This fundamental fear was born of the observation that at least one prophet quite successfully demonstrated an utter disregard for the king's own bully gods. Moreover, that prophet proved to be immune to the indignant wrath of those gods, which wrath presumably was aroused by the prophet's insulting attitude. So, while directly denying the power manifested by this new messiah, the king intuitively subscribed to it, and feared it even more than he did the wrath of his own bully gods. He was wholly unaware of his error in attributing this non-rationalized intuition to his relationship with his own gods rather than to the power motivating the prophet.

Spinoza (1632) said: "This is the reason why each man has devised for himself, out of his own brain, a different mode of worshiping God, so that God might love him above all others and direct all nature to the service of his blend of cupidity and insatiable avarice."

The effect on the populace of the monarch's temerity was to awaken a suspicion that there is a power greater than any temporal ruler's. With this recognition there awoke a sense of freedom, though ever so slight, from the temporal ruler's dominance. The Christ demonstration of non-fear of death and his subsequent resurrection was highly convincing in the matter of their intuitive ability to sense a life continuity replacing their superstition that life-after-death is the only worthwhile area of existence. This made it important for the populace to win emancipation during life-on-earth.

Exultantly (though hesitantly) they claimed the shrine-shelter as OURS.

Turning to the artist, they commanded, "Stop painting pictures of faked exploits for the king! Paint for US!" Within the framework of his painting for the king the artist had interspersed an abstraction of his harmonic articulation necessity quite unrecognized by the king.

The artist arose to the new opportunity and obeyed the popular command. It soon became self-evident, however, that although he could paint a lie about a king, he could not paint a composite lie about a whole population's exploits, which must be universally satisfactory as "deed" illusion to every individual of that population. Wherefore, he painted allegorical subjects dealing with morals or mind-over-matter subjects of universal appeal. Into these allegorical paintings he also wove his interspersed abstract harmonics. El Greco's paintings are a strongly suggestive demonstration of this abstraction compounded with picture.

Thus emerged the beginning of a POPULAR LIVING patronage of the artist-scientist, signifying the birth of an one-for-all and all-for-one objective activity, albeit rampant with confusion, glittering camouflage, and stenches.

Immediately, however, there appeared a new necessity.

The "author," being an artist, discovered that he, too, must articulate for many. Under the impetus of this compelling urge the first printing press materialized,—primarily to print the Bible, which was the most useful subject of universal interest for writers to articulate under the new popular patronage. This instrument of literacy-promotion actually proved to be the primary emancipating means of man from his then current matter-over-mind, or might-makes-right, status to that of mind-over-matter dominance. The development of the individual mind was brought about by the printed word.

Man, when printing the Bible, produced by inanimate machine extensions replicas of a product which evoked an understanding between author and reader, by virtue of the inanimate printed symbols of the implicit word meanings identical to that called forth by perusal of the original manuscript, although this end-means was non-identical to the manuscript of the artist. This is in juxtaposition to the popular patronage first developed by the painter wherein the many eyes of the populace viewed directly the *original* articulation of the artist. The machine extension, as first apparent in book-making, is now highly integrated in the mass production of the visual art as demonstrated in the motion picture industry, where the original concept of the artist is amplified for scanning by hundreds of millions of eyes.

What a thrilling indirect result this is in contradistinction to the mind-over-matter retrogression implicit in holy rule-making by the disciples of the prophets! The superstitious or intuitive shunning of disciplehood by members of industrial society today, which grants new leadership but for an instant lest the "leaders" fall into a retrogression of method, is dramatically emphasized in the rise and fall of such idols-for-a-day as Lindbergh, Pickford, Hoover, MacDonald, and others.

Because of the very high percentage of illiteracy at the time of this initial demonstration of industry (book printing) industry was "manifested" in a *seemingly* unimportant category. But this very seeming unimportance and the apparently limited potential field of the product's distribution hoodwinked the temporal monarch and the organized church into allowing its uncontested inception. Otherwise, this first wedge in the ultimate unseating of both the monarch and the church would have been bitterly resisted. The doom of the monarch and of the church lay not only in the establishment of mass production but in the EMANCIPATION of man THROUGH KNOWLEDGE,—of which the printed word was to become the instrument.

The monarch probably said, "This is a fine idea! Now, I will have a lot of books to give to my courtiers and important colleagues!" The book was to him just a bauble. To the church, it was at first a new mechanism of control. While the populace was kept ignorant, the clerics found it important to read ever more widely in order to browbeat any heretical revolutionary.

The authors of that day—seeking subjects of wide popular appeal—printed more than forty almost identical tales based on the Faust legend, interspersed with their own particular moralizations and dogma. But the Bible continued to be the most popular product of the press. Its universal appeal was due to its sustenance of the credit of potential mind-over-matter, which was certainly the only possible constant, in those days, for the prevention of factual retrogression from mind-over-matter through the absurd dogmatic end-results of professional discipledom.

The monopoly of printing an English translation of the Bible was retained even to a comparatively recent day; it remained a King's "patent" until the War of the Revolution in America emboldened the colonists to print Bibles without royalty tribute.

The reproduction of universally satisfying products to meet the demand of a popular patronage (which we currently call mass production) was particularly significant as being the first manifestation of the new era,—the ultimate far extension of which is not yet even remotely realizable.

INDUSTRY was BORN.

By "industry" we mean the phenomenon of scientific human-effort-coördination of three or more beings which, through the selected activity of the two-or-more beings, is made possible by the third being in whom the two-or-more divided-activity-performers have faith that: he truly has divided the effort and will coördinate that effort to the end that: mutually profitable resultant compositions are obtained, within a reasonable time limit, beyond the physical ability of any being, or group of beings, non-mentally coördinated, to obtain within all time.

Industry can concern itself only with the reproduction of those designs which adequately satisfy the "standard," and are reproduceable in a quantity directly proportionate to their time-liness and adequacy; in relation to which industrial satisfaction "standards" improve (include and refine), and without which satisfaction "standards" cannot improve—such is the human progress responsibility of reproductive design, being based on our philosophic interpretation of LIFE, to wit, that whatever is ideal enough becomes reproduceable in its own image in direct proportion to its adequacy.

STAGES OF "PATRONAGE" AND OF SHELTER DESIGNING ATTITUDES

1. ARCHITECTURE UNDER THE PATRONAGE OF DEATH.

   "I know that thou will bring me to death, and to the HOUSE appointed for all living."

   Job XXX:23.

   (The conception of life only after death.)

2. ARCHITECTURE UNDER THE PATRONAGE OF LIFE,— BUT A SINGLE, VAIN, SELFISH LIFE.

   "It is the curse of kings to be attended by slaves that take their humors for a warrant to break within the bloody HOUSE of life."

   Shakespeare, *King John* IV:2.

Patrons of Art: Death and Life

3. ARCHITECTURE UNDER THE PATRONAGE OF LIFE,—
ONE-for-ALL and ALL-for-ONE. POPULAR USE PATRON-
AGE:

"Let the houses be changed and arranged in order and this will
easily be done when they are first made in parts on the open
places and then the framework can be fitted together on the
site where they are to be permanent. Let the country folk
inhabit a part of the new houses when the court is not present."

Leonardo da Vinci, *Notebook*, 1515.

"The building which was fitted accurately to answer its end
would turn out to be beautiful though beauty had not been
intended."

Moeller, *Essay on Architecture*.

"HOUSES are built to live in, and not look on; therefore, let
use be preferred before uniformity, except where both may be
had."

Bacon, *Building*.

THE UNIVERSAL ETERNAL ARCHITECTURAL
VIEWPOINT:

"Happiness DWELLS not in herds nor in gold; the soul is the
dwelling of happiness."

Democritus.

"Beauty is the purgation of superfluities." Michael Angelo.

4. NATURE'S ARCHITECTURE THE SCIENTIST'S EXPLO-
RATION.

"Beauty rests on necessities. The line of beauty is the result of
perfect economy. The cell of the bee is built at that angle
which gives the most strength with the least wax. The bone in
the quill of the bird gives the most alar strength with the least
weight. . . . There is not a particle to spare in natural structures. In rhetoric this ART OF OMISSION is the chief
SECRET OF POWER. In general it is proof of high culture to
say the greatest matters in the simplest way,—veracity, first of
all and forever."

Emerson.

"A structural gelatinous INVESTMENT of the anterior part
of the body is the beginning of the HOUSE. It increases, assumes a peculiar fibrous structure, and in the course of an hour,
in a vigorous animal, it is separated as an envelope in which the
whole body is capable of free movement."

Huxley, *The Anatomy of Invertebrates*, p. 514.

13

Span-Spinning from Abstract Thought to Physical Science

TELEOLOGIC alacrity enabled man to fashion empirically, seemingly by prestidigitation; for instance, there was the Yogi who could, by means of cultivated figuring talent, mentally extract in a few seconds the cube root of an 18 digit figure. Such ability gradually engendered the false popular conclusion that mechanical experimentation is not scientific unless obviously correlated with and preceded by the use of mathematics or at least drafting board activity. These latter media of science seem so profound to the only slightly rationalizing "public" that it has come to acclaim as scientific only those who visibly utilize these means and, conversely, to discredit the teleologic "handy" inventor. Nevertheless, the intuitive teleologic fashioner consistently precedes the calculator in the functioning process of invention; in fact, the simplest superstitions of the teleologic inventor intuitively pursued have led the way. Occasionally, individuals have demonstrated an ability to encompass both the intuitive postulation ability and academic finesse and skill.

This is not to impute spuriousness to those who employ calculus in their computations. It is intended simply as a protest against the erroneous impression that calculus is indispensable for creative achievement and that valid scientific postulations cannot be set forth by relatively non-erudite persons. Calculus is simply a tool, as is a pencil, a method of calculation. What you *do* with the pencil, or with calculus, is quite apart from the instrument; likewise, merely to understand how to use calculus or a pencil does not automatically change one from a dolt to a scientist or an artist. It is necessary in objective science (invention) to proceed from an original intuitive assumption which, by the use of calculus as a checking process, may either be forwarded from "possibility" to "probability," or dismissed as untenable. Indicated results may be accelerated through calculus, just as the electrical calculating machine may be an accelerating means of checkage.

Once the philosopher had segregated the sail from wind, and wind from a personalized God, he had of necessity to graph abstract force lines before he could comprehend what it was he himself was "sensing." In this process he first noted down two lines of force, one representing the momentum and direction of the sea waves and the other the force and direction of the wind when the latter had shifted to a new direction from that of the momentum persisting in the waves of the "old sea," the direction of which had been determined by an earlier wind. Then he noted a third line which was that of the line of direction developed by the keel and rudder of the ship due to its ploughing in a groove of least frictional resistance. These three forces (sea momentum, wind momentum, and least-frictional-resistance direction), were represented by an angular convergence of lines, the length of each representing the quantity of force involved. The philosopher then drew a fourth line from the convergence of the other three to represent the resultant of force, both as to direction and degree. This fourth line was recognized as a dictatable variable as a result of the man-controllable rudder angle relationship to the keel (the latter a diminutive beginning for "free will" latitudes.)

The great significance of this abstract line development was that the prosaic philosopher realized therein that he could evolve not only a scientific demonstration of mind-over-matter in the realm of direction of force utilization, but could gain mechanical advantage through its application; he could apparently make the boat go up-wind by the angular control of sails and rudder.

Rationalization of these forces ultimately called for their segregation into two additional categories: pure tension force, and pure compression force. The classic demonstration of these angularly intersecting lines was subject to static interpretation, as the scientist-philosopher carelessly failed to indicate the pushes and pulls which were evident to him.

Incidentally, his segregation of the newly discovered force phenomena, first into wind and then into ship momentum (later into force *per se* manifesting in directly oppositional ways,

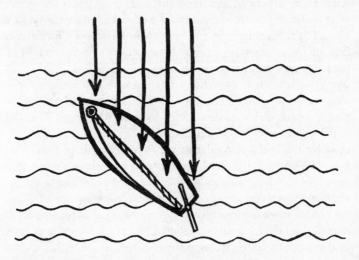

namely push and pull) is typical of the infinite progression of science and mind. For every new concept of mind there is promised an ultimate segregation into seemingly opposed categories, each of which in turn, when its special characteristics are thoroughly comprehended, calls for further segregation. The seemingly balanced oppositional characteristics, in due course, are found to have non-balancing oppositional identities.

14

Dogmatic Toll Takers: Detour Via the North West Spiral:
Triangles and Squares

DOGMATIC disciples of the mind-over-matter philosophers immediately converted postulations of the original truth evolved by the early geometrists into graphic formula, and, in consequence, participated with the *fans* of the unselfish-to-death-degree prophets in the bogging-down of man. The scientist's dogmatic fans carelessly accepted "points" and "straight" lines as matter-of-fact static realities, without troubling to discover for themselves the inherent principles of relative *progression*. This satisfied their "traditional" concept of life as non-improvable and changeless except for seasons, a concept then as yet unchallenged by any scientific instrument progression such as man has witnessed in the last century, which progressively breaks down time and space. Their interpretations were made in terms of a "world" not much greater than a day's walk from the hamlet of the thinker, which "anyone could *see* was a flat plane"; hence they evolved a static geometry with an apparently static material line as its essence.

After assuming this quasi-factual line, they next supposed a plane which was representative of a series of touching parallel lines. They admitted, naïvely, that their plane was theoretical and, therefore, non-sensorially existent. This contradiction, far from bothering them, was easily explained away. To demonstrate the static sensorial world in which they thought they lived, they next imagined a stack of planes, thus demonstrating, in effect, the cube upon which they based a theory of sensorial solid geometry.

Partly as a result of their endeavor to justify this rationalization and partially due to pure arithmetical coincidence, the dogmatic philosophic school discovered the principle that the product of units of length multiplied by units of width equaled the sum of square units of the posited linear module of the area of a right angled quadrangular plane. They further multiplied the number of square units of the plane by the height of the cube, as determined by the number of the same linear module units in a third perpendicular line at right angles to the plane, and so arrived at the volume of the three-dimensional cube. Thus far the process *happened* to coincide with their purely abstract multiplication system.

Finding it impossible to discover a fourth perpendicular to the cube, that is, one that would not be coincidental with one of the three lines of perpendicularity already established, and assuming through the coincidence of its occurring in squaring and cubing that it was a constant and requisite property of all dimensional appraisal, they were unable graphically to realize the mathematically indicated fourth dimension—not to mention the infinity of dimensions beyond the fourth. Consequently, a cult was developed, the subscribers to which pretended a mystical awareness of fourth and infinity dimensions and "squaring of the circle," *et cetera*. They overlooked entirely the philosopher's geo-metry (measurement of an expanding sphere) and used, instead, as a yardstick for the interpretation of the spheroidally and radiantly expanding energy universe, a static, structurally unstable, static line-cube, unstable because it lacked triangular diagonals and was, therefore, collapsible.

The fallacy of this dogma is readily apparent. First, a dot was hypothecated, out of which was evolved a supposed line, out of which grew a supposed plane, and out of two non-realities a reality in the form of a cube that was objectively insisted upon as factually truthful, though actually non-existent. If the dogmatists had been logical they would have been compelled to admit that since it had *no longevity* it *did not exist in time*, (without time dimension) and consequently not in their own life-time-reality. This compromised cube was satisfactory enough to them, however, because it coincided with their empirical building block of stone which seemed real enough and which was from their viewpoint quite eternal. Non time-dimensioning, they, of course, conceived of no *relative* longevity.

The cube thus arrived at by arbitrary inclusions and exclusions, which coincided with the building blocks of their physical world, made it possible for the dogmatists to calculate "practically" in shelter design. The then-current satisfaction of this integration of their geometrical interpretation and every day requirements dismissed from the tradition of academic geometry the true characteristic of the original thought demonstrations of the scientific philosophers.

The original *dynamic* demonstrations allowed of concept extension into coincidence with that concept recognized by modern physicists of an expanding energy universe. The self-satisfied dogmatic exclusion of the time-energy-geometry and confinement of rationalization to a relatively static concept (leading to the building by the populace of temples and cathedrals that required seven to ten generations for completion under the misapprehension that they would stand forever, which misapprehension has underwritten the fallacial economics of collateralized debt) has caused the academic imposition upon new students, throughout 2000 years, of a static concept in their cultivated knowledge which has made it almost impossible for the population now considering itself fairly well educated to comprehend the logical significance of "relativity" implicit in mathematics as re-cited by Einstein and his contemporary physicists.

If those long ago embryonic *academicians* had been more accurately observational, as was the scientist Democritus when promulgating the atomic theory, they would have realized that their dot, if graphed at all, could be but an aggregation of a myriad of primarily spheroidal particles (Democritus's "worlds"). Had they been more earnest and persevering in their research they must have been forced inevitably into a scientific study of the phenomenon of radiation into which the modern scientist has penetrated, by the difficult elimination of their presumptive errors.

They would have realized that there is only *one* dimension or infinity of the *one* dimension: TIME, or HOW FAR (or more properly "FAST") RADIALLY OUTWARD, IN TIME AND SPACE, INTEGRATED AS RATE FROM THE CENTER OF THE SPHERE. Such a conception would have brought them success in their attempts to graph the implied progressive dimensions of simple mathematics in terms of the perpendicular, for an infinity of perpendiculars (radii) may be applied to the surface of a sphere without any impingement, one upon the other, and the progression of volumetric increase in the terms of any uniform radial division modulus as $\Pi.R^3$, is identical to the progression of new dimensions of the expanding universe. Moreover, the infinity of radii in a sphere permits graphing their multiplicity in time, together with a coördinate symmetry of unity in the universe by virtue of the directional coincidence of all radii in a sphere. Each radius extends to the outermost boundary (the radiant surface of the sphere) from the only true point (the radial convergence directional center of the sphere) in the shortest "distance" possible, i.e., in the shortest "space" of time.

A sphere is *unit*, but a line is not because the terminals of a line must represent *arbitrary* cut-offs. All lines, except when abstractly considered as "direction," are somewhat curved, and all curved lines must eventually intersect,—no matter how remotely. Not even a graphed spiral is forever possible because the errors in a graphed line constantly dislocate the line and insist upon an ultimate intersecting contact. This, quite simply, is the essential concept in Einstein's "curved space." The only possible *symbol of unity* in plane geometry is the CIRCLE.

There is incontestable evidence that those who were central in the mind-over-matter emergence era comprehended the infinity of progression and glimpsed, at least, a truthful system of graphic formula. The evidence is found in the peak reached by symbology, in mathematics, words and decoration. In particular may be cited the evidence that occurs in navigation, in which the angle $\angle$, an abstract unit of a whole, *abstract* because it is the *space between the converging lines*, is used for measure. The rounded wheel, which at first was solid and later became compression and finally tension *spoked*, and the "HALO" in decorative art as the unit symbol of the energy or power God "radiantly" expansive above man, is empirical testimony of long existing knowledge of a radiant time dimension. The wheel is centra-mechanical to time-space-relativity evolution and popularization.

When starting their academy, the dogmatic mathematical prophets set in motion a retrogression in knowledge of almost twice the duration of the retrogression initiated by the religious disciples. Consequently, only through individual pioneer inventors and a small band of true researchers has there been maintained a body of amplifying knowledge which has, however, been continuously the source of the momentum of industrial growth.

The vast majority of "educated" people will have to unlearn almost all that they "think" they know in order to divest themselves of vocabularies so largely embodying words of a static nature: "basic," "good," "bad," "is," "distance" (as miles), *et cetera*. (San Francisco 3 minutes from New York telephonically, 20 hours aeronautically, 150 days ambularly; it all depends on relative satisfaction requirements of man.) These static words will have to be dropped from current usage before society can be happily synchronized through comprehension of the phenomenon of the energy-expanding universe.

An indication of society's intuitive awareness of the need of this throw-off of old meanings reveals itself in many ways. For instance, it is to be amusingly witnessed in the quickening shift from one fashion to another in women's hats and gowns, the fashions of which are predicated on satirical exhumations of forms earlier evolved in earnest pomp and circumstance. These current adornments come under the classification of "costume" and in no way indicate that the wearers today think of themselves alternately as a harem gal and the Empress Josephine. The originals, however, were worn in all seriousness not as fashions but as empirical developments (as various materials became available) of the most alluring feathers-for-female-survival.

The failure of the academies founded in the wake of the great Mediterranean scientist-philosophers to recognize "time" as a prime factor of mathematics was primarily due to man's relatively stationary position in his environment, caused by limited means of transportation. Popularly speaking, man could travel only so far as he could walk. He had little or no communication with the world beyond his hamlet unless he were a bully leader and had a "horse." Even then travel was highly confined.

The world was apparently flat. Anyone could see that it was. Each isolated hamlet thought itself egotistically to be "it"—the center of the flat universe. Strangers beyond their horizon had best be wary lest they fall off the edge. The evening sky was a decorative panorama oscillating above a flat static stage. Ego "stood pat." Naturally, in terms of this flat world, men thought that two or more perpendiculars to the earth's surface (columns or tree trunks) must be parallel. Thus was fabricated the delusion of parallelism. Seeming parallelism (for instance, that between two sun rays [radii] an inch apart upon arrival at "earth") is termed parallax in astronomy. The seemingly parallel columns of the ancients could be capped by lintels, if the span were not too great and if the column height in proportion to girth could support the additional load. So quadrangular openings appeared. Ere long the square became the fundamental architectural (arch) module limited in proportions only of weight and width for stability in a factually non-static universe erroneously treated as static. The lack of panoramic background in early painting is indicative of the confinement of early scrutiny.

The "square" illusion, which coincided with the cube module concept, was so seemingly true, real and practical that square-blocked ramparts were erected about the static towns of square blocked buildings inflexibly jointed. This architecture was diagnostic of "fear" of molestation and disrupture, and of an inability to face the facts of a world of time, change, and motion. Even to the present this "fearful" tradition survives for the static realist not only in his architecture but in his economics—he is so proud of being a "square shooter."

Fortunately for progress, there have always traveled across the flat scene a few who were fearless. Travail, "work" and "hardship" were part and parcel of travel at that time in contradistinction to luxury-travel-cruises of today. Travel was then as popularly shunned as it is today courted. Then a traveler was a "nut" to undertake such ill-conceived hardship. Weight-and-width-for-stability shelters (obviously grossly inefficient) were incompatible with travel. So, of necessity, the traveler invented portable, readily pitchable tents, structurally formed of *pure compression members* in triangular *flexible*-jointed stability, covered with pure tension webs. These were directly and unmistakably a manifestation not only of highest scientific mental segregation and re-ordering of elements, but, also, of the longing urge for experience and knowledge, derivable through explorative travel.

The triangle, through the ages, has been the symbol of the architecture of motion, first in tents, then in the rigging of sailing ships, thereafter in trestles, and most recently in airplane wings and radio masts. It is found as the primary module in the decorative design of mobile people, as, for instance, the American Indian.

In the early days of travel, mobility involved a high mind-over-matter conquest of the elements in the non-environment controlled wilderness. The ingenuity and wisdom of the leaders who empirically evolved light mobile tents, *et cetera*, was essential to the welfare of tribal followers.

If a succeeding true mind-over-matter leader was not to be found in the tribe after the death of a mobile leader, the tribe intuitively dared not to move further than the last locality to which the leader had brought it. This must have occurred time after time throughout ages. (We find reference, for instance, to the ten "lost tribes" of Israel, bereft of their leaders.) Fearful to travel further, such people excused their fear complex by a myth. Superstitiously there evolved wide subscription to legends of a "promised land," a goal, a destiny, an arbitrary terminal to a line, to which leaders had brought their "faithful followers." This self-backpatting conceit disguising fear and inferiority to circumstances still characterizes all localized, static people. It is the root of swollen-locus-vanity and ego of the misappropriated and paradoxical self-styling "conservative." Only pioneers have conserved society. Satisfied with their destination theory the "statics" proceeded to dig in. With new generations the old triangular forms, formerly necessitated by travel, disappeared, and the static square, consistent with a flat earth, automatically appeared. MObility degenerated into NObility.

The Jews are a seeming exception. They were and still are an involuntarily wandering people, their symbol being superimposed equilateral triangles (✡). It is known as the "seal of Solomon's highest wisdom." (King Solomon designed his throne upon wheels.) Involuntarily do the Jews wander. Bereft of unified leadership, they long and try continuously to settle down, but their hereditary development of high survival ingenuity as an originally cast out and forced to travel minority, non-submissive to temporal rulers, that very same survival ingenuity (that eschews and evades the majority-adopted "ethics" of materialistic societies compounded with an ingenuity to effect permanent settlement), renders them too disruptive a force for staticizing societies and inevitably they are cast out once more. Their casting out has, throughout history, coincided with the impending decline and fall of the society which cast them out. Oddly and sadly the "outcast" complex inclines them perversely to excel in the very pursuits to which they were originally and still orthodoxly are most spiritually opposed, to-wit, the exploitation of social essentials. It may be said, then, that the cause of their proverbial "wailing" is paradoxically their linkage to survival, their contribution to mankind's welfaring and environmental conquest being the preservation of those arts and proclivities which may be kept alive only through economics of intermittent emergency mobilization.

The history of static, bogged-down, leader-bereft hordes is

fraught with the saying, "This is the place to which HE brought us. It is good enough for us. We shall let well enough alone."

"Letting well enough alone" has precluded exploration of physical phenomena other than in terms of surfaces, superficialities and superstitions. Of necessity such inadequate explanations have had to be maintained by "ethics" and "hands off" laws, which initiate a progression of divestment of attained knowledge ultimately shrinking demonstrations of intelligence to zero.

There is quite possibly a scientific truth to be evolved from the fact that motion, particularly rhythmic motion, is highly provocative of thought objectification. Certainly travel provides perspective, broad angles, and accelerated progressions potential of clarification of the experience trend. Most authors will testify that thoughts come to them in profusion as they speed clickety-clicking over the country in a transcontinental train, and in even greater profusion in droning flight. It is the writer's experience—noted because we are all our own best laboratories—that he unconsciously paces the room while objectifying thought in dictation, puncutating by sitting down and becoming aware for the first time of the pacing that has occurred.

It is to be noted that historically the mobile tribes were primarily present in the areas northerly to, or altitudinous above, the isotherm of mean low temperature of 32° F., along which isotherm the large majority of the world's people dwell. In Eurasia "invading hordes" came from the area north of this isotherm. In America, the cubical pueblo dwellers lived south of, and the triangularly tented mobile Indians roamed north of this isotherm, though all were genetically at least partly Indian. The most southerly were pure Inca and Mayan Indian. The border-line and northerly Indians were cross bred with Mongolians who had coursed over Bering Strait and down through Alaska.

In testament of this history, the static or square architectural habits are found mainly along and to the south of the popular isotherm. Very far north the simple hemispherical igloo is witness of an innate sense of the radiant universe amongst northerly people. The hemispherical, conical, cylindrical, and hexagonal hut forms may be widely found in all semi-nomadic "light traveling" primitives: African or Indonesian. They are primary dynamic-sense forms.

Populations originally existing in warm climes but which dared to penetrate colder realms or higher altitudes have been abetted further in their progressive "thinking ability" by the abatement of the myriad of parasitical infections with which they were originally afflicted in warmer regions and which still persist rampantly in populations south of this isotherm. This "delousing" of the cold climate pioneers yielded a relative physical calmness which, compounded with the hibernation necessitated by a cold climate, has favored carrying through mental concentration into effective thought. The science of mathematics and the central philosophies have come from the high places and from relatively cold climes. Currently, as an end result, almost the complete body of what is classifiable as "industrial society" is found, in America and to a considerable degree in Eurasia, to be wholly north of the isotherm of 32° mean low temperature. (See chart.) The "outs" of the great progression of man's events and mind-over-matter emergence from stale-mated settling down are always clockwise around east to west and spiralling up toward the North Pole. This spiral tends toward an integrating of the world populace by the industrial people of North America and North Eurasia *over* the Arctic. Canadian Airways are now carrying 40% of the world's air freight, their eight main airlines being north and south, not east and west, with more terminals in the Arctic circle than over the U. S. Border. In the summer of 1937 the Canadian Government sent 50 geological expeditions "into the north" to roll back the map of Canada.

The long sought "north west" passage dreamed of by early explorers is coming true by air as it spirals ever north west finally to leap back and forth directly over the Pole. Russia's scientific colonization of the Arctic and pioneering of the North Pole air route, compounded with the Canadian activity, promises integration by 1942, punctuated meanwhile with certain political integrations and developments. This north west spiral is directly instrumented by mind-over-mattering, and the latter's current extensions, aeronautics and radio, are central to its graduation to industrial magnitude.

15

The 2000-Year Streamlining of Society

THE longing of individuals and minorities to journey from known to unknown territory was amplified, after the early human "delousing," from a longing to journey bodily, to a longing, on the part of a few, to journey mentally. It was discovered that the mind can explore without bodily accompaniment through teleologic projection of analyzed past exploration experience. For instance, a child who has never been outside New York City can reasonably comprehend movie scenes of Alpine skiing as an extension of the experience of sliding down the banister compounded with memory of snow in the streets, albeit very dirty snow. There emerged from the early masses certain central thinkers who, teleologically traveling, ushered in the mind-over-matter emergence era.

These mind-over-matterers attained de-selfed rationalization by virtue of integrity of thought, readiness to include, and persistence in penetration and analysis. This was furthered, as the social front in a succession of north west "outs" established itself on the Mediterranean stage, by objectifying thought into mathematical forms. Once away to the concept of "time," through mathematical thinking, the persevering-with-integrity mind-over-matterers must surely have been impressed with wonder at their having the time in which to THINK, especially to think effectively.

Undoubtedly and in consistence with the caliber of their demonstrated thinking, the early successful scientific philosophers must have comprehended the fact that sufficient *time* for rationalizing had accrued through man's environment conquest. This environment control was not available to their cave-dwelling forebears, whose time was fully consumed in defending, replenishing and reproducing themselves, or in the subsequent primitive objective science of recording experience with pictures. It was not until a large enough number of human forebears, stimulated by leader-minds, fortuitously banded together in coöperative effort that a degree of sustained environment control became possible, providing the potential isolation of a modicum of *time* for rationalizing. This event marked the beginning of science which, as defined by Edington, is simply, *"The sincere attempt to set in order the facts of experience,"* with the implied goal of ordering future experience.

Setting in order the facts of their experience, the mind-over-matterers of the great mathematical emergence era (known to *us* as having occurred particularly in the Mediterranean lands 700-200 B. C.) must have realized that their environment control was *maintained* by dint of *animate* slavery. Human slavery was at its historical zenith when geometry was incepted, both in the numerical proportion of society involved and in the smooth functioning of the system, and in sheer cruelty.

Our "thinker," pursuing causes and effects with integrity, must further have rationalized that he had evolved a thought progression, i.e., from arithmetic, to geometry, to trigonometry, to force analysis, and, finally, to certain laws of force, including leverage, the application of which would give the user a practicable mechanical "advantage" over human work ability.

"In effect," he must have realized, "I have unwittingly established a progression, the further extension of which indicates that the utilization of the mechanical advantage principles will result in more work being done than could possibly be accomplished by the use of animate slaves without such extensions."

Continuing to reflect, he went on: "Although man has for long empirically demonstrated 'mechanical advantage' in work through the hand prize, and other simple instruments, the distinction here is that I may now anticipate results even in compound leverage design through the instrumentality of mathematics, geometry and scientific laws of force. The farther the extensions of these truths, the greater the acceleration of time control and work saving in the matter of attaining environment control with an ever diminishing use of animate slaves. The end result must be the complete replacement of the animate by the inanimate slave. The power for the operation of the inanimate slaves will be derived from mechanisms motivated by inanimate forces such as I have detected, segregated and charted in kinetics of wind and water phenomena."

The scientist-philosopher realized that until man should conquer his environment with the indicated inanimate slaves, he should not in integrity be entitled to discover new cosmic knowledge; but if and when he should succeed in such conquest, then in leisure and conscientious freedom, new central philosophies for the enjoyment of that environment would undoubtedly accrue. However, until the accomplishment of environment control by the inanimate slave, man's mental activity (the philosopher perceived) must be confined to the amplifying, by rationalization of the physical processes already evolved through the scientist-philosopher's mathematics $<$ geometry $<$ laws of force progression. This amplification would transit two periods: one of retrogression of every characteristic of the old society based on personal slavery down to a low point of almost complete zero, and another of evolution from central chaos to a society based on an inanimate slave sustenance.

Wherefore, ever goaded by integrity, the rationalizer must have foreseen that society would mandatorially be designedly streamlined by himself to chaos in synchronization with the (uncomprehended-by-the-old-society) evolution of the inanimate mechanism; chaos, because bereft of all comprehension of meaning in its traditions and uncomforted by experienced knowledge of the new. Divining peril to this streamlining design in any pronouncement of so devastating a procedure, he resolved that no new cosmic concept should be evolved until this evolution attained majority. Accordingly, he declined to broadcast clues or set down formulas involving any human or personal equation. He did, however, reveal certain laws of inanimate and impersonal properties, for instance, the law of the proportion of weight displacement of water by floating bodies. (Archimedes, 280 B. C., Syracuse, north westward of Greece.)

These impersonal laws, interpreted through the central-attitudes of the attained philosophy and deriving from scientific observations of inanimate phenomena, were the first of many in the realm of science upon which man could "hang his hat" without fear of disillusionment. They are to be differentiated, however, from those set down by the prophet's disciples, who romantically cited promises in equations of personal performance. The reason the philosopher-scientist refused to state laws or formulas for attainment in the terms of personal performance was that these would preclude man's "thinking through" to results, a popular mind-to-over-matter progression that must not be interrupted if mind were to dominate. By the non-availability of laws of "how" to rationalize, man was free to rationalize. Thus free, and simultaneously compelled to rationalize in order to survive, man was bound to perform the myriad of extension developments of the mechanisms essential to attainment of that thrilling day when environment control would be structured upon an inanimate slavery of objectivized self-mechanics extension into a from-self-segregated family of mechanics.

In 1632, Spinoza reviewed well the single "life preserver" of civilization which the scientist-philosopher had provided for use during the flood water period of the era of chaos:

"It was looked upon as indisputable that the judgment of the Gods far surpassed our comprehension; and this alone would have been sufficient to keep the human race in darkness to all eternity if mathematics, which does not deal with ends, but with the essences and properties of forms, had not placed before us another rule of truth. In addition to mathematics other causes also might be assigned, which it is superfluous here to enumerate, tending to make men reflect upon universal prejudices and leading them to a true knowledge of things. . . . The wise man . . . is scarcely ever moved in his mind, but, being conscious by a certain eternal necessity of himself, of God, and of all things, never ceases to be and always enjoys true peace of soul. If the way which, as I have shown, leads hither, seems very difficult, it can nevertheless be found."

16

The Zero Hour

Iᴛ ɪs fascinating to discover that in the nadir or zero hour of society's Greek streamlined course, the mathematical symbol "o," zero, entered our particular civilization factually for the first time. That low point may be said to have been from 1000 to 1600 A. D. Although the Arabs had contributed to civilization not only a simplified form of mathematical symbology—their Arabic numerals, whereby every number was reduced to a unit symbol—but, also, algebra, which sped up calculation to a high degree, the Arabic numerals, as first introduced, did not contain a symbol for "nothing." The invasion of Spain by the Moors, popularly thought to represent a retrogression of society, actually carried with it the great gift of number simplification somewhat as the bee carries pollen for inadvertent fertilization. The Arabs pollenized the growth of science and industry with the cipher.

At this point of history (1176) the ability to calculate was the gift of or was retained in the custody of a talented few. The art was primarily confined to monks or other members of the organized church.

Calculating was done then in two ways: one, by doubling numbers, which is an arduous method; the other, a superior method, with the abacus. This is a frame containing parallel wires or rods mounted with sliding beads. It is still used by some Chinese merchants. It was closely guarded by the church because, through its control, the church was profitably able to act as the calculating intermediary in transactions or undertakings in general. Obviously, this was a power-building privilege. Common to both methods of calculation was the lack of a symbol for "nothing" which made it impossible even with the superior abacus to write down the result of any problem that developed a "blank column." For instance, seven million three hundred and seven (7,000,307) might, also, have been "737."

It is a valid reflection that the non-inclusion of the cipher is accountable by the fact that the people had been so materialistic in their viewpoint that they had not conceived of any necessity of a symbol for intangibility, infiniteness or abstraction. Man had not yet penetrated the non-sensorial bands. The cipher (called *cafrun* in Arabic) had been imported by the "pollenizing bee" from the Hindus, but the Arabs did not bring it into the western world until approximately two hundrd years after they brought to that world their system of simplified numerals and their algebra which latter were indeed limited without the cipher.

The repercussions of this introduction of the cipher were tremendous. The first Italian translation of the Arabic work that included the cipher was done from studies of the mathematician, al-Khowarazmi of Khiva, who indicated in his treatises a new facility for calculation afforded by a cipher, for instance, by using ciphers for the "blank" columns. This positioning of numbers immediately developed the method now daily used in multiplication, namely, the shifting of each successive line of product one column to the left. Originally a cipher was carried in the space now left blank. With the simple new arithmetic, instrumented by the cipher, any educated person could complete, in a few minutes, calculations that had hitherto required weeks, months, and even years. Try for yourself a multiplication problem using Roman numerals and you will realize the significance of this new development.

So important to commerce and the teleologic development of knowledge in general was this introduction of the cipher that merchants, who until then had been limited to laborious calculating by hand or by the employment of the priest and his abacus, discovered that they could now do their own calculating. However, the organized church chose to take an attitude of prohibition toward the new method of calculating by means of the cipher. So, throughout the period from 1200 to the late 1500's, the church used its mighty power of political alliance with temporal rulers to outlaw the cipher, which in every country of Europe, was threatening church "privilege." A bitter fight was waged for three and a half centuries by the "abacists" against the "algorists" (cipherists). Meantime, however, scientists and students throughout Europe had begun to calculate in the new manner. This proved to be so important that the populace began to call all calculating "ciphering." The cipher was the key.

Merchants, especially needing the cipher, used it in stealth lest they be heavily fined. This led to the cipher's acquiring a special meaning, namely, "secret code." Popular ciphering, in general, and the "secret code" connotations so vulgarized the word "cipher" for the scientific world of the day that the Italian scientists were obliged to evolve the new name "zero" for the symbol.

The Arabs did even more in the pollenizing role than bring in Arabic numerals. They kept alive and now introduced into Europe the mathematical and geometrical attainments of the early Mediterraneans. The latter's mathematical treatises, together with most important writings of the Greeks including many scriptures about the acts of the apostles and the prophets, had been filed in the great library of Alexandria. All of these works were destroyed during two successive vandalizations of the great library. Unfortunately, all of the eggs of science and religion seemingly had been placed in one basket. We have no known New Testament of earlier date than approximately 150 A. D.

Considering the chaotic state of society and its low mental rationalization ability in the early centuries A. D., it is safe to assume that the Bible testifies in a highly erroneous way to the doings and sayings of the prophets, which entitles us, in the light of scientifically revealed history, to latitude of interpolation such as outlined herein.

The Arabs had saved some eggs (the best of the scientific eggs) because of their need of mathematics and geometry in overland navigational problems. The Arabs constituted the transportation system of the times between Far Eastern and European civilization. They applied mathematics externally in their caravan navigation and found the use of angular measurement sights reliable. They learned that this conferred scientific prognosticating ability.

Being a mobile people, not only did they simplify their architecture (to the triangulated tent) but also every instrument and mechanical extension that they were under necessity of constantly transporting with them. They had to do all things with devices of the least weight and size and so quite logically reduced number symbology from multiple forms, derived empirically from tallying, to singular. In their mathematical coursing they invented algebra, which derives, etymologically, from *aljebr*, the reunion of broken parts, or *jabara*, reunited, in effect teleology.

In demonstrating the exquisite timing of evolution, it is interesting to observe that the Arabs, having borne the mathematical gifts in their mobile storage to European civilization, to which the front had again moved north-westward, were dispersed from Spain (the then dominant culture center of Europe) the verisame year (1492) as the discovery of the new continents of America. This latter event has effectively obscured the former in our egocentric histories.

The North American continent was to furnish the stage for the enactment of the drama already possible of formulation through the phenomenon inherent in the invention of printing (the Bible), compounded with the resurrected mathematics, as the mechanical extension means of society, a drama which was to world-unfurl the principle of industry instrumented by mass production and scientific leadership.

Just as the popular historical textbook has missed the main point of the Moorish invasion, stressing instead the names of princes and battles, honors and horrors, so, also, has it failed to stress the all-important industrial significance of the scientific progression in this event of great discovery.

The discovery of the new clean slate of the American continents was, incidentally, a complete inadvertence so far as society's volition was concerned. ("Inadvertence" is now a specific factor known in science as the "random element.") If they had had sustainable mechanical refrigeration in Europe at that time, it is possible that the Americas would not have been discovered until much later. Spices were employed, then, in lieu of refrigeration, to preserve foods, and spices were available only in the Far East. The Turks had closed the way to the Far East via caravan, and were exacting high toll from Europe for the precious spices. Columbus, employing the already established theory that the world is round, set sail to the Far East (India) by going west. That he did not discover a western passage to India, Columbus never knew; he died believing he had, and indeed he was the first of the bees to pollenize the new continent with scientific instrument extractions.

One more scientific factor entered the scene during the zero hour of the Mediterranean philosophers' streamlining. That was the concept of time as a segregated philosophic entity. We have already seen what an important factor time is in Einstein's formula, where rate of energy combines time, as pure abstract, with space, as pure matter. TIME entered the picture through poetry. Many, if not most, of the important scientific events that have occurred have appeared first in fun and play, as for instance the suspension bridge which appeared first as a Chinese tight-rope-walker's frame. Funambulist = rope-walker; *funis* = rope; *ambulare* = walk. "Fun" — "rope" — Will Rogers — line — tension — the "fun" of life.

Many scientific events have also appeared first as "tricks" of the organized priesthoods, though the inventors may quite readily have been laiety, conveniently "bumped off." The priesthood employed the scientific gadgets to convince the populace that the priests had contact with unseen powers and anthropomorphic gods. The principle of syphonage was first used by Hindu priests to bewilder the populace. They used christening cups in which syphons were hidden. The cups would be filled with water almost to the brim and then, suddenly, at the critical level the water would disappear from the cup through a syphon inlet and outlet concealed in the base of the legs of a statuette priest holding a statuette baby. There is not only comforting thought but great import of vast future indispensability involved in contemporary radio's 90% low "circus" programs.

TIME was first mentioned as an entity by Sappho, and from Sappho's day was kept alive by the poets (by Goethe, quite prominently), pending expression in scientific formula. In this connection, Dr. Charles Beard, historian, has listed for the writer for incorporation at the present point in this book a list which he considers to represent the epochal changes in man's social growth:

1. Man discovers himself—*Antigone* of Sophocles.
2. Christian idea of tragic conflict between ideal and real.
3. The idea of progress (15th century); unfoldment in TIME.
4. The Christian-18th century idea of worth and value of human personality—not to be used for alien ends of slavery and exploitation.

The factor of TIME entering at the zero hour emerged eventually at the opening of the "twentieth century," with Einstein's formula signalizing the termination of the down-and-up streamlined course of society designed by the scientific philosophers of the Mediterranean. Throughout the intervening centuries man's outlook was statically confined to the scientific formulas provided for him by those philosophers. This static viewpoint itself, which we now strive to break down, seems to have been included in the streamline design by the scientific Greek (despite his own secret awareness of time) almost as a hypnotic necessity to keep man's nose to the grindstone until such "time" as the fixation of his attention upon mechanisms had developed self-extension into a satisfactory inanimate slave demonstration.

The emergence of the time concept as something more specific than the vague thing which a clock ticks away, a concept in which time is as essential a component or unit of the physical world as is oxygen, came with the advent of the cipher, the enabling instrument of time's calculability.

At the instant in history when the demonstration of the sustainability of society by inanimate slaves had been potentially accomplished, as revealed on the continent of North America, Einstein announced his theory of relativity. This is a concept of the universe, all parts of which are in constant motion, as powered by unit energy in relative rates of speed of motion proportional to the frictional relationships of all the parts—a concept of LIFE as TIME itself. Einstein's relativity concept was actually the first new thought of cosmic calibre to emerge since the 200 B. C. termination of the scientist philosophers' declaration of social streamlining.

The "theory of relativity" marked, then, the birth of an extraordinary era, newly unfolding, in which man must expand the principle of inanimate slavery from out of its cradle in the industrial portion of society until it embraces and serves all people.

Sad as is the current warring in the orient, the inanimate slave is inevitably penetrating that vast area of the world's population majority. As Miles Vaughn so aptly said: "Manchukuo is really the world's last great West."

When the inanimate slave is omnipresent for the world's populace, science predicts the maintainance of full-flowering bloom, after maturity, for man to his last days, and even the possibility of a continuity of living within the same mechanism when and if, in the fulfillment of this new era, this is desired by all men.

As soon as the full complement of inanimate slaves has penetrated the Orient, the rationalizations which started among these very people, in their mountains, the thought that originally evolved mathematics and invented fundamental structural principles will have girdled the world. It will have returned home, completely objectivized and, freed of all contaminations of interim personal equation tradition imposition, and the gap in the great circle will have been closed.

17

Baby Industry Is Kidnapped

At the crucial point of the Middle Age, two strongly contrasting figures emerged. One was the RATIONALIZER; the other the BELIEVER. One represented the artist, scientist and philosopher; the other was the essence of confused devotion to romance, dogma, and the surface traceries racketed by the fans of the two original abstract leader-types, the philosopher and the prophet.

One was LEONARDO DA VINCI; the other, SAVONAROLA.

The fans (fanatic followers) of the original *prosaic* or scientific philosophers had exploited the popular credit accruing to them through their proximity to the SOURCE and thus became the embryo academicians. The fans of the prophets, through like exploitation, became the priesthood, going in for esthetic, intrinsic and moral exploitations.

Leonardo, builder of useful instruments, sculptor, painter, author and architect, conceived, amongst his many inventions, the aeroplane. Although the means of its construction were not yet at hand, its conception was none the less rationally and scientifically formulated. Likewise Leonardo foresaw the application of industry to his current activity, architecture. He perceived the necessity of mobility, popular use and the efficiency of centralized manufacture, and he created designs, similar in many ways to the form of the *dymaxion* house, that is, hexagonal in contour, triangularly sectional for wedge assembly.

Savonarola, a victim of the mental confusion that characterized the old animism, evolved beautifully poetical but futile *bon mots*, or lashed his flock into a horrific, groaning mesmerization. Whatever he bludgeoned out was imbibed by the priesthood as fuel for the inculcation of a blindly, fearfully obedient spirit in people.

We cite Leonardo and Savonarola as opposing types to accentuate the *status quo* of the Greek streamline at this point in history, but will digress for a space from discussion of them.

By the middle of the period 1500-1600, ushered in teleologically by Leonardo, the coördinated management of machines for the reproduction of popularly consumable products had spread from the making of books to the manufacture of all kinds of commodities, particularly such rapidly consumed articles as fabrics for clothing, in the manufacture of which unaccountable "time" was saved.

Soon the efficiency of the industrial mechanism produced more than sufficient to satisfy the wants of the people in the locality of the factory. The surplus was offered to people in foreign parts where there were either no factories at all or no identical manufacture, and so commenced the export of industrial products.

Transportation was so slow, however, that a long period elapsed before a manufacturer could "realize" on his production. This offered a particular entrepreneuring advantage for the feudal landlord, who was the legal beneficiary of the land-grabbing kings. He was well accustomed to collecting tithes from his tenants in a *fiscus* (basket, origin of the word fiscal) at the end of each season, with the physical power to dispossess those tenants who had no tenth to contribute, which act was known as "finance" (*finis*, business).

Observing that the industrial factory was far out-distancing, in productivity, the capacity of hand-to-mouth workers in his arts-and-crafts land plant and wishing to "chisel" into the new, the feudal landlord volunteered to underwrite the TIME interval required for the business of export, by supplying goods from his land to support the workers during the interval. (Workers in plants must eat.) In return, he asked a *commission in kind* (profit) from the manufacturer. *Kind* originally meant heads of cattle, marked off in units to supply the underwriting security.

Baby Industry Is Kidnapped

But inasmuch as cattle are alive and reproduce "after their kind," their number normally multiplied. The feudal landlord claimed—and was conceded—the excess new-born stock. This was the origin of the phenomenon "interest." The feudal lords were not the first to practice it. The Greeks and Phoenicians originated the idea in agrarian export-import trading. But the feudalists were the first to wed the interest phenomenon to inanimate industrial production. The word "pecuniary" comes from *pecus*, which is the Greek name for cattle, which the Phoenicians employed as *interim* collateral. Practically all finance terminology comes from agrarian sources: "stock" or shares of an industry derives from cattle; the farmer owned a "share" of stock meaning a share of cattle, or capital. "Watering stock" originated in the deceptive practice of causing cattle to drink prior to weighing for sale.

Money had, of course, been in use for trading long before the birth of industry. The Phoenicians, by ship, and the Arabs, by caravan, had early developed this perquisite of trade. The demand for money increased infinitely under the impetus of industry, its increasing productivity, and the specialization of production. When goods were shipped to foreign destinations, where a strange language was spoken, there was little possibility of credit of buyer by seller. Very often the produce of the buyer's land was not desired in exchange for the exported goods. So it became necessary to devise *currencies* as an abstraction of trade, in order that payment might be made for goods purchased by the foreign customer in some *temporary* medium subsequently and universally convertible by the shipper in acquisition of other types of product, or produce in other places.

It was a natural sequence of events for the feudal landlord to become a capital-furnisher. He had, through necessity and tradition, specialized in trading with precious stones and minerals originally extracted from the land, or from tombs of wealthy dead where they had been laid away with the bodies because of their "eternal" quality, and the possibility of their being needed by the deceased to pay his way in heaven, an acknowledged strange country.

147

To keep abreast of the ever-accelerating amplification of industry, with its high manifolding mechanical ability, as well as the rapidly multiplying requirements of money for trade, the capital-furnishers made overtures to the priesthood. The priesthood was already surreptitiously anxious to speculate the vast riches that the church had accrued through exploitation of the people's fear and as the successor to the pagan temple riches and vast surreptitious tomb robbing on their own part. The money-lenders found it expedient to make their headquarters, like current theatre-ticket speculators, near the churches (out of which they had been fired at the inception of Christianity).

Together the feudalists and brotherhoods systematically and piratically explored the tombs of the Pharaohs and the habitats of ignorant wild people in the vicinity of sources of precious stones and metals. This necessitated the establishment of the dignifiedly entitled "foreign trading posts," where managers could be counted on (through fear-bullying by the financiers) to handle local credit "situations." Often this exploration-buccaneering was done directly by the priesthood, whose outposts are still to be found in all pioneered lands. The greatest vandalism was probably done by the cross-bearers. In the foreign trading posts, the "managers" of the moneylenders' affairs came, in due course, to handle credit by a bookkeeping abstraction in lieu of coincidental shipments of gold and other specie for every transaction. This expedient was occasioned by the increase in high seas piracy, a hi-jacking racket intramurally underwritten by the same feudalists who underwrote the export-import trade of goods. Efficiency was developed through the seasonal balancing of trade by an occasional or periodic transfer of actual goods or bullion.

So bountifully prosperous did the industrial phenomenon become to the landed feudalist and to church racketeers that they were tempted to finance ever greater and more able equipment for the manufacturers. In a relatively short time, therefore, the industrial equation, which started with and was first managed by the artist, inventor and mechanic, came under the control of exploiters, by reason of their financing of equipment, debt manipulations and foreclosures. The *industrial* managers (leader crafts-men), being of the longing type, were imbued with pleasure in the mere act of production of goods for people and, as such, were readily exploitable.

The moneylenders (disguised agents of the feudalists and church) represented the quintescence of materialism and non-science. They hesitated fearfully, however, to accredit ma-chinery due to their lack of knowledge of its potential mechan-ical ability. Unable to speak the language of the scientific indus-trialist, they could not check for themselves, except in a ludicrous trial-and-demonstration manner (for instance, by thumping, kicking, listening to and smelling a piece of machinery)—the potential adequacy of the ever more complicated equipment which, in their greed, they wished to patronize.

To meet the situation, they created and subsidized richly a *business manager* who was authorized to watch over the indus-trial enterprises in their stead. To be doubly safe, they utilized their temporal power to influence, through patronage, code-makers (lawyers) to the end that rules of state or precedence might be enacted for the protection of their investments.

As their wealth rapidly increased, the feudal rulers and money-lenders yearned to enjoy the amplifying profits and earnings of their investments. Satisfaction of vanity being their prime source of enjoyment, they desired to travel and display their riches before other feudalists. Travel necessitated their absence as watch-dogs over the source of their earnings. So they created corporations or abstract legal entities, the management of which could be entrusted to several men or *directors*. The feudalist's cupidity trusted no one man.

With passing years, the efficiency of machinery and its com-plexity gave promise of earnings greater than any early feudal landlord had dared to dream of, provided a relatively tremendous investment could be made in "capital" equipment. The required investment was larger than any feudalist could or would venture to underwrite singly. So, despite mutual fear and distrust, and coerced by avarice the moneylenders pooled their resources for investment, each receiving "shares" according to his contribution. These "shares" carried votes of director-election proportionate to their *prima facie* value.

Since the principle of mechanics-accrediting involves ever increasingly complex and costly machinery, it is obvious that ever greater and more popular credit of its performance is necessary, thus inevitably bringing the number of participants in the original pooling to thousands of shareholders, through the sequence of friends of friends of friends.

The progression perforce carried the sharing outside the bounds of the feudal leader class into the realm of courtiers and *petite bourgeoisie*. Although this increased sharing appeared to a minor degree during the nineteenth century, it was actually not until the World War that the knowledge and, therefore, the credit of the worker-populace was articulated in industrial sharing. The people had long "shared" the ultimate products and services of industry, but in the 1920's the workers really took over the numerical majority of "shares," albeit the holdings were individually minute dollarwise.

The inequity of the vote attached to the share suddenly became apparent through wide participation. It would be quite inequitous to have a vote attached to every dollar bill. This vote-per-share enabled small groups of men, through proxies and the law of average, not only to control the election of Boards of Directors and thereby the affairs of a corporation, but, by much surreptitious ability, to affect indirect earnings without direct peculation.

This "milking" is effected through continuously interlocking directorates, third and fourth-hand indirect earnings being thus utterly undetectable. Such earnings are based simply on contiguous effects, i.e., the third or fourth-hand effect of some elective operation of one industrial property upon the value of the property of others, the amplification of which serves, in turn, as collateral for credit liquefaction. With such liquid credit a sufficiently large capitalist can agglomerate a 3-1 liquid credit of others "on call" for eventual market speculation, into which, of course, he would never enter without pooled assurance of coöperative manipulation for profit.

Murphy, being a minor speculator owning one share of TEL. & TEL., can say to himself, "I have a unique way of voting. If I like a share, I buy and keep it; if not, I sell it! This action is taken on the basis of my crediting or not crediting the industrial activity involved. I don't care who runs a particular industry so long as when I invest in it, it seems good to me."

Murphy may buy TEL. & TEL. twenty times a year and sell it as often. He is not interested in the management of the company beyond his attempt to anticipate its solvency or insolvency. Quite evidently, Murphy does not care about the voting power of his shares.

This indifference is true of most small shareholders with the exception of a few, who, suffering from an inferiority complex, enjoy a sense of importance when deviling the "great" at annual stockholders' meetings. This seemingly lax attitude on the part of the great majority yields proxies which, although for a relatively few shares so far as individual holdings are concerned, permit a behind-the-scenes control by those privileged to vote the proxies. This is particularly facilitated by wholesale quantities of proxies for shares held by estates, banks and trust companies, which latter often send in such proxies on the "instruction" of the prevailing financial "big shot" of the situation.

Inasmuch as the votes not wanted by the small shareholders are used against their interests by secret manipulation on the part of the stealthy watch dogs of doubt-and-fear and all the army of subordinates of the "big shot" chiselers, it is reasonable to expect that this voting appurtenance of common shares will be removed in the evolutionary willy-nillying of democracy. In this connection, Stuart Chase once said that the populace could free industry from Finance-capital's manipulation by the bold stroke of having the government call in every share of common stock extant and supplying in exchange shares with non-voting power, though participant in all other ways. This thoughtful suggestion is one of "reform" and it is probable that the change will be mechanically brought about as later to be outlined.

It was by means of abstract devices of laws, votes and high-sounding morals that infant industry, of, by and for the people, was kidnapped by cupidity. But science, rich in infinite treasure-trove, is serenely able to pay the ransom.

18

Longing Crosses the Sea

THE period now under consideration, in our history of essential motivating forces and the economics of creative art, is that which began with Columbus's discovery of a new continent and ended with Copernicus's postulate that our "world" is not a standing-still center of the universe. The dates relative to this most arbitrarily selected point in history are unimportant. It is always NOW.

The center of the considered period was approximately 121,000 earth revolutions ago. Rays originally emanating from each and every star, then reflected from earth-events of that time, have in the meantime expanded outward 2 quintillion miles from earth, or about 1/500 of the distance to the farthest currently discovered star. Possible persons with able telescopes on planets of that neophite star member will actually see the events happening 15,000 years hence from "now," which we now preposterously call "330 years *ago*." Those events are actually sensorially and mechanically occurring, at this instant, upon the surface of a sphere only 330 light years radiantly out from earth, for, remember, radiation includes all ray types, and whereas *light* rays reflect from the surface, other rays penetrate to and reflect from each and every physical depth outward at the same rate as the light reflected from the surface.

The mind, when comprehending events of 330 years "ago," is merely exercising its limitless function of jumping outward into the universe to that series and area of expanding time spheres to intercept the events *now*. What we sometimes call "ghostly" phenomena may quite scientifically be "assumed" to be events which have rebounded off other heavenly bodies, with the same certainty of angularity impact as that involved in the impacting of billiard balls, back to earth in the highly ephemeralized form of their interim expansion. It is to be noted that fictions of lying or imagination subsequently interwoven into "past" events cannot be reflected because they did not happen.

During our now considered period, which covered slightly more than a century, Galileo presented scientific proof of the postulate of Copernicus. Vasco de Gama and Magellan added empirical proof, the one by voyaging southeast to the Orient around the Cape of Good Hope, and the other by sailing southwest around the Horn and girdling the globe. Despite Magellan's physical death or abandonment of self-ship one half way around, Magellan's phantom captain completed the trip of his original undertaking, for his thought momentum was convincing enough to his successors to persuade them to continue westward into the unknown instead of "turning back," which is always eastward from the viewpoint of the "overall" trend of man migration. Man follows the source of his energy, ever westward.

In the very center of this century, which was of tremendous significance for popular industry then incubating in Europe, Leonardo wedded science, art and mechanics, the first stable matrimonial triangle. Leonardo, the artist-scientist, and Savonarola, the dramatic, dogmatic, fear-inspiring priest, were symbolical of the intersection of the new road of civilization emergent and the old one certified for death. The world of Leonardo, the world of truth, was usefully emergent; that of Savonarola a hoax, uselessly recessional and dissipant.

The world of Savanarola was one of surface glamour, highly sensorial and popular. In it, the religions of materialism found fertility for their seeds planted in the fearful popular credulity. The great churches developed the surfaces of their edifices, in an utterly time-wasting manner and with complete lack of consideration of the barest necessities of living beings, especially children. The result was an exquisite intricacy of lacy craft workings of academic art, for which the age came to be particularly famous, and nothing more. Filth, disease, torture and pillage rampaged while ignorant beings were taught to "embroider" their souls.

The feudalist, seeking industrial control, fought hypocritically behind the period's romanticism; the fighting was carried on in the romantic guise of great wars of religious principle.

"England" and "Spain," in quest of new lands and people for exploitation sent out ships with great crosses on their sails. The word "nation" represented at that time the financial ruler in contradistinction to the idea that a nation is its people. The "nation" captured new lands in the name of the cross, actually planting its symbol with great solemnity. England, seeking to reopen and control the way to the Far East by land, found it expedient to send crusaders through Europe to the eastern Mediterranean. Mayhap many crusaders were quite romantically intent upon recapturing the Holy Grail from the infidels, and the many incidental *en route* pillagings were accounted as gestures of God-given beneficence. The Holy Grail, though a physical prize, was quite possibly symbolic of a longing urge to recapture the secret well of thought sealed up with the passing of the Greek and Yogi scientist-philosophers. But behind the romance and spirituality of the quest and the cross-emblazoned shields, there was an economic causality, namely, the necessity of controlling far-flung elemental sources and export markets by overland route to the Far East. While England and Spain vied for the control of these, Holland and France, participating to lesser degree, strove primarily for control of the money exchanges complementary to the traffic.

England, wresting such maritime victories from Spain as the sinking of her Armada, emerged victorious in the struggle for control of the industrial colonies in North Temperate America. She took off, also, India and African Centralia, Australia, *et cetera*, and became the greatest export-import trade empire ever established.

Leonardo, harbinger of a new world, demonstrated in his thinking and activity an element that was unnoted by the exploiters. Through simplification, scientific analysis and the harmonious articulation of his philosophy, he demonstrated to humanity an "out" from rampant selfishness, materialism and exploitation. This "out"—no matter how diminutive and random it then appeared—became, by virtue of far-time-ahead sightedness and the abstract quality of truth, ever more tactically important, as the progression in all lines of efficiency approached ephemerality. The "out" was to be attained by a new and more effective way of thinking and doing, i.e., by teleology.

The new era, so brilliantly budding in Leonardo, had inevitably to become dominant through successive teleologists. Leonardo, the longing-motivated teleologist, was the interpolator, partially from the findings of academic specialists and pagan art, but mostly from scientific contemplation of nature, into goods, mechanisms and harmonies essential for the re-encouragement of humanity during its transition into an ultimate kingdom of Life Heaven from that of a Death Heaven.

Until the personalization in da Vinci of the forces presaging emancipation of man, through mind-over-matter control, the only "out" for popular man was death. Only after death, life being so bitterly hard, could he conceive of attaining heaven.

Synchronously, North Temperate America, new stage for industry's transplantation, is seen to have been not only relatively clear of any static civilization that, unknown to us, may have thrived upon it in prehistoric days (there are more Indians now than there were then), but it was also rich in almost every element essential to the highest development of the industrial principle. The impact of the Spanish invasion on Central American static civilizations, coupled with will-o'-the-wisp intrinsic values of pillaged gold which debilitated Spanish pioneering, certified industrial supremacy to the north.

Remembering that we have assumed man's motivation to be only through either longing or fear, although neither in pure condition, and that the longing type is wont to include and refine whereas the fear type tends to exclude and confuse, it becomes apparent that the fear-motivated feudalists were forced by circumstances of the trend to patronize the longing-motivated, industry-incubating individuals of that time such as Leonardo or Columbus in order to survive. Otherwise, we may be sure, feudalists' ships would never have billowed forth on fear-bestirring voyages of discovery. Certainly the fear type would not have dared in the poor little vessels then available, to cross a sea of unknown hazards, the terrific dynamics of which were so often reported in lurid misaccounts, which included such fabrications as sea serpents. (Such hardship folk tales as "Sinbad the Sailor" are typical.) It is certain, also, that the slothful, fearful, organized feudal servants would not have essayed to run away from their bully masters, let alone make initial crossings of the awful sea.

Colonization of the new continent was accomplished, therefore, by an extraction of a relatively "pure" longing type from out the confused, "Middle-Ages" world. The colonizers longed for liberty; longed for freedom of philosophic thought, or physical exploration, and for economic freedom, either by deed or invention. They longed, too, for freedom in which to breed a new race, no longer enchained by confused religions, traditional esthetic art, and superficial, material, intrinsic values. There was likewise manifest a longing to articulate physical might, such as in high seas buccaneering. This latter may not have been a very pure form of longing, but it was nevertheless longing.

Broadly, the combined longing of the many types was pure enough in strain to provide a colonization that was predominantly mental, for longing is a mental trait. It is the essence of mind-over-matter proclivity, even though it be only employed to break down, capture or annihilate space in order to be in the living presence of a loved one.

America was colonized, on the one hand, by communes of thinkers, and, on the other, by buccaneers who "blackbirded" slaves from Africa to till the soil of Virginia. It is significant that the mind-over-matterists, the Pilgrims, and others who in due course developed the inanimate slave, landed in the north, whereas materialists who perpetuated the animate slave settled in the south. This was in accord with the northwest progression of the mind-over-matterist and industry. Here was a clear trend indicator.

Shiploads of immigrants, eschewing all raiment and gadgets reminiscent of the decadent artistic glamour of the civilization they had left behind, landed *en masse*, and, with equanimity, faced the hardships and difficulties of communal survival. Being of the longing type and embodying in large measure the scientist-artist, they succeeded rapidly and efficiently in industrializing their survival problems. They differentiated wisely between difficulties arising from the special and personal causes of their pilgrimage and the requirements of their common welfare.

The colonies became commonwealths, the geographical layout of which bespoke in every way "common wealth." The town was planned as radiant from a "common" center for special buildings, typifying the tolerant recognition of all specific philosophic proclivities of the individual. Churches, representative of the gamut of philosophic tenets, were erected side by side upon this "common," together with a town meeting house which stood for the from-philosophy-segregated common interest of civil affairs, and, most exciting of all, there was included a public school designed to nurture the mind-over-matter abstract minds of new beings on the verge of coming into existence. Erudition, objectively obtainable through reading, writing and arithmetic, was the universal longing of all the colonists. It was revered as the positive emancipating force of mankind from the religion-bogged philosophy articulate in Old World churches.

Dwellings were reared around the "common," all hands taking part in their construction. A tolerant allowance was popularly accredited either to the prospective occupant or to the town carpenter for structural design invention. Incidentally, the carpenter of that period, who transported books of "stock" designs from the old country to the new, was the forerunner of those architects who, for two succeeding centuries (though still humbly entitled "carpenter") copied European styles, and, for still another century professionally, as architects, "worked" their styling trade. This "architect" fad was not to die out completely until a quarter century after the "World War" of 1914-1918.

The area of land surrounding the early commonwealth dwellings was apportioned for individual tillage, each allotment being within the tiller's ability, and the total product being used for the sustenance of the community. (Incidentally the word "till" as a depository of money derives from the depository of the fruits of tillage.)

In the course of time, intelligent efficiency discerned that the ability of some persons was greatest in carpentry, or in metal work, or in some other craft. With gradual recognition these abilities came to be tolerantly patronized by all the community. Those of craft skill were released from the primary necessity of field tillage; others were singled out because of a strategic ability to organize youths with a proclivity for military activity into armed units for mutual protection against the ravages of nomadic and curious savages, whose land they were "settling."

So efficient was this communal life that it was not long before it became a materially fertile field for the engraftment of the best mechanical characteristics of "industry" so recently emergent in renaissance Europe. Be it noted that the Pilgrims did not come to this country as conscious pioneers of the industrial principle, but by segregation through longing happened to be its most able progenitors. This is another demonstration of the persistence of inadvertence, or the random element, in the industrial progression.

19

Machinery Follows Longing and Carves a Trend Pattern

IN THE development of mills and factories machines were first located in rear rooms, sheds and storehouses. The latter shelters were haphazardly adjusted to the requirements of the machine. Subsequently, however, the profitableness of the machines required the extension of their scientific efficiency to buildings specifically designed for the various mechanical processes.

The history of machines and factory designs has been an inside-out radiant one, in sharp contrast to the evolution of man's dwelling design. Man has designed his shelters for dwelling, worship and play from the outside-in, for it was first necessary to be shielded against the elements and marauder attack in the shortest time possible. This expediency overlooked and obscured the fact that the man-mechanism is vastly superior, in exquisiteness and inclusiveness, to the industrial machines of man's devising. Not understanding himself as physically a machine, man has failed to extend radiantly from his machine-self with the efficiency that he has devoted to his industrial mechanisms, viewing which he has had greater perspective, and relative to which more daring in prophesy of use-satisfaction.

In the space of a comparatively few years the American colonies traversed every step of the industrial development which, in Europe, had required 1500 years. Mind-over-matter demonstrated itself with exquisite acceleration in the new country, and man rapidly conquered TIME.

Whenever man's industrial mechanism has moved westward, the new mechanical colonization has *not* repeated the earlier mechanical schedule of development of the locality from which it migrated, *i.e.* through successive crude mechanical stages. The new westward mechanical colonization has always imported the *latest* mechanical devices from the east. This is currently demonstrated in highly advanced form in the Orient where warring planes are not the old Jennies of the last World War, but the latest Douglases, *et cetera*. In other words, the westerly takes up where the easterly leaves off.

It was not long before the industrial productivity of the American colonies—despite manifold handicaps—attracted from the Old World an even greater extraction of longing-dominated people, though of lesser longing-domination than the first settlers. The new colonizers were agglomerated to a colonization that was already so scientifically pure that the efficiency of the hardy originals quickly communicated itself to the newcomers. The latter, inspired and emboldened to further longing-pioneering, pressed onward into the wilderness of the rich new continent and discovered more of its resources to abet the centrals of communal productivity.

Ocean transportation, of a diminutive character but adhering to more or less scheduled regularity, was established from the Old to the New World. Colonization increased as a geometrical progression.

Extractions from widely divergent Old World sources pooled in new unit communities in the New World. These pooled units resulted in the cross-breeding of the members of the longing type of various races until, by the advent of the World War approximately three hundred years later, there was in the United States a longing type embodying, in potentially numerically equal proportions, all white "nationalities."

Although colonists from the Old World still represented highly districtized units of populace extraction, they were indicative, nonetheless, of America's potentially integrating a white race of the longing-domination type with rapidly diminishing specific nationalistic traits and traditions. This was made possible by the absence of hard-and-fast national boundaries to keep the Old World extractions in continued separation.

Not long after their establishment, the high productivity of the healthy American communes as well as their need, in terms of efficiency, of goods and mechanisms of the Old World's industrial specializations, attracted the trader, and, consequently, his feudal capitalist. (Even up to 1917 cotton mill machinery was primarily imported from England and France and was superior to any obtainable in America.)

Now that the trans-Atlantic voyage was less fear-arousing, due to its having been successfully negotiated a number of times, the fear-dominated traders and their crafty capitalists dared to come to the new continent for the purpose of appraising its geography for the expedient location of trading centrals. Since their particular exploitation ability was in the field of maritime commerce, they chose locations that were most central and which simultaneously were consistent with the best anchorage facilities and best transportation means to and from the hinterland. They found New York particularly adaptable to their purpose, with Boston and Philadelphia next in importance.

The Dutch—the moneyed bankers whose specie was so essential to the feudal trader—colonized New York. Hence it is not surprising that New York is, in its town plan, eloquently articulate of an old materialistic civilization penetrating a new one. Manhattan Island necessarily called for a water-front street paralleling the curvature of the island. Back of this curving thoroughfare, however, the land was not laid out after the radiant plan adopted by the philosophic Pilgrims in the design of their communes.

Not only is the materialist's flat earth static concept, with its resultant square designing, in marked contrast to the triangulated structures of nomads, as earlier mentioned, but it is the opposite of the radiant town-planning of the philosophic-minded. In the early plan of Boston, for instance, there was a communal radiant design. As Boston came under the dominance of trading exploiters and capitalists (the materialistic-minded) the radiant town plan was encompassed by sections of square blocks (Back Bay, *et cetera*). Detroit, also, was laid out on a radiant plan which broke down into smaller triangles, having been designed by engineers of the army. It was not long, however, before materialistic exploiters superimposed a square plan upon the original design, and so Detroit today, as a city, is the oddest of directional hodge-podges.

It may be noted in passing that highways, which are in effect mechanical extensions of the communal phantom captain, just as is the dynamo, were, by the indirection of the random element, brought into being as a militaristic instrument. As the great highways of Europe were laid down by the Romans entirely for army utilization, so, also, are the wide arterial avenues of Washington of military origin. They were designed in their great width—now so seemingly by-chance suitable for automobile traffic—to provide gun vistas that guns in the central part of the capital might have clear shooting at an approaching enemy. The untutored in this knowledge remark upon the sagacity of the planners of Washington in anticipating automobile traffic, which was not invented until the lapse of many years. When disillusioned in such matters, the majority exclaim, "Oh, everything has such a morbid causality!"

Upon inspecting enough of man's instruments, "inadvertently" provided by original causes seemingly at great variance with ultimate use, one often discovers a planning-intelligence or sagacity beyond any ever demonstrated by man with pre-professed objective. It would seem that true intelligence must ultimately have its way and that those who oppose it, or wait upon destruction or stitch-in-time provocation, are ineffectual. Society may just as well set about doing intelligent town planning at the outset and, wherever possible, correct old town plans to conform to what intelligence alone may dictate. For instance, aeroplane depots should certainly be in a town's center. It is ridiculous for Bermuda air passengers to spend only five hours flying to New York, and then "waste" an hour and a half or two hours traversing the few miles from Port Washington to Times Square, New York's "town center." Chicago has had a remarkable opportunity for airport placement in the area on which the World's Fair was constructed, that is, on the midtown lake front, but is still vascillating about it (probably retarded by R.R.-emanating propaganda, as Chicago is America's largest center of this obsoleting mechanism) while bemoaning "another depression" as they creep through fifteen miles of traffic between the present airport and the city's center.

New York, today having revolted against the spoilage system, is to be commended upon having acquired its formerly "private" North Beach airport, which is central to all of greater New York, as a result of its "fiery" Mayor's four year fight. Mayor La Guardia has literally brought about the construction of an airport out of a vast, mountainous dump-heap island in Flushing Bay. The latter has been spread out to fill in the bay and flats. Little did the dumpers dream of winged ships to land upon their reeking load. This area adjacent to the "Fair" grounds will constitute the largest airport in the world, with facilities not only for land planes but for sea planes in protected waters. Although obviously less in size as a project, this great airport plan has involved an engineering vision equal in brilliance to that which conceived our new age wonders, Grand Coulee, Boulder Dam and the Tennessee Valley operation where an entire regional revamp has taken place. Although ninety per cent of all American millionaires' yachts have "steamed" out by this rubbish mountain island, Flushing's "Fujiyama" at the mouth of Long Island Sound, none of their minds envisioned its speculative purchase for revamping into the world's largest airport.

It goes without saying that an adequate airport could not have been inserted in the center of New York City by any conceivable manipulation of private enterprise and "condemnation," or underwritten solely by any local or state authority. This project was of necessity locally subscribed to in direct proportion to the local benefit, although primarily federally accredited, since airports are subject to national prerogative. Many are international in scope of efficiency-required jurisdiction. The newest and most important must be intercontinental, or, better, world-considerate, and ergo of world-wide patronage requirement not only of establishment but maintenance.

Airports are within the category of de-personalized, de-localized, de-nationalized universality of dependability which included earlier the aquatic era's "aids to navigation": buoys, charts, lighthouses, radio beacons, *et cetera*. In "aids to navigation," idiosyncracies-of-nations and personal-pride-perversions have been progressively removed in equal measure to the removal of their inefficient and ofttimes fatal imposition upon ships themselves (the rococco crippled Armada), or upon 'planes, or most recently upon radio circuits, since disaster makes the whole world kin (notwithstanding mystery maniacs such as faked the Amelia Earhart S.O.S.'s), because the "ole debil sea" is too historically vivid and dramatic in man's commonweal to allow of such jeopardization. A sailor making a landfall in a fog and storm must not be confused by "tricolor"-painted "can" buoys or "swastika"-shaped "spars." The time element in the fast-moving liquid estate allows of no measure for interpreting such "fool"ish business. International law and maintainance of the "aids" has supplanted the kindly but fatally inadequate personal contributions of the good Abbots of Aberbrothoc and their errant "bells" on the "Inchcape Rock." The time lag for navigational-aid recognition is exquisitely lessened in the gaseous estate's aerial navigating. As machinery follows longing it certifies success to the commonweal integrating force.

San Francisco, too, is planning a World's Fair for 1939 and has arranged that at the conclusion thereof the 400-acre exposition site will become the "Air Crossroads of the Pacific," capitalizing surely on its strategic convenience of location by serving the greatest number and those in the greatest hurry: 10 minutes by bus or cab from the air terminal building to downtown Oakland or San Francisco.

The phantom captain is indeed extending his mechanisms of mutual interservice in a magnificent, hope-inspiring manner at the start of the integrating era.

20

The Warehouse Era

WITH the arrival in America of traders and feudal capitalists, the erudition of the literate colonies, though eventually to prove prime emancipator, became a matter, for the nonce, of important exploitation. A battle of wits developed between the shrewd, materialistically-inclined newcomers and the freedom-loving pioneers. The outpost centrals, Boston and Philadelphia, as well as the primary trading central, New York, provided the exploitation schemers with many academically exploitable persons, who were won over by a variety of temptations.

Boston and Philadelphia, centers of advanced education, began to develop a vast crop of "lawyers" out of second and third generation colonists, who used their learning to espouse the cause of the intrinsically wealthier and pleasantly patronizing Old-World bully, which "cause" was the acquisition of control over the industrial productivity of the new land. The academies and universities became paradoxically endowment-won tools for *mental* attitude conditioning in a manner suitable to materialistic exloitation. Matter had successfully counter-attacked to momentary re-dominance over mind.

Innumerable legal contrivances were effected to divert the profitable fruit of the colonies' production into a channel of revenue, coursing back to the Old World. England—ruler of the maritime trade, to whom the Dutch, with their moneys-centralization, were inherently and expeditiously subservient—became the chief revenue extractor. Before long "she" set up the colonies as "sovereign" estates which "she" controlled by the titular deeding of properties through the spaded "Crown"—that Crown in the name of which original discoveries upon the continent had been piratically claimed with sanctimonious cross-planting in, paradoxically, "God's *own* country."

The Pilgrims had settled in common weal, heedless, in their fervor, of the piratical claims of vast lands, because they intuitively felt themselves to be unaffected, from a practical viewpoint, by such an untenable assumption, i.e., that the land belonged to the king and must be especially deeded to them as accessory-after-the-fact of settlement. A bit nostalgically, however, they "took it" gravely as God-given red tape, and through the same sentiment renamed their new communes after the town which they voluntarily abandoned. So transcendental to material power was the pure Pilgrim element that it was "above" physically resisting bullying tactics. This spiritual aloofness, coupled with realistic and vastly novel emergencies and the swelling of the ranks by the fearful, sheepish "witchcraft" sabotaging and propagandizing slaves of Old-World control, caused the colonies popularly to forget the European "depression." Moreover, the fact that the colonists' children had not experienced the European chaos allowed of the latter's becoming materially intrigued by the glamours of the sovereign estate.

Eventually, however, the offspring of the cross-bred longing colonizers became surfeited with the in-valid "sovereign" claim. Annoyed and taxed beyond endurance, they burst the bonds of the Old World. The American Revolution was the revolt of a new mind-over-matter, longing-dominated scientific element, not only from England but from the WHOLE of Europe—and more understandingly from that streamlined interim chaos of the Greek teleologists.

Fate played a high part in the success of the revolt. Although our academic historians have romantically featured Lafayette as the in-the-cause-of-freedom representative of France, coming to the aid of the Colonists inspired by their beauteous necessity, the truth is that French participation was precipitated by the racketeer's-necessity of France to protect her "sovereign" claims in hinterland America. Two sovereign expeditions, paid for or manipulated by France's feudal capitalists, had penetrated into the

North American continent both to the north and to the south of the English and Dutch colonies. These two expeditions had staked out for France all of the central continent between their north and south lines of exploration, viz., the entire valleys of the Mississippi River and the majority of the St. Lawrence.

Spain, the first nation that had asserted sovereign claims in America, was entrenched in the land south and west of the French dominion, that is, in the West Indies, Mexico, and Central and South America, with penetrations from Central America north-ward along the west coast of North America. Spain, therefore, warily weighed the question of forcibly protecting her sovereign claims and decided that they were well insulated from the British by the French. So, through statecraft intrigue, she abetted the French in their aid to the rebellious British colonists. "She" (Spain) thus avoided direct participation lest she be involved in open combat with a traditional enemy which would have jeopardized her domain in the event of failure of the revolution.

The colonials emerged triumphant over England. Despite the victory, however, and despite their continued success in dealing with Europe through the statecraft of rebellious, erudite Boston and Philadelphia "lawyer" delegates to Europe (playing European interests one against the other so effectively as to put over, for instance, the "Louisiana purchase" from France in lieu of pressing the colonies' claims in French-English Canada, which were quite potential of "proof"), they were naively unable to remain aloof from the insistently infiltrating trade and social traditions. It was impossible not to be influenced by the back-stroking of resident servants of feudal capitalists who disclaimed any "realistic" sympathy for the "mother" country. Moreover, it seemed expedient to adhere to the money habits of trade as imported by the Dutch. Hence the American colonists, having started with a no-property idea, became highly propertyized.

An extensive coterie of Boston and Philadelphia lawyers found such profit in protecting materialistic habits that, ignoring the spirit of freedom that had utterly permeated the Declaration of Independence, they schemingly saw to it that the Constitution, adopted subsequent to the revolt, was well pitted with loopholes for exploitation use. The "unearned-profit" disease, as with syphilis, has taken years of patient researching on the part of a few, and long-suffering and blatant balking on the part of many to become potential of extermination.

Fortunately, one democracy-saving factor survived the "Old World" contagion continuity. Primary education remained socialized.

In consideration of the then extreme isolation of trading centers and the poor means of transportation and communication, it became an easy matter for the capitalist to exploit the new industrialism, now so potentially productive of social weal in America. The exploiter-virus needed only to make two moves: first, to finance the exploration and discovery of elemental sources of such raws as were vital to the manufacturing processes, and, secondly, to employ lawyers to arrange transportation and communication franchises and to seize the monopoly of transportation, both to and from sources, and between centrals of increasingly necessary intercoursing.

The "bought for a shilling" sources of raws were non-revenue producing, however, without some primary conversion by refining and fabrication into forms that would lend themselves to economical transportation to manufacturing centers and into convenient units of trade classification and small manufacture purchase.

So the capitalists established refineries and mills at sources as well as great warehouses in the trading centers to which they brought their converted-at-the-source raws. These warehouses were akin to concentrated "mines" located conveniently near both the small manufacturer and the merchants, and the masses of population essential both for operation by the manufacturers, and as an initial consumer-outlet for the end "goods" so produced.

Hence the period between the Revolution and the World War, although characterized by an ever-improving mechanization of transportation facilities, as a result of greed for profitable revenue from the monopolies, may be called, popularly, the WARE-HOUSE ERA. An analogy is not untenable between the practices and attitude toward human beings involved in this appellation and substitution "ho" for the letter "a" in the period's "name."

Despite the journeys of trade managers and political servants of capital, scheduled travel was not *popular* in the warehouse era. The migratory, pioneering movements consigned themselves to "covered wagons," and did not patronize the commercialized routes established under transportation franchises.

The warehouse era was provocative of the establishment of ever greater and greater CITIES, having five primary elements: CENTRALIZED CONSUMER PRODUCT MANUFACTURE, WAREHOUSING, CLERKING AND TRADE, EXPORT AND IMPORT, and, the INTERSPERSED DWELLER, WORKER, BUYER OF THE CENTRALS. The last mentioned composite element was of least calculation consequence to the capitalists except as an animate machine to run teleologically the inanimate machine extensions; to serve as a machine of clerking, and as a machine of consumption of product.

These cities, through economic profit-efficiency, evolved within their bounds concentrated marts or exchanges, all embodying the foregoing five primary elemental constituents. But an export and import city's strategic sub-divisions are disposed by geographical considerations of warehousing relative thereto, calling for a sub-segregation of the whole phenomenon "city" into specializing marts, such as those of produce, leather, spices and metal.

Logically, the manufactories requiring water power decentralized themselves somewhat from the city toward available rivers, but they did not detach themselves further than a day's horse-haul from the warehouse centrals.

In the warehouse era, no matter how ingenious young and erudite minds may have been in the invention of processes and mechanical tools, the ultimate fabrication of the inventions was necessarily limited to the warehoused materials. Most typical of this era, in which metals were becoming of increasing consequence, was the familiar sight of *rust* everywhere. Capitalists interested in tonnage-of-metal-turned-out were not concerned with making better end products for ultimate consumers. Conversely they served and profited by the tenet that: the faster products rust and deteriorate, the greater the revenue.

RUST was characteristic of the inferiority of goods which it behooved the capitalist to produce in his ever more efficient, behind-the-scenes, industrial plant. The capitalists' gleamingly equipped powerhouses stood in marked contrast to the rusting pots and pans, the manufacture of which he was instrumenting.

Equally great was the contrast between the business buildings designed for the efficient clerking and accounting of trade and the shabby dwellings of the bifunctional, biexploitable worker-consumer, as the warehouse era matured.

The fact that the "skyscrapers" were primarily the "show windows" of multitudinous rackets, partially accounted for their lavish pretentiousness of design. Thus, late in the warehouse era, the gigantic Equitable Building, the largest business structure in the world at the end of the World War, as well as many lesser structures, provided the strangest of paradoxes. The Equitable was furnished with the finest of plumbing and fixtures, because it had been found conducive to highest efficiency to have the clerks housed, *while working*, in the most orderly, resistance-eliminating and harmony-breeding surroundings. Thus housed during hired hours they could put their best endeavor into their "accounting," *et cetera*, without the loss of a single dollar. A large percentage of stenographers at that time commuted from hovels with "outside" wooden privies "or equal" to heavens of sanitary luxury. Little wonder that the clerks of those days enjoyed giving "company" parties in their offices!

Before the introduction of first-class plumbing into the "house of business" one could readily distinguish by accoutrement and deportment between the feudalist's traveled debutante daughter and Miss Murphy, the local "stenog." However, the business-plumbing-heaven, with its attractive rest rooms, precipitated first a rapid evolution in the standards of dress of the clerical working girl and subsequently all working girls. She accelerated her transition in accoutrement to a compatibility with standards of plumbing experience. Within a few years, this transition, abetted by movies and "style" publications, made it impossible, superficially, to distinguish the "deb" from the typist.

As a business scheme the warehouse era may be "boiled down" to a one-way flow diagram in which the exploiter grabbed off sources with whatever minimum subterfuge was necessary as well as control of the transportation means of the down-hill flow to the dump heap. The faster the element of the original source of exploitation reached the dump heap the better. Ergo, the rule of thumb was the perpetuation of the lowest possible degree of efficiency in products and consumer life—"thumbs down" to *improvement*—orthodox bankers always say "No." Anyone who entered into a ringside executive's seat in such a business economy had perforce, as a "realist," to subscribe to this rule.

Since, evolutionarily, man is ever more intelligent, even the modicum of rationalization obtaining in the "inner circle" evoked the conscious recognition by its members of the profits inherent in the "principle of inefficiency." What they lacked was sufficient intellect to comprehend the inherently greater debits. These did not show on the books in good times and were otherwise (usually politically) accounted in bad times. Some boldly laughed it off; others, intuitively awake, sought sanctimoniously to salve their consciences through sympathetic benevolences—church charities, *et cetera*.

Once more it is to be pointed out that despite so ruthless an attitude, the exploiters inevitably established high efficiency in the behind-the-scenes essential productive mechanisms while pursuing the superficial rottenness. These mechanisms had the potentiality of becoming, granted a random element emergence, directly available to the industrial communal society growing up in the North American continent. This rising society with its extending industrial mechanism despite exploitation camouflage actually was *the* guinea pig of the "New World" laboratory.

The Warehouse Era

The exploiters had one great vulnerability. This was their dump-heap-bound scheme itself. The progression of cupidity and waste had ultimately to amplify into an attempt to engulf the whole world in accelerated destruction. Wherefore:—the World War. The random element involved was socialized education in the United States. Those in command of the business of public economy were able to prevent the high initiative of the cross-bred longing type from articulating its cultivated knowledge in end-product efficiency or in efficiencies of personal environment. They were not smart enough, however, to stop popular education itself. Not smart enough to stop the abstract and all-important mind-over-matter progression. Not being mind-over-matterist-minded, they failed to appraise this "theoretical" progression as so powerful as ultimately first to dominate and then to eliminate their "materialism."

21

Not in Vain Did They Die

THE 1914-1918 World War marked not only the high point of the warehouse era but the "peak" and crisis of many other force trend curves. Its outbreak signalized the attainment by feudally capitalized trade of a saturation of export markets within the geographical limits of the world.

The discovery in 1909 of the North Pole, and in 1910 of the South Pole, signalized the end of man's pioneering penetration within sensorial geographical limits. A World War within a few years to divide up the now *limited* spoils of land claimage was certified by these polar discoveries. If trade had been established with Mars, presumably providing ample outlet for all of the feudal capitalists' exploitation of Earthians' productivity, there would not have been a World War.

It is to be noted that these terminal physical discoveries coincidentally overlapped the nativity inventions of the new era, penetrating into, and structuring upon, the 96% vaster and noncompromisable riches of the non-sensorial forces of the universe, discoverable and employable only through intellect and faith.

The War concluded the colonization in-flow to the American continent. Shortly thereafter, and for the first time in the four hundred year history of the colonization, immigration fell below emigration. Cross-bred, longing, industry-incubating America had become outflowing, deliquescent.

Constructively, the War initiated the application of the industrial principles to machines for *consumer* use in contradistinction to the dominant manufacture of scientific "behind the scenes" machinery for the production of non-mechanical consumer goods. Particularly notable among the mechanical products for consumer use were the telephone, electric light, and automobile, which made possible the populace's individual turning of night into day, miles into inches, and the coursing over roads theretofore used primarily by the trading exploiter and his servants. The end of the War marked the ascendancy of passenger miles *per capita* transported by automobiles over passenger miles *per capita* carried by the railroads. Today, only twenty years later, the auto carries U. S. man 26 miles for every 1 that he rides on the R.R.; and air travel is fast rising and already carries 1/30 the U.S. passenger mileage of the R.R.

The Chart of Inventions at the end of the book reveals strikingly the abstract inventions at the turn of the century and up to the World War, as well as the contiguous mechanical inventions of the same period attained only through high intellectual activity and imagination which inevitably presaged an entirely new, world-populace-integrating era of scientifically dictated survival.

The advent of popular intercommunication signalized the breaking down of the Time-and-Space that had intervened between consumer-workers, and which, by isolating them as individual units, had hitherto rendered them highly exploitable by the feudal capitalist.

All three—the automobile, telephone and electric light—were products of the most extraordinary mathematical calculation and high scientific rendition. Of the three possibly the automobile—which Ford conceived of as mass-producible for a popular market (while other producers lingered over their manufacturing on a tailoring basis solely for the feudal lord and his well paid trustees)—was the most significant. At the time of the World War the automobile was a crude vehicle and its quantitative output relatively small, but it was none the less an attained phenomenon. Throughout all prior ages no one thing so symbolized dominance by the material overlord as did the horse. By virtue of his control of the horse, the overman had been able to traverse more space, capture outlying undiscovered sources, win wars, and accomplish more work than was possible by any on-foot peasantry. Anyone who could claim a horse was a potential feudal leader.

Early feudal leaders, fearful and arrogant, arrayed themselves in armor that was ever more impregnable, but at the same time was so increasingly complicated and heavy that the picture of Alice and the White Knight, which seems ridiculous and amusing, truly represented the ultimo fact of the progression. These men actually had to be hoisted by a group of servants onto their horses, also armored, that is, about their tops and sides. Despite the clumsiness of their paraphernalia a few feudal leaders, thus armed and mounted, could ride upon serfdom certain of easy conquest.

The Battle of Cressy marked an historical turning point in the overthrow (much later to be made irrevocable, however) of mounted feudalism by serfdom. At this juncture the serfs put their addled but survival-activated heads together and evolved the idea of a deployed line, armed with pikes. While the enemy was charging, these pikes could be swiftly implanted in the ground, their points pitching forward at an angle that would impale the unarmored undersides of the oncoming horses. The "pikers" were successful in unseating the armored knights who, lying helpless on the ground, became the easy victims of the meagerly and light armed serf.

The 1914-1918 World War marked the end of the traditional mounting of military pawns of feudal leaders, i.e., the cavalry, although a *nouveau riche* "aristocracy" still confusedly goes "horsey" on the first "one hundred grand."

With the inception by Ford of a mechanical vehicle for mass use, not only was the populace suddenly provided with one "horse," but 30 to 100 "horses" each. With one fell swoop the serf, if he had a job and could drive, was made the physical equal or superior of his historic master without the latter's vain display. This mechanical end product irrevocably broke down the class system in America despite petty pretense otherwise.

The World War established additionally, beyond all possibility of elimination from the social progression, the already invented attainment of the airship and aeroplane which, by their war-extensive successful use, gave to man the practical realization of his through-all-time-dreamed-of ability to fly, the potential of which, in man's thinking, certified his inevitable victory over ALL space and time. The significance of the REALIZATION OF FLYING is so far-reaching as to be beyond calculation, though it may be dimly appraised in the world-wide, nation and breed surmounting, exultation and "god" making of Lindbergh's achievements.

The War marked, also, the attainment of the popular recognition of the superior practicality of communication by radio, though like the aeroplane the radio in 1918 was still not popularly available. The radio conferred to all an eventual ability to communicate across world-spanning and even star-spanning distances, instantly, wirelessly.

Both AVIATION and WIRELESS were INSPIRATIONAL to a popular REVOLT against MONOPOLY dominance.

Another result of the World War was the attainment of *popular* participation in "higher," or college, education, leading youth into realms of physics, chemistry, medicine and engineering on a remunerative basis. Prior to 1914, despite a plenitude of popular higher educational establishments, no means of teleologic pioneering was practically open to the student other than to increase the entrenchment of monopoly through the application of acquired knowledge to the improvement of the efficiency of the mechanism of exploitation, by means of which the exploiter was turning out cheap, rustable and breakable end products.

Feudal capital, unwitting these emergences, was now fighting for *supremacy* in the no-further-extensible world markets. During the War, capital profited drunkenly from the fabulous outlet for source-monopoly materials involved in the destruction attending war:—thousands upon thousands of tons of sunken ships called for thousands upon thousands of tons of metal for replacement. So secure did he feel in his power to manipulate "scarcities" and governments by controlling them with legal "frame-ups" concocted by his lawyer-servants out of the rules of the "divine right" of property, that he had neither worry about nor intimation of the inevitable emancipation from his exploitation which he was unintentionally accelerating, with his high-profit World War activity, for his former victims.

The myriad of ramifications of this destructive war-"out" blinded the monopolist to the potentials involved in the wedding of general scientific erudition with the mechanical end-products introduced by Ford, Edison, Bell, Singer, et al., which were destined to overthrow his monopoly dominance.

Although the capitalist sensed the character of the profit involved in world warring, his imagination was too circumscribed to encompass the enormous proportions to which, once started, it had necessarily to expand. He had expected to maintain the war as a nicely controlled destructive activity with assured results. Not so the reality! The holocaust ran into figures involving a credit necessity to cover manufacturing and transportation time-lags that far exceeded the combined extant and on-paper-accounted-dollars value of the property controlled by all capitaldom.

Wages alone of workers and fighters called out of the vast unemployment cumulatives of machine replacement were far in excess of the total of private capital or "credit" coverage. Wherefore, capitaldom was in a predicament of more than momentary duration. However, the "lawyers" found an "out" through the medium of capitaldom's political control of governments, which made it possible arbitrarily to expand government credits WITHOUT COLLATERAL through the apparent sanctity of the good old "sovereignty." Little did they realize that, in a semi-industrialized era, the invocation of non-collateralized government credit was the invocation of popular credit, of which governments are the acknowledged legal representatives in contradistinction to the "private" characteristic of credit in early "sovereign" days.

So accustomed was capitaldom to the notion that it could manipulate government through political gangsterism that it was a matter of no concern to it—if it thought of it at all—that it was drawing on true per capita credit, for, in its own terminology of "interpretation," it was only multiplying the potential and in-due-course-to-be-accounted *per capita* "debt" to itself, capital-dom.

This governmental credit to finance profiteering was so grati-fyingly adequate for the nonce that capitaldom drank deeply of it, even to the point of inebriation. Hence by the time the world's populace had sickened of warring to the extent of insisting, by popular demand, on cessation of the slaughter, the governmental or popular credit which had been invoked and which, therefore, had been irreparably set up on the books in accountants' figures, was three times as great as the total of capitaldom's war-swollen private credit, which had previously been the sole source of credit for "industry" as well as for "government."

The debt system as it previously had worked out constantly increased in size, due to capitaldom's maneuvering of the activi-ties to which it had loaned its "credit," and reached such a state of inability to refund the liquid credit that foreclosure was always inevitable. Inasmuch as the collateral was at least a two to one value against the loan, the debt structure was amplified on a pro-gression of two to one against liquid activities. Thus capitaldom's amassed credit structure, which we now call "debt structure," was accountingly established.

DEBT STRUCTURE not only sounds like DEATH STRUCTURE, but even in the words of trade is actually so: MORT-GAGE, MEASURE-OF-DEATH, MORA-TORIUM, HOLD-OFF-THE-DEATH-BLOW. Popular credit is far dif-ferent from capitalistic private credit which, in fact, is not credit at all, but a collateralized pound-of-flesh debt mechanism.

Popular credit, on the other hand, is the very essence of life. It accredits potentials of life behavior. It accredits the progressive ability of men coöperatively to improve their commonwealing. It accredits science with the ability to instrument and with the ordering of men's coöperation in the betterment of its common wealth.

As a result of the World War a three to one ratio was established of the accounted living credit dominance over debt accounting.

Not in vain, the sacrifice of millions of lives under the dishonestly propagandized, yet sincerely populace accepted, notion of a war to save democracy! Not only did capitaldom release dominant popular credit from Pandora's box when it lifted the profit lid of the World War chest, but it let out, also, a set-up of mechanical principles and scientific attainments destined to prove the means for sensible speculation of the popular credit and the establishment of a working mechanism for democracy's eventual emancipation.

22

Enter Alloy: Exit Rust

SCIENTIFIC discovery is invention, and *vice versa*.

We say "discovery" because scientists (sometimes called inventors) simply bring into physical, tangible relief, energy properties of the universe which are and always have been latently present. There is herein inferred no credit of "scientific attitude" in the fussings of millions of tricksters of mechanical rearrangements who are popularly called inventors. However, even after "discovery," inventions often remain popularly unrecognized and unemployed for long periods. For example, chrome-nickel, an alloyed combination of elements of special proportions for toughening of steel, was scientifically "discovered" in 1898 but was not put to practical use until the World War.

Alloying of basic metals in general had not attained to broad use prior to the World War because the finance-capitalist, herewith "dubbed" Fincap for short, was interested in *tonnage* not in *quality*, and failed to envision the value, even in his own production-machine monopolies, of alloy employment that might afford higher longevity in service of mechanisms.

In fact, it was quite counter to Fincap's interest to achieve such high longevity even in his own mechanisms for, through such devices as interlocking directorates and widespread holdings, he apparently reaped higher revenue from the production of gross tonnage of erosive disintegratable raws than out of the production of improved machinery.

By instigating the War, Fincap unleashed popular man's educated ingenuity (theretofore but minutely and fearfully "valved off" for Fincap's competitive ends) into the people's own service to demonstrate its survival worth, in defense of family, nation, idealism and honor in the broadest sense.

Fincap, busy with profits, did not dream of the change of attitude toward machinery and its basic manufacture that would transpire during the War. Educated man's ingeniousness, waging war, was limitless. Men fought defensively for their freedom, their "democracy." The ostensible "offensive" was simply the means of "defense." Better, ever better, guns were required. Guns wore out with terrific rapidity, which intensified their scarcity and called attention to the necessity of designing guns that would last longer. English ordinance men demonstrated that steel alloyed with chrome and nickel which, as stated, had been originally invented in Germany, was so tough that it could withstand disabling wear twice as long as could the gun steels till then employed.

The utilization of chrome-nickel-steel in British guns was only one of a myriad of innovations designed to provide increased longevity of service of man's extension-mechanisms of predominant survival. Chrome-nickel-steel not only provided a metal that was relatively rust-proof, but one with increased *hardness* and *toughness* and one with twice the tensile strength of ordinary steel and with 50% more than the tensile strength of the best gun steels in use prior to its inclusion. Specifically and matter of factly, *this increase in the tensile strength of steel symbolized the great transition from the matter-over-mind to mind-over-matter dominance.*

Prior to the War, ordinary steels and cast iron, *et cetera*, were approximately *identical* in compressive and tensile strength. These two stress categories of "compression" and "tension" comprise essentially unique stress satisfaction segregations of all structures and mechanisms. They are selectively employed by scientific man to balance the two primary (and otherwise unharnessed) energy characteristics: *push* and *pull*. True, there are other stress and structural characteristics such as "hardness," "elasticity," "elongation," *et cetera*, but these are figuratively speaking, children of the parents: *compression* and *tension*.

The pre-War steel-iron family averaged approximately 60,000 lbs. to the square inch, "ultimate" in either compressive *or* tensile strength, and was representative, broadly speaking, of the most "efficient" of all man's materials-of-design-satisfaction and synthesis. ("Efficient" connotes an integration of the weight-strength, availability, coincident longevity-workability-under-standability factors as it applies to structuring of the inanimate slave. [It might also apply to appraisal of a spontaneous inamorata.]) Not only was the steel-iron family *balanced* in its *compressive* and *tensile* strength, but up to the World War its *compressive* strength was still only the equivalent of the top compressive strength of masonry and stone which was likewise 60,000 lbs. to the square inch.

Stone and masonry, however, have a tensile strength relatively far less than their compressive strength. Moreover, the stone and masonry tensile strength (of 50 to 500 lbs. per square inch) is inferior, by cross-sectional area comparison, even to that of the best fibrous members of animate structures—that is, of wood, hemp, *et cetera*. Wherefore, steel, although equaled *compressively* by masonry, was 120 times stronger than the latter (pre-War) from a tensile viewpoint. That is why we say that in steel lay, broadly speaking, the most important by man synthesized advance of materials for structural design satisfaction up to that date.

Immediately following the war-born institution of toughened, hardened and non-corrosive alloys and their inclusion in heat-treated steel products, further refinements of the alloying process occurred.

Subsequent to the War, industry advanced the *tensile* ability of certain special production steel products ("piano wire," *et cetera*) to 400% *more* than the compression-resisting ability of any steel,—"production" or "research"—by equivalent cross-sectional comparison, i.e., to 300,000 lbs. to the square inch *tensile* strength.

Proof that these changes factually symbolized the transition to popular mind dominance over matter is to be drawn precisely from this structural and mechanical tension *vs.* compression history.

It was postulated earlier that the tension line is a fitting symbol of intellection, being practically unlimited in length with relation to its cross-sectional area. Being also flexible, the tensed structural member is instantly adjustable to load changes and may, therefore, receive *eccentric* loadings at any point along its surface, because *it tends to pull true and, with loading, becomes more cohesively taut.* It is more "intelligent" to "play" a great fish with a delicate tension line with which one may tire and ultimately reel him in (despite his superior size, weight and speed to like characteristics of the fisherman) than, irrationally in a might-makes-right bully manner, to jump into the water and attempt to push the fish out with a fishing pole of possibly 100 times the cross-sectional area of the line.

Vertically and statically employed structural compression members have "advantage" over any other equally dimensioned compression member employed horizontally, slantwise or otherwise. Vertical compression members of masonry are limited in height to 18 times their diameter. This is the old Greek column formula. The compression stress-satisfaction members of steels and woods are allowed a little better than this proportion of diameter to length.

Structurally speaking, eccentric or working loads *must* be applied to compressive members only at their terminals, in the line of the longitudinal axis; otherwise their fundamental tendency to deflect from that axis will be amplified toward failure through collapse, or sheer.

Although the compression member is thus highly limited in its functioning in comparison to the tension member, granted equal cross-sectional strength, the "practical" structural advantage was nonetheless held by compression-employed materials, as in the stone arch bridge, until the U. S. Civil War (at which time the Bessemer and Kelly processes of economical steel manufacture were invented), due to the high economic availability in these earlier days of inanimate, unsynthesized stone with its simple pounds-per-square-inch compression resistance highly superior stressively to the tensile strength of vegetable or living tissue-structured fibers. This compressive advantage was then symbolic of the superiority of might-makes-right throughout all the days of pre-mechanized society.

In the post-Civil War synthesis era, stone was supplanted by a metallic extraction from stone itself which, as a primary structural and instrumental material, made the machine possible. This extraction had obviously called for functioning of the selective mechanism of intellect.

Following the analogy of tension representing "right" and compression "might," this intellectual functioning developed not only a *parity* with might in the commercial or warehouse era prior to the World War as symbolized by an equal balance of the compressive and tensile ability of the then most able structural materials (as demonstrated in the Brooklyn Bridge with its stone compression masts and steel tension cables), but, also, a slight edge over "might," that is, approximately 70,000 lbs. per square inch in compression and 75,000 lbs. tensile strength in alloyed steel, which latter was 10,000 lbs. more than the "best" *compression* strength of stone (60,000 lbs.) and 500% greater tensile strength than in the stone structure days. This 14 2/7% *compressive* gain of steel over stone represents approximately the sum total of advance of the pushing bully of the 20th century A.D. over his 3,000,000 B.C. stone age forebear, and the 1500% gain of steel in tensile ability represents the practical "intellectual" gain over the stone age.

As mentioned above, tension members are much more versatile functionally in relation to working loads than compression members, where either is developed to its most satisfactory or efficient extension. Wherefore, in cross-sectional tests of one cubic inch units the superior metals of the tension or compression categories may show only an equivalent resistance to ultimate failure. They are not at all equivalent as practically disposed in their respective extended "best" structural employment.

To lift a weight mechanically to any height, for instance, to the top of the Empire State Building, there is required either an elevating plunger similar to that of the old push-up elevator, or a tension cable suspended and reeled overhead. If a push-up elevator were to be used, it would call for a horizontal cross section *diameter* almost as great as that of the Empire State Building itself to avoid dangerous deflection, though the load be but one pound. So effective, however, is metal in tension and so unlimited is it in cross-sectional ratio to length, that a steel cable of $1''$ diameter would be sufficient to lift a several ton load to the top of the building.

In the giant suspension bridge, the roadway (or "working-load" receiver) is directly connected by hanging (a tension function) only to the tension members, the roadway being threaded through the compression masts without touching them lest the latter be deflected. In a weight-for-weight comparison of compression members *vs.* tension members, in balanced structure relationship, each disposed in the manner of greatest efficiency of service, as demonstrated in the modern suspension bridges, the steel even of war vintage was six times more *useful* when employed in the tension than in the compression function. This latter comparison is in "versatility" and is not to be confused with pure push-pull ability. Pursuing our analogy of "mind" being represented by tension and "matter" by compression, it would seem that the post-War industrial era started with a ratio of mind-over-matter dominance of 6:1.

With the inception of alloys and their post-War higher development, metals in their most suitable state for tension use jumped further, that is, to four times the ability of steel in the most suitable state for compression, or 280,000 lbs. tension *vs.* 70,000 lbs. compression. This statement, be it remembered, is made on the basis of tests of cubic inch blocks, and is not to be confused with the 6:1 greater ability of steel used in its most efficient tensile disposition over steel used in its most efficient compressive disposition. These static and dynamic advantages must be integrated to assess the increasing economic advantage of tensed over compressed steel. There was, therefore, a 24:1 total use advantage in the steel used in tension over steel employed in compression at the opening of this decade (1930). Our teleologic

Enter Alloy: Exit Rust

designer is cautioned that steel should be employed tensilely wherever mechanically appropriate. This is done with efficiency in the great suspension bridges already mentioned, in which the cross-sectional area of the steel in the direct compression of the masts is 24:1 to the cross-sectional area of the cables, although both members participate equally in supporting the ultimate working road-load.

Current industrially producible steel is not only 24:1 more economically useful in *tension* than in *compression*, but compared to the structural ability of stone it is *compressively* 1½:1, and *tensilely* 240:1, more useful. It is also 6000:1 more *tensilely* useful than the mortar used to join the stones together.

Although mind and matter have become, in the industrial era, apparently of equal compressive importance, mind has attained a distinctly superior tensile ability. This corollary of man's progress, revealed in structural ability, seems to be justified by comparison of these figures to those developed in the early chapter: "$E = Mc^2$" = "Mrs. Murphy's Horse Power," indicating an approximate gain by man of 29 inanislaves.

Man's scientific or intellectual control of his environment is specifically indicated by his progression in tensive cohesive flexibility of adjustment, as directly demonstrated in the ratio of increased tension ability of materials extracted from his environment for that environment's structural encompassment. Structurally speaking, if stone has a tensile strength of 1000 lbs. per square inch and commercial steel has 240,000 lbs. per square inch, then man in the stone age had only 1/240 of the ability of man today. In other words, modern man has advanced by intellectuality 2400% beyond his stone age ancestor in ability to conquer environment. This is *potential*, rather than actual, of course, because man still structures his homes in stone, brick and mortar, hiding with an inferior-complexity his steel ability under tons of stone "facing." Furthermore, that hidden steel in building has not yet been segregated into efficient tension and compression elemental balance of "best" possible service, as demonstrated in the suspension bridge. A beginning may be noted in the tension diagonals employed in the large one story light frame steel structures—such as in the temporary buildings of the world fairs.

It is interesting that nature's structures—whether tree, human, fish or fowl—long ago took cognizance of the fundamental tendency of the elements in their solid state to do more efficient work in tension, in which state their molecular forms are arranged in a most adequate manner, to-wit: The life cell in each of nature's creatures not only indicates cognizance of the superiority of solids in tension, but also of the fact that every element is transmutable energetically into solid, liquid and gaseous states, being converted progressively from the solid to the gaseous state by energy radiation with usual volume increase as passaging from solid-to-liquid-to-gas. (There is one marked exception to this progression, most fortunate for man. H_2O has greater volume as ice than as water.) A progression of *mutability* or flow is evidenced in the progression of solid-to-liquid-to-gas, i.e., as the transfer is made from solid>liquid>gas a higher degree of plasticity and elasticity is progressively attained.

Nature fashioned her primary structural member, the life cell, as a globule in which elements in their liquid and gaseous states are compressively enclosed by elements in their solid and tensed state. A small proportion of elements in a gaseous state are enclosed within the liquid that is held within the tensed solid estate globule. The ball skin of solids is always in tension (due, partly, to its being filled with liquid, and, partly, to the fact that it is pressured outward by the inclusion of the relatively highly compressible gas under pressure within the relatively non-compressible liquid) except at load transfer points, that is, at the portion of its surface upon which the ball rests, or at the point at which it is push-contacted by the life cell arrangement. Any applied load or work is distributed equally to all of its solid tensile surface, through the medium of its contained relatively non-compressible liquid, which is a highly mutable load-disbursing design-member. The *shock* of contact of eccentric loads upon the life cell is absorbed by the small quantum of the already compressed but still further compressible gases pregnant in the liquid. The life cell may be likened to a "sausage" balloon filled with carbonic ("fizzy") water.

Mechanical science is slowly comprehending this vastly efficient structural principle of nature. Its partial observation and teleologic application to the design of the pneumatic tire has made possible potentially safe, superior-to-horse-speeds in motorization which could never have been attained by compressively employed steel tires of the horse-drawn vehicle's wheels.

Until the advent of the age of marked superiority of metals in tension over tensile abilities of natural fibers and "raw" stones, it was useless for man to overcontemplate this structural efficiency of nature.

Leonardo da Vinci was apprised of the natural principle of mechanically functioning structures, but he had neither the precise materials to be highly use-effective teleologically nor the possibility of evolving them out of anything at hand to correspond with their efficiency as observed in nature.

As a result of the service improvement of machinery during the World War and the many discoveries in processes of alloying, heat-treating, and electro-chemical analyses, it is now not only suitable but essential to efficiency for man to incorporate in his structural and mechanical designs the efficient principle which, in nature, enables life-celled-structured birds and insects to fly, and the tree, the largest living unit mechanism, to rear itself to colossal heights relative to trunk diameter, and, adjustingly, to withstand storm and change through life continuities in some cases of several thousand years.

The microscopically observed structures of "worked" steel and tree trunks are, alike, comprised of myriads of sausage-balloon-fibrous units. The science of the determination of the electrical-frictional affinities of molecules in lubricants, cohesives and aggregates, and the ratios of these agglomerations is known as colloidal chemistry. Colloidal chemistry, coupled with thermodynamics in its advanced stage (comprehending general characteristics of the energy phenomena in chrystalline, liquid and gaseous estates) currently constitutes the central objective of science which seeks structurally to employ the primary electrical polarity specifics of radiation.

In compression, a tangential agglomeration of spheroids is structurally the most satisfactory cellular arrangement since cellular elongations under compression tend to wedge and split asunder their agglomerations. In tension, however, fibrous crystalline surfaced elongations of the globular cells are most frictionally cohesive.

The foregoing discussion of structural function may seem to be unrelated to a discussion of the forces unleashed by Fincap when he encouraged, during the World War, the ingenuity of young, educated minds for what he conjectured, at the time, would be his own profit production. Nevertheless, it is not only pertinent but it precisely typifies the myriad of enrichments, intricacies and niceties of penetration-for-use-purposes which the popular educated mind attained in the World War and which creates the irrevocable chasm between business minds still focused upon surfaces and the science-led deeply-penetrating-by-mind social trend. The widening breach demonstrated itself dramatically in the '29 and '37 panics.

The geometric progression of intellectual complexity of industry engendered by the War made it devastatingly evident—when the War was concluded—that Fincap (excepting only his hazy awareness of the names of broad fields of activity such as that of the "chemical industry") was completely devoid of any tactical comprehension of the industrial mechanism. Until the War, Fincap had been able in a general, workable way to comprehend relatively simple industrial mechanisms which were gross and easy to see with the naked eye—for example, in a cotton mill, where Fincap was familiar with the cards, spindles, slubbers, spinning frames and other equipment.

Ford, the true industrial-principle leader as distinguished from Fincap, tried to stop the War but found his peace-ship gesture absurdly inadequate. So, with the ingenuity that had inspired his

Enter Alloy: Exit Rust

earlier conception of the production of automobiles-for-people *vs.* automobiles-for-the-individual, he plunged into the industrialization of war machinery to speed war's end. True, many other highly ingenious industrialists entered the war-machinery field, but Henry Ford represents the most efficient and progressively intuitive of the group.

Ford's unique "principle of service" had already differentiated him from other financially hamstrung industrialists. His positing of CONTINUITY *vs.* STATICISM had evolved a continually moving production line in lieu of the antiquated "batch" method of production. Realizing that continuity is logically integrated with service, Ford became highly concerned with the longevity of reciprocating parts in his products and processes. He was more concerned about this than was any other industrialist in the world.

Through his contact with war ordinance engineers such as the British gun designers who ushered in chrome-nickel-steel, Ford became thoroughly apprised of the alloying and heat-treating of metals for higher service. This interest in the special alloying of metals to provide the highest specific satisfaction under any of an infinity of conditions of speed, loading, frequency, *et cetera*, with infinite frictional or energy considerations, precipitated an intensive research by Ford into electro-chemical metallurgical analysis. The results guided him in evolving hosts of special alloys.

The first application of these alloys occurred in Ford's production machinery, and even more exquisitely in his tools-to-make-tools. Eventually the principle was extended to the finished product, namely, the automobile itself, designed and fabricated for popular use. Within a very short post-War period, Ford structured into his automobile 54 different types of alloyed steels which, under microscopic or electrical analysis, were individually as different as are rubies, diamonds and emeralds.

Despite this *new* steel world, the "business man" still speaks of steel with the general notion that there is only one such article. "Steel is up 3 points," *et cetera*. He is lingering in the warehouse era of mental activity during which steel companies rendered almost any kind of malleable ferrous product into sheets, tubes, and other sections, and shipped them as "steel" to warehouses in cities for the take-it-or-leave-it use of the manufacturers of rustable goods.

23

Ford Consolidates the Scientific Emergence

THE "direct" effect of the use of alloys scarcely needs further detailed mention; it was, simply stated, a progression of inevitable research efficiency. There was, however, a far-reaching "indirect" effect of its use which can best be demonstrated by a further discussion of Ford as the most prominent servant of that indirect result, evolution.

"In the first place," we may imagine Ford conjecturing, "if I am going to alloy my steels in a multitude of ways, I certainly do not intend to buy already manufactured-into-use-form units of sheets, tubes, H-sections, *et cetera*, and then have to resmelt and reprocess those steels in order to introduce the alloys. That would mean paying additionally to my own work for the original processing, transporting and warehousing, plus a probable inordinate profit to the steel monopoly manufacturer. So I will make my own steels. Moreover, since I already know of a multitude of metals that may be used with specific advantage, I can conceive of a sudden shift to the employment of metals outside the iron-steel group, where the weight-strength-economic factor shows a specific advantage; for instance, the aluminum alloying group. I am not inclined to tie up my capital in any one mine or source because, in my case, capital is freedom of ability which obviously involves dependence on no one mine or source."

Ford's principle being CONTINUITY, he inferred (by intuitively understanding the truth of the flexible adjustment of the tension line and its superiority) the necessity of recognizing that his capital was primarily "intellect," compounded with a *credit* of his intellect and capability by vast numbers of workers and consumers.

"As there are many as yet undeveloped sources of the materials

I currently need," he probably continued, "I will have to be the temporary operator of such sources. However, I shall be only too glad, when I have these under control, to sell these sources to competitive material monopolists who unquestionably will run after me in the hope of procuring the monopoly of such sources.

"Let them hold the bag; I wish to be free with all my capital to pick and choose continuously. Logically, if I do not subscribe to the ownership of sources, I cannot tie my capital up in advance anticipatory inventories in warehouses. Warehouses are in effect transplanted highly concentrate mines. Before I may have exhausted my warehoused supply I may find cause to redesign; by having to eliminate the material so stored I should lose that much capital, which I have no right to do.

"In view of these rationalizations, there is only one course to pursue, i.e., develop a TIMING system, a time-coördinated planning. Through such a time control plan I can so organize my efforts (energy) that I shall be able to take from sources daily only such materials as I need to maintain the daily flow. Having made an original postulation of what my first day's run should be, I must order forward that run on pure assumption just as I reasonably assumed and proved my first mass market without waiting for orders, as did the others.

"In this manner, my whole inventory will be in motion, with the exception of a small fraction in the form of finished parts visible in stacks adjacent the final assembly line."

In an amazingly short time, after the War, Ford had ships loading and daily sailing out of Iquique, and other ports of all the countries of the world, as well as caravans, trains and trucks in every land, to the tune of some $70,000,000 worth of materials *always in motion*, with the exception of final visibly comprehensive accumulations at the assembly line.

All who have dealt with Ford in the supply of materials will attest the fact that, when buying, for instance, a carload of ground limestone at Joliet, Illinois, etc., etc., etc., he insists upon —and this is well understood by the supplier—the rolling of the car of lime TODAY. (Incidentally he pays for it *today*.) Once the shipment starts on its way, Ford's checkers, who constitute part of the extraordinary mechanism of his shipment-motion-time plan, not only keep constant check on the position progression of every item, but, also, see to it that it loses no time en route.

Ford, carrying out his idea of efficient continuity-service (SERVICE because it WORKS) in all likelihood continued reasoning as follows:

"In connection with my design of a world-encompassing, continuous 24-hours-a-day 'moving picture' operation, I had better study my world map with great care and see how I may route shipments to avoid penetration through costly centers. (Freight differentials are so inequitous that it costs me as much to move a freight car across New York City as it does to move it 800 miles across open country.) Moreover, since I originally wrote OFF the books all cost of plant and structure, not carrying this for bonding purposes as does Fincap in a debit or debt column—I am perfectly free to deploy my materials and fabricating operations (whether for the fabricating of parts for ultimate product, or of tools to make tools) to logical locations, world wide in scope of placement (indifferent to sovereign boundaries), i.e., to mean centers between the sources of material, available power and shipping facilities, and shifting consumer geography.

"I shall, also, not overlook the favorable fact that, since I have popular man (the worker) driving an automobile, the politicians by pointing an accusing finger at motoring Murphy and calling him a 'plutocrat' are extracting exquisite road taxes from his pocket. However, to justify this hi-jacking, the politician is having to furnish the worker with roads on which to ride. This cycle of events makes it possible for me to establish my assembly plants at theoretical locations of greatest efficiency, without regard to the fact that they may be highly decentralized from railroads, with the certainty that the workers and goods can reach the plant by truck and car."

The result of Ford's rationalization—granted that it may have been highly subconscious and intuitive although inevitable to his postulation of the principle of continuous movement along the production line—was so highly efficient that it forced the entire industrial world to follow suit. Until that time the industrial world (90% of which, exclusive of Ford, was controlled by Fincap) represented the pole opposed to continuity, that is, the warehouse era promotional scheme of inefficiency and discard. Break down the other fellow. A broken down fellow is exploitable. In pursuing competitively the old principle of survival of the fittest, Fincap had tried, of course, not to eliminate himself, a possibility he always fearfully suppressed by "morale." COMPETITION is a FEAR-MOTIVATED word. Ford, on the other hand, was motivated simply by LONGING for GREATER-EVER-GREATER EFFICIENCY OF SERVICE and longing to realize his early dream of an integrated industrial and agrarian society.

Ford has often been accused of ruthlessness in his evolutionary tactics, but the accusation stems primarily from the propaganda of the finance capital world. It would be inaccurate to say that it emanates from his competitors, for Ford quite sublimely acknowledges no "competitors."

The propaganda inferring Ford's "ruthlessness" was primarily evoked in the following manner. When Ford decided to evolve his time-plan of operation to replace static capital investment in sources and inventories, he not only had to posit an assumption of daily need, but to underwrite one complete cycle of operations from the furthest reaches of his original shipment through to assembly, delivery and repayment by the automobile wholesaler, thus replenishing his "ability" or credit.

Inasmuch as this assumption involved a mobile inventory of some $70,000,000, augmented by a tremendous outlay for decentralized manufactories and assembly plants at central points of consumption instead of in one plant (Detroit), Ford went to Fincap in New York and asked to borrow $70,000,000.

Was Fincap glad to lend it to him?

"INDEED . . . *INDEED*, Mr. Ford!"

Not only was there unfettered collateral in his unmortgaged plant, but should he fail to repay the loan Fincap would be enabled to conquer this disturbing random element which continuously defeated his own so-called principle of "conservation." In such an eventuality, the staticism principle would, in effect, continue to yield high revenue without attention to service for the populace, and without altering Fincap's retardation of progress.

Now, Ford, in establishing his principle of continuity production for popular consumption, developed so profitable a business for local wholesalers and retailers (the commercial "small fry" or would-be little Fincaps of the warehouse era) that they considered a contract with Ford worth great effort to obtain and almost any temporary inconvenience or hardship to retain.

Ford, having abandoned many attempts at reform because he found them futile, including his famous "peace ship," also gave up the idea of preaching idealistically against "competitive profit" even to the small fry capitalists. He retained the notion, however, that ultimate efficiency would eliminate the unwholesome factors of an unearned profit economy. This efficiency made him "hard boiled" with his wholesale-retail outlets, but he did not become at any time underhanded or unscrupulous.

Knowing the degree to which a distributor valued a Ford car distribution contract, Ford foresightedly and forthrightly included in his agency contract a clause that was quite thoroughly understood by each and every distributor at the time of signing the contract. This clause was to the effect that Ford was empowered to demand the licensee's acceptance, at any time within the year, of the full quota of cars stipulated by the licensee annually in advance, and in relation to which his earnings were proportional. Furthermore, Ford, when agreeing to license the distributor, received the written promise of the licensee to pay cash upon demand for any or all cars delivered to him as part of his (the licensee's) annual quota.

This agreement was in effect between Ford and his licensees for years before Ford had recourse to the employment of this clause. The fact that he had not enforced this stipulation (fairly arrived at because the licensee sought the license from Ford and the license paid the licensee well) established by habit in the brains of many licensees the notion-precedent that Ford did not expect ever to put the precautionary provision into operation. It was just "one of those things."

Then, quite suddenly, Ford found himself unable to make his turnover realize a return sufficiently rapidly to meet the date line of his $70,000,000 debt to the finance capital world. This was because the time control plan and its gargantuan expansion had involved a multitude of theoretical postulates of performance.

The payment date drew near. Only one week to go! Fincap's mouth began to water. The biggest breakdown of progress in the whole course of history, by means of debt, was within his fore-closing grasp.

To meet the issue, Ford set in operation his emergency licensee clause. He shipped rapidly to his distributors every car that could be processed out of his mobile inventory and demanded cash in payment therefor. Of course, an animal howl went up, but alignment with Ford and his principle of continuity service for popular patronage was so truly profitable for the widespread army of small fry capitalists and distributors, that the vast majority of those whose credit with local banks was sum-totally adequate to produce the necessary $70,000,000 borrowed the required amount from their local banking institutions. Thus, Ford was enabled to pay off his debt to Fincap. The little capitalists—themselves indirect debt merchants—passed on the debt to the little local banks, which, in turn, due to the necessity of integration and integrity within the capitalistic system itself, could and did borrow from the big banks. So the debt was returned to its starting point, the central capitalist finance world.

Ford had established in reality for all people, for all time, the principle of industrial synchronization with "TIME."

The production of people's goods became synchronized with what mathematics had long before pointed out to be the true scientific state of affairs: a TIME-RATE world, a calculus world. Until the Ford incident, industry had been managed and ac-counted solely by static arithmetic, despite its existence in an eternally factual time-rate energy radiant world. Einstein's "relativity" reached the Murphys through Ford.

Ford's "ruthlessness" was no greater than the "ruthlessness" of Leonardo da Vinci when he insisted upon actually measuring in truly scientific manner (that is, in degrees, minutes, seconds and thirds of a circle) every art object, every living entity coming within his sphere of contact. Leonardo's efficiency of observation evolved a mathematical "perspective frame" and brought about the disillusionment of every pagan romance, of every Christian bigotry credo, and of every academic scholar's pretentiousness. Conversely, it enabled him to design great networks of irrigation canals and to invent the wheelbarrow and countless other commonplace instruments and processes then currently in high use-state, despite the complete lack of inanimate power means (other than diminutive water wheels). In consequence, Leonardo's contemporaries called him not only "ruthless" but "heretic," which had a real and awful meaning in those days of horrific religious inquisition. Pretentious scholars hurled "ignoramus" at him, and the people knew him as a "sorcerer." But most wounding of all to the immortal painter of The Last Supper and Mona Lisa was the epithet "feelingless prosaic trickster" so unjustly applied by the esthetic coterie of stingingly eloquent, chi-chi "artistic" earthians of his day.

Until Ford's irrevocable victory over staticism and debt, he had been primarily concerned with the *process* of production, and only secondarily with the improvement of its end-object, the automobile. Although he had had a considerable hand in the inventions comprising the total-invention "automobile," he had not been its sole inventor, and, in common with many other inventors, he was momentarily satisfied so far as the end-product was concerned with having attained an invention that "worked" and was popularly acquirable and useful.

When the "forces" of debt-and-exploitation realized that Ford had emerged signally victorious from the "corner" in which they thought they had him, they had further recourse to a deceptive form of attempted competition. The car of the non-competing

Ford which, in its mechanical parts, had been the beneficiary of the alloying science and was, therefore, a highly reliable and popular instrument, was, also, a relatively uncomfortable and "grotesque" contraption in the popular, functionally-unseeing eye. This had not been remedied by changes in outward appearance, general structure or dimensional design for the reason that its superficial general changelessness allowed of its being manufactured at progressively lower and lower cost, with a concomitant depletion of profit to imitating competitors. The populace, with the infiltration of Old World commerce and esthetics, had long since lost its pristine simplicity of perception-of-essentials which was so characteristic of it in the first days of communal settlement in the new continent. Therefore, the people were readily responsive to Fincap's next deception.

The exploiting-competitors, through the media of advertising and the formation of opinion through the Fincap-allied press (Ford did not advertise at that time), set about fostering a public sense of dissatisfaction in the comfort, luxury and pride-of-ownership aspects of the Ford product. They called attention to the fact that they themselves were furnishing seemingly far more luxurious, bigger and "classier" designs than any exhibited by Ford. They appealed with unerring thrusts to the vanity of the consistent suckers of such propaganda as the "own your own home and become one of us property-stable citizens." The nationwide competition in miniature coach making by boys, sponsored and conducted by Fincap's Fisher Body Company, was typical of the retrogressive propaganda. They did not mention that their diversions to surface attraction had to be paid for, and that the "cost" was being taken out of the mechanical efficiency and longevity of service of their product, which could ill afford such depletion, having already been functionally outclassed by Ford's scientific alloying processes and his "service" principle. Paradoxically $25,000 Rolls Royces of that period developed their svelte beauty through functional revelation in design, whereas the cheap, popular cars were "tricked" up to hide function.

The propaganda succeeded—at least for the moment. Ford's

patronage by the populace fell off markedly and Ford became the victim of utter unappreciation on the part of his beneficiaries. He was torn between the temptation to close-up shop forever and his life-long-dominant longing-necessity to pioneer once more. Being an artist (an intuitive dynamic senser) and remembering his years of fight to establish the vast principle of scientific service-by-the-people-to-the-people, he inevitably chose to pioneer again. He designed an improved car that would be not only more efficient mechanically than any other theretofore available at any cost, but one that would conform to the popular "notion"— standards of "agreeable" and "happy" use.

While evolving and thoroughly testing his new car he shut down his world-wide plant. Every step of the process was carried out under his own DIRECT supervision. When he was personally assured of success in design and operation, he ordered his time-planning department, his production machinery designers, and his designers of tools-to-make-tools, to return to work. He invested a fresh $52,000,000 in the new unit. This was, however, exclusively an outlay for process machinery and is not to be confused with his mobile inventory investment. The expenditure for machinery, he wrote down as usual—to zero.

The new car was a success—faster and, of scientific necessity, safer, than any other on the road except an inconsequential .1% of special custom machines. It was the first popular car to go a mile-a-minute. When these initial Model A's came out, an amusing anecdote described how the driver of an expensive, imported Mercedes observed that he was being overtaken by one of the new Fords. He stepped on the gas and went faster and faster until finally he attained his top speed of 70. The Ford drew alongside and its proletarian driver earnestly shouted, "Hey, can you tell me how to shift into high? I just bought it!"

Popular patronage reconverged on Ford. But he did not halt, as Fincap would have done, to reap the maximum profit return from the new product. Ford is quite willing to make the worst of blunders *once* because he is a true trial-and-error artist and scientist. Despite public approval, no sooner was the new car in full production before he evolved an even better car—one that was more able and more efficient than any transportation vehicle ever produced in the world, the "V8." This new progression of product evolution was consistent with Ford's own behind-the-scenes evolution and testifies to his maturing. Ford's attention had become focused upon end-product and he observed with delight the popular repercussions to the new model which indicated public appreciation of his having paid attention to the people's utilitarian requirements and their advancing harmonic evaluation. Human dignity was involved.

When Ford had completed his 10,000,000th car (he has now produced over 27,000,000) he observed that inasmuch as a car has an average longevity of five years (now approaching seven due to the inception of additional scientific alloying possibilities) and that inasmuch as 2,000,000 Fords a year constituted the largest production he could envisage attaining, relative to known factors, he realized that his maximum production would probably be but 10,000,000 cars in every five years, only sufficient to replace those already rolling. He realized that the majority of his customers were coincidentally his own workers, direct and indirect. Actually there obtained then a cycle of people producing their own transport media through industrial coördination and simultaneously the means of acquisition not only of the transport media, but also of all other essentials.

There has been a vast amount of propaganda by the Communist Party against Ford. Through ignorance of science and industry they improperly identify Ford's motivation and activity with Big Business. For long the American Communists have also improperly identified *Big Business* and *Industry*, erroneously assuming the *unearned increment* corollary of the former to be generic to the latter. Two factors "seemingly" substantiate their criticism of Ford: his lowering of wages in the early '30s and "regimentation" of the workers in Ford factories.

The lowering of the wage scale of the Ford Company workers, they maintain, was a flagrant retraction from Ford's earlier program of then-unheard-of wages for the lowliest worker in the Ford plant. Many will remember his establishment of a minimum $5 a day for even a "sweeper" at a time when the theme of a song "A dollar a day is very good pay when you work on the boulevard" was still popularly true. Ford progressively amplified minimum wages from this $5 level for a number of years. Despite the seemingly lower wages established by Ford in the instance particularly referred to by the Communists, Ford has not actually ever lowered his workers' income.

Thinking in terms of production by workers and of the workers' ability to acquire the product of their coöperative effort, Ford realized that the dollar-buying power of the worker's dollar had increased enormously in proportion to the specific satisfaction attainable in product to be purchased. Therefore, he understood that lowering the *number* of dollars does not of necessity mean a lowering of the worker's wage-ability to acquire goods and services.

As an example of his reasoning, one may cite vegetable produce in the improvement of which—both in standard and availability— Ford's tractors (as cultivators) and trucks (as a transportation medium of universal distribution) and passenger automobiles (as transport of worker-purchaser) played a major role. One cannot regard the present vegetable product as being the same as that which the worker could obtain with his "dollar" prior to or early in the establishment of the automobile as a popular instrument. The stringless fresh green beans available the year around today when compared with the stringy, half-wilted product infrequently obtainable in fresh form during a short season prior to the advent of the automobile is unquestionably worth, in specific energy to the consumer (by actual calories and harmonious nutriment) many times its predecessor.

Ford had consistently reinvested capital gain into improved process and ability, safety, comfort and service of end-product, the automobile, with the result that the latter continually lowered in cost and price. This happened throughout the years he continued Model "T." Wherefore, a given wage dollar bought increasing trackless individual transportation facility. On this basis alone, considering his workers as his primary customers, Ford would have been justified in lowering wages progressively, after announcing his $5 a day minimum, were his aim the maintainance of a *level* rate of compensation. Ford did not lower wages at that time, however, but continued to improve his automobile. The current Ford car, retailing for approximately $700, could not have been duplicated 15 years ago for $700,000. Twenty years ago, when Ford first announced his $5 a day scale, neither Mr. Rockefeller nor Mr. Morgan could have acquired, at any price, a vehicle comparable to the present Ford car.

Soon after Franklin Roosevelt became President all gold was withdrawn from circulation, and the largest quantity of bullion in all history was impounded. The dollar was actually almost halved in *specie* value, but actually it bought a greater number of shirts because shirts had already dropped from $3 to $1. Being on a world-wide operation basis, Ford was compelled of necessity to maintain a wage rate that took into consideration the international devaluation of the dollar.

In reality Ford did not reduce the proportion of wage ability when he reduced its dollars and cents figure; on the contrary, he allowed wage ability to increase enormously, for in so doing he developed a continuity of employment that supplanted his earlier intermittent employment with a resultant higher annual wage. Furthermore, it is probable that the proportion of dollars paid out in wages to dollars invested in materials and power (none goes into rent for, be it remembered, Ford writes off plant immediately upon its establishment) has increased consistently.

The reason the Communist confuses the motives of Ford with that of Big Business is that Big Business's scientific behind-the-scenes researches constantly ape, or, through the fraternity of the engineers, participate in the technical data for which Ford sets the pace. The General Motors plants seem visually to be on a surface par with the Ford plant. This visible similarity of these two mammoth automobile producing industries causes the Communist to say that they are identical activities. The "Big Business" automobile manufacturer is, however, still exploitation and profit-minded and extracts profit for dividend-distribution-purposes which does not go back into the business to create greater service or wages, whereas Ford is specifically motivated by the service principle, turning all profit back into the establishment of an increasing mechanical serviceability, ever amplifying his principle of better product and more work.

Inasmuch as the primarily-for-profit world is still so factually existent, it continues to be impossible for the Ford principle to be isolated and popularly demonstrated all the way through to the consumer. When it comes to the distribution of product, Ford must contend with multitudinous factors of the old exploitation world; for instance, with the distribution station's "real" estate impositions and the distributor's political and financial relationships in local marts. So unreasonable, intrinsic and intricate are the ramifications of the latter that Ford considers it inefficient in most instances to vie directly for local popular patronage. This intrigue which he avoids was demonstrated in the ability of ex-Mayor Walker politically to prevent the introduction of Ford taxis in New York, under Ford Company operation, at one-half the then-current taxi tariff. Although a service of evident benefit to people in efficiency, cost, size and safety would have resulted, Walker vetoed it because the taxi privilege racket was a major revenue producer for his sponsoring political machine.

It is because of the existence of this local racket condition that Ford cars costing the Ford Motor Company 10¢ *per lb.* completely assembled at Edgewater, N. J., the assembly plant for New York City, and including a reserve for evolutionary scientific change in plant and product, retail in New York City, just across the river, at 22½¢ *per lb.*—a 120% gross overtake by the entrepreneur profit world. Of course the net overtake is much smaller. Possibly 50% must be deducted from the 120% for service station maintainance, *et cetera*.

Ford became intent some years ago on reducing to some extent the superusurious finance charges attendant upon "time purchase," the popular mode of acquiring an automobile which, incidentally, makes it a fact that the majority of people "rent" transportation rather than "buy" their automobiles. To bust this multiple fee finance racket, he created a finance company of his own known as the Universal Credit Corporation.

This venture into the field of banking mechanisms proved a second inadvertent life-saver for Ford and his popular service principle when the banking crash of '32 occurred, which latter may be traced throughout this discourse and later chapters to the direct influence of the Ford time-control principle and, therefore, indirectly to the World War and the experience gained therefrom by Ford. When the '32 bank moratorium was imposed by the Administration, shutting off from Ford vast sums of credit on deposit in banks—jeopardizing his continuity of operation—the Universal Credit Corporation proved itself the means of continuing. So tremendous and potentially profitable to bankers was the Universal Credit Corporation (it was considered to be the major competitor of their amalgamated legally sustainable but nonetheless highly usurious time-payment organizations) that, overnight, Ford was able to sell Universal Credit Corporation for $50,000,000 cash. This sale to Fincap spanned the time-lag until his credit could be released from the closed banks.

The specific rationalization that we wish to bring into relief at this juncture is that Ford's unending process of doing more with less had the effect, relative to any given product standard, of deflating the cost of acquisition of that specific standard, which is another way of saying increased wage "dollarability."

The Ford decentralization and mobilization and service process so rapidly reduced the prices of fixed standard, and even deteriorated standard, real estate relative-purchase or rental "values" as well as prices, for instance, of #1 Prime Western hogs, that just before the bank moratorium, 1¢ meals were actually being sold in New York City, which, albeit poor in quality, were sustaining thousands of people. The progression of prices was so precipitously downward and man work was being so rapidly supplanted by the scientific industrial progression that work was scarce for all but a few. There were, consequently, fewer wage earners to spend. Those who had dollars, however, could buy a given stand-ard for an acceleratingly lower portion of their dollar.

This is to say that if the true standard of the dollar is what the worker may exchange it for, i.e., the cost of a meal or the price of shelter, then a meal which cost 25¢ in 1920 was selling in 1930 for 1¢. A man still receiving a dollar-an-hour from the industrial world had, in fact, increased his rate in 1930 to $25 an hour in 1920 dollarability. This being so, even though the number of workers was reduced, the number of dollars still being distributed by the industry of Ford's leadership increased 25-fold in the post-War decade which was a far greater increase than the amount of worker reduction. Therefore, more dollars of food-buying ability were available for circulation than before, and the depression was in reality a lack of ability to account a high relative devaluation of the intrinsic cost of the land which was the debt base of Fincap.

Another trouble was that there was no way to make the one man who was getting a proportional $25 an hour increase, dis-tribute or circulate his earnings to those who had been replaced by the machine. The only way to do this would be by the system outlined in the chapter, Dollarability, wherein work would be distributed on a minimum stint basis so that all people might have a chance to work and be self-supporting.

Ford was quite aware that dollars accruing to the static stand-ard world from rents and other non-productive sources were diminishing so rapidly in relative volume to that of industrial pro-duction as to threaten with bankruptcy those whose income was mainly an unearned increment from intrinsic properties.

Since, however, the entrepreneur and profit world still con-trolled politics to a marked degree, it was possible for the politics-controlled government temporarily to halt the '29-'32 reckoning. It did this through government by increasing the so-called popu-lar "debt" to absorb the property bankruptcy while arbitrarily pegging its further ravages. It is not yet evident to the layman that this complete bankruptcy of Fincap did occur in 1932, wherefore the Communist is "railing" against an in-fact "dead" system. Thinking the system still alive (as do, indeed, many of Fincap's progeny) and not being able to sense by personal contact the Ford industrial service principle because Ford has not been able to articulate completely through to the customer, due to the entrepreneuring contamination, and unaware that Fincap is being maintained in dead dummy form by politics and government for the sake of a framework of popularly understood means of transaction, the Communist continues to confuse Ford with the beheaded chicken's run-around of the axed entrepreneuring profit system.

It is paradoxical that the spokesmen for Communism in America should have so bitterly attacked Ford while the mother country, Russia, developed a worshipful religion of Ford, whose industrial mechanisms the Communists in Russia perceived, through distance perspective, to be essential to their success in the attempt permanently to establish socialism—a political theory which necessitates an abundance of primary essentials in a country of scarcity of essentials. Russia, through isolation by statecraft from the sovereign nations of Fincap, at first had non-available the abundances which might otherwise have provided earlier success in her realization of socialism.

No one man, organization or principle has been so utilized by the in-Russia-Communists as Henry Ford. There is nothing in any way incompatible between the industrial service principle of Ford and Russian Communism. The fabricated-by-illusion differentiation is "optical" only as viewed through the arbitrarily imposed and soon quite-evidently-to-be-removed rusting screen door of Fincap's legal debt contrivance.

With regard to the second criticism leveled at Ford, namely, regimentation of the workers in Ford establishments, it is to be noted that the specific focus of the criticism is actually a single personality, namely, Ford's production manager.

Probably no one factor has beclouded the Ford "ideal" more than has the hard fisted management of this production man. The production routine of the world-encompassing Ford establishment is so utterly vast that its Captain, Mr. Ford, has of necessity o attend to the *progressive* aspects of his service in the further extension of his principle. *Irrevocable* establishment of progressive principles is of far greater importance to him than is any remedial attention to personality idiosyncrasies of his workers. These are personal limitations, and personalities die. So Ford has wisely continued to rely on the proven production-routine ability of this man, which is great. There are multitudes of stupidity factors contemporaneously to be contended with which no amount of namby-pamby philosophizing can deal with successfully.

Ford himself is so heavily engaged in the scientific improvement of process and product that the personalities participating in the running of the by-Ford-created-machine to reproduce the by-Ford-created-product seem of no more importance to him than whether a gentle tongued lady or an oathsome truck driver purchases and drives one of his Ford cars. Ford has given up "reform." He earnestly tried plenty of it and found it did not work. He is now consecrated completely to new form production.

If Ford's production mechanisms or end-products can be run by bullies, they certainly can be more ably run—and will eventually be so run—by more tolerant and intelligent characters evolutionary to the intelligent popular scientific inter-service. Needless to say, the bullying of the production manager is effective only in the Detroit headquarters. There is little evidence of it elsewhere in the vastly decentralized Ford operation. Its existence even in Detroit, however, is no justification for a misappraisal of the service principle which Ford pioneers for man.

Before leaving this discussion, it is important for our continuity of thought to remark that Ford's first important breakaway from Fincap's control occurred many years ago, soon after his successful establishment of his principle of a "moving line" of production for popular consumption. This principle, it will be recalled, involved the assumption that if enough cars were produced to justify a production line, they could be produced at so low a price that popular man as well as Fincap could purchase them.

This being an unproved principle, it took a large pioneering credit to underwrite it. After several bitterly discouraging failures, involving complete bankruptcy, Ford finally was successful—with the financial aid of friendly Detroit capitalists—in raising enough money successfully to complete the postulated cycle. Although the principle demonstrated itself healthily, it soon became evident to Ford that the shareholders in his undertaking, thinking that they had hit upon an eternal gold mine, wished to EXTRACT profit in inordinate proportion to their original investment rather than subscribing to reapplication of the returns to an expansion of service.

Sitting alone and thoughtfully on his back fence—where it is said he still considers all important matters—Ford concluded that the rapid credit amplification of his activity was born of popular spontaneous subscription to his principle. So he determined that all credit amplifications should be continually set to work again in the improvement of production and service until extended to all the people of the earth.

To effect this determination—and to avoid forever interference in his singleness of purpose through legally-established minority stockholders' rights (a capital finance contrivance designed to make possible a minority's guidance of vast earning activities), Ford was forced to buy-in all outstanding shares. He paid what was then a fabulous sum for them. Had he procrastinated in this determination, it might have been many more years before our industrial emancipation from feudal chiseling would have occurred.

Many people laugh at Henry Ford and his hobbies—his Americana and his folk dancing and his fiddling. We might laugh similarly at the paradox of Leonardo's designs for whorehouses and mausoleums. It is highly credible that Ford is so non-egotistical as to think himself artistic *only* in the matter of collecting antiquities or in "twinkle" dancing. Little does he perceive himself to be the greatest artist of our day.

Nevertheless he is, for, single-handedly, he has conceived and painted the greatest picture that has ever been painted for mankind, a continuous animated motion picture that encircles the whole world. When there is time perspective on Ford equivalent to the 400 year interval between ourselves and Leonardo da Vinci, which enables us to appraise da Vinci as the greatest artist of the Middle Ages, Ford will undoubtedly be acclaimed by the people of that later day as certainly the greatest artist of the 20th century.

24

Accounting Subterfuges of Capital's Bankruptcy

Up to the time of the War, 1914-1918, the wage-earning popu-lace as a whole, the world over, had not understood the amplifica-tion of credit to be obtained by placing their excess earnings in share investments. Even industrialized America had, until then, simply hidden its money in its sock, or had BOUGHT land (the only way it could acquire land to till without molestation unless it went to a wilderness homestead) or had deposited excess credit in savings banks or life insurance policies to protect families "against a rainy day."

The vast government (popular) credit invoked by Fincap to underwrite war production (to end the War, the incendiary costs of which had exceeded private capital's participation limits) had, however, legally to be accounted. This was necessitous to Fincap in the practical extension of property and debt laws already interpretatively imposed by him on the Constitution. Debt must always be legally accounted under Fincap's "system."

The government had increased its debt limit and had financed business—"war" business. This debt had to be passed along to the people whom the government represents. An arbitrary and forthright statement by government that every one of its citizens had unwittingly established an indebtedness to some abstract lender, or to Mr. Morgan *and* Company, of $105 *per capita* would have been, on the one hand, too "ephemeral" an accounting, and, on the other, unnecessarily "morbid." It would have been legally insufficient and could not have been assessed.

As an alternative to such abstract financial "nonsense," the banking fraternity, long accustomed to marketing issues to petty capitalists as well as to his own director-directed trusts, conceived the notion of selling government "securities" to the people as a means of assessing the debt.

Abetted by popular press propaganda and the momentum of patriotism, the gloriously termed "LIBERTY" and "VICTORY" bonds were promulgated. Glorious, yes! but how paradoxical the conjunction of such words as "liberty" and "bond"; "victory" and "bond." At any rate, the indebtedness of the government was definitely established as "owing" to a vast portion of the populace, and the short term notes to Morgan & Company were repaid to the extent that "the boys" had at first advanced the credit to help get the war going.

"This scheme," reasoned Fincap, "will allow me, as the bonds mature, to take over the handling of the debt. I shall be less busy, then, with consolidating and reinvesting war profits and can, myself, sell the refunding bonds at a neat turnover to my controlled institutional trusts, *et cetera*. Incidentally, I sha'n't have to make even a selling effort. It will be perfectly delightful! The legally controlled trusts will HAVE to buy what I legally hand them so long as I synchronize the refunding to their portfolio requirements." (The mechanics of this will be recited later in detail.)

That is how Fincap's brain worked. As usual, Fincap failed to realize that he had inadvertently let loose a new popular phenomenon. Through the propagandization of people into the purchase of their own government's securities Fincap not only made the populace security-and-investment minded for the first time, but also simultaneously and unwittingly (which we will later amplify) shifted the credit command potentially, though not yet actively, into the popular realm from out his own walled estate.

Subsequent to the War, the Ford-led "industrialization" occurred through the RELEASE from war to peace activity of SCIENTIFIC INSTRUMENTS and PROCESSES, invoked by the War. The American people, as a result of several factors, developed a credit of their government not only as a united whole able to do things in a "big way," but as a major, if not the major, world power. These factors were (1) the government's wide mobilization for the War, (2) the uprooting of the people's sons from their agricultural and factory-static homes, (3) their transportation oversea, (4) the world-involved-news integration inherent in the War, and, subsequently, (5) the attentively read news relative to the gargantuan industrial activities attendant on the War. Moreover, the people acquired the habit of investing in the industrial mechanism, of which the government was during the War apparent manager. Subsequently, due to the first high earnings of industrialization and the erroneously-postulated building activities by bewildered Fincap, the public delved ever more deeply into industrial share investment. "Liberty Bonds" were quickly converted into common shares of industrial enterprises. An era of "speculation" set in. The people bought industrial shares instead of refinancing the bonds as they were expected to do. Government bonds were selling at that time at "discounts" that today, when recalled, wring the heart of Fincap's progeny (questionably granting that organ to exist in his progeny).

A large portion of the invoked and expanded American government "debt" could not, however, be legally pinned upon the populace through the sale of "LIBERTY" and "VICTORY" bonds despite all aid of patriotic hysteria, yet it, also, had to be accounted. The dollars had been spent and the profits had been reaped by Fincap. So the latter endeavored to keep the eyeglass of debt firmly fixed upon the noses of people and government. The people were brought, through the press, to SEE that something HAD TO BE DONE about international war debts.

It was through this international war debt contrivance that Fincap accounted the government's—or the people's—invocation of credit to pay for his war profiteering. Through his political control of government, Fincap had, during the war, sanctimoniously dramatized, as an holy of holies affair, the ambassadorial statecraft or borrowing of "sovereign" France, "sovereign" England, and "sovereign" everything.

So impressive did the "NAME GAME" become that, in the hysteria of patriotism and of the dramatic romance of World War, the right of holy of holies sovereign France to establish a non-collateral credit in the U. S. for the purchase of U. S.-produced goods was popularly approved. These neat "national" titles positing eternal isolation policies in a potentially world-integrated populace (integrated through the War-born necessity of a common protection of their slowly-established degree of emancipation from utter slavery) were as useful to Fincap as it is essential for Fincap today to retain the practically meaningless (from a factual viewpoint) "individual sovereignty" of the 48 States of America. The important issues of the trend are still being confused by national titles: *anti*-Chinese, *pro*-Japanese, *et cetera*, instead of *anti*-hodge-podge, or *pro*-industrial emancipation.

Americans are so highly intercoursing today (as a result of automobile and abstract radio, motion picture and newspaper travel) within regional areas vastly larger than those delineated by "state" boundaries that they have to be continually propagandized into their "state" and "town" sovereignty-vanity sustenance by rekindled sectional ire against "damned Yanks," "effete easterners," "vindictive crackers," or by fear-invoking notices to the effect that "SECURITY" of home and family is "THREATENED" (no explanations given) by the central government's looming mutual-interest-efficiency control as an obvious all-for-one and one-for-all necessity.

Industry, itself, takes no heed of "state" or, for that matter, of "national" boundaries other than to pay tariffs when transiting arbitrarily imposed border lines. "Tariffs" are maintained by the constitutional-interpretation-in-Fincap's-favor on the part of such machine-run organs as low calibered state legislatures. These non-significant, from the industrial or popular viewpoint, sovereign border lines are still utterly essential to the political gangdom control of government by Fincap and constitute the only reason for their press-advocated continuance.

How appealing to the intelligence is the I.C.C. license plate now to be seen at the rear of great trucks and buses, yet so paradoxically surrounded by three or four "sovereign" state licenses! Which, in the case of conflict, is more appealing to the intelligence as a tactical criterion—a U. S. Bureau of Standards scientific codification, or a local town council's politically devised ordinance?

Eventually, the automobile which through its popular adoption has made industry what it is will probably blaze the way, by popular vote, to the obliteration of all state borders. The trend in traffic problem solution already indicates the breakdown of special traffic lighting systems in Chicago *vs.* special traffic lighting systems in New York or Podunk. National driving standards and a national license are inevitable. The racket of the small incorporated towns and villages making game of the transient automobilist to fund local administration and patronage has been almost stamped out through centralization to higher geographical stages of government. There is herein a practical inference of the elimination of ultimate state borders and, through continentally centralized traffic regulations, of the multitude of subterfuges in driving-license procurement now so well known to millions of drivers who, losing grace in one state, may regain it without question in another, the majority of the population having a part time residence in at least two states.

When the War ended, the integration of the debt indicated that all other large "sovereign" nations were in debt to the United States. With the obvious irrationality of a clown, Fincap attempted to impose a refunding schedule of this debt, pyramided upon the sovereign victims of sovereigns—Germany and the Central Allies.

Until the outbreak of the War, "big shot" henchmen of Fincap had their headquarters in Europe. These heirs, successors and assigns of the original feudal racketeers, who had financially followed the American pilgrimage in a partially successful attempt to profit-harness the new continental development, continued to reside legally on the European continent for obscurity and long-range untaxable manipulation. Although the tricks of sovereignty and statecraft had been theoretically evaded by the successful 1776 secession, the business-trick-habit inculcated by the feudalists in the new continent enabled Fincap continuously to enjoy exploitation of the highly productive, longing-inspired American colonials who had through evolution extracted the vital essence of the industrial principle from Europe.

This feudal finance gangdom schemed for and precipitated the World War and, through financial agents, drew America into the embrangle. These European feudal chisellers had controlled world-productivity by controlling the specie medium essential to trade until the 1914 saturation point of world-encompassing export outlets occurred. This signaled the European feudal chisellers' inception of the War. Theirs the greatest surprise, when, at the end of the War through unforeseen ramifications, the credit monopoly had passed over from them to the American people, not to their American banking branch houses.

Astutely recognizing that the American populace itself was unaware of the capture, and desirous of recapturing this credit dominance which became exquisitely centralized in the American government, Fincap attempted futilely to impose great reparations payments upon the "sovereign" losers. Granted the reparations could have been carried out, these payments would have released European people from the yoke of their involuntary indebtedness to the American people.

A schoolboy could have foreseen the inability of Germany and her Allies to pay off the War's debts, but Americans, still wearing the debt-lenses clamped on their noses by Fincap, puppetishly clamored for payment. Whereupon the American agents of European Fincap ordained that the apparently popularly accredited Americans, Dawes and Young, should descend upon Europe and "arrange" schedules of the debt refund. If this impossible and typical Fincap debt refunding, "from frying pan into the fire" *plan* had not been saddled upon the Central Allies we should have had no Hitler, and the Fascist bogy would probably have been amusingly confined within the geographical limits of the boot of Italy instead of developing so broadly that the latter is kicking the pants off the whole world today. "T'anks," incorrigible boot-lickers of Fincap,—Mr. Coolidge, Mr. Hoover, Mr. Young, Mr. Dawes, Mr. Morgan,—nice plan.

Laughing up his sleeve, Fincap did everything in his "power" to "aid" the American emissaries in arranging enormous schedules phrased in nomenclature designed to be utterly incomprehensible to the American people. Said he, sanctimoniously, "I have quite obviously done my part in helping to arrange repayment to the American people. When it becomes apparent that the various sovereign holy of holies have no intention of meeting their American obligations, the failure will be blamed on the carelessness of America's emissaries. Having enjoyed the profits of war, we can easily dispel—in the smoke of sovereignty—the fable of this debt by which we have gained, and on account of which (since it was simply a trick of ours) we have no intention of losing through legal bankruptcy—ha, ha!" Sovereign states do not go bankrupt legally; they simply "change political color."

Nonetheless, *quasi* credit had not only shifted from private to popular prerogative, but inadvertently had become real credit and the industrialized American people became its master. The cat was out of the bag. The world of people in America gained credit control beyond recall, a decade later to be demonstrated as inadvertent popular control of the accrediting of industrial advance.

This nascent credit mastery was not, as Fincap would have it, "in the role of creditor nation," but inherent in that sector of world populace leading the industrial advance; freed of indebtedness to any outside source; wealthy in capital instruments and goods of industry 100 times over any internal accounting-out of the ravages of the old debt disease; isolated on a continent relatively safeguarding it from attack till popular realization and consolidation of the man-emancipation could inevitably develop, and governmentally unified in a healthy young democracy, the latter a time-limit and publicity safeguarded administrative scheme self-adjusting to the scientific acceleration of evolution which had already, through hydraulic damming and power conversion, harnessed *in-continuity* the unlimited ceaselessly replenishing wealth credit of star-emanating energy.

25

Indirect Effect of the War: Death of the Warehouse-Commerce City

BEARING in mind the evolution of physical decentralization in industry, as articulated by Ford, it is evident that necessity to keep up with such pioneering pace setting must have inevitably resulted in an exodus from the city of a multitude of manufacturers. Furthermore, the "tin" (sheet steel) pan manufacturer, *et al*, whose products formed part of the general rust heaps of inefficient profiteering belittering the countryside, began, also, to avail themselves of brought-into-use-by-the-War alloyed and alternate metals. The force that motivated Ford to decentralize operations toward sources of raw materials motivated these smaller competitors. This *decentralization* of *physical* activity (work or play) and the cityward *concentration* of *mental* activity (work or play) was facilitated by the contiguous war-born improvements of transportation and communication.

Thus the general warehouse necessity within the "gates" of great cities ceased, except for the accommodation of certain seaboard imports and highly transient consumer products such as food, clothing, stationery, *et cetera*, and faddish appurtenances for city distribution.

So, too, abated the vast clerkage attendant upon warehousing commerce. Concurrently and moreover, new and able accounting machinery began to infiltrate the ranks of such as remained of the clerks, despite the fact that the capitalist, fearfully detesting machinery, was less inclined to install it in the personal environment of his centrals than in his distant manufactories.

The current "capitalist"—at least 99.9% of the aggregate—is in no way comparable predatorily to his prehistoric savage forebear. He has become, in fact, a relatively delightful, hearty and emotional being, with the exception of certain minority capitalists who still continue, with shrewd and powerful super-brains, to scheme for means of grandiose exploitation, manipulation and monopoly. The retention of the profit-way of thinking by the majority of Fincaps is attributable far more to habit and petty vanity and lack of courageous imagination of other ways of survival for dear ones, than to fundamentally malevolent instinct. We might better nominate the cause as the *habit of non-thinking*. Years of great prosperity are productive of the converse of the phenomenon, *thought*, in those discouraged in such activity by early environment. So it was quite natural that inevitable friendly relationship between clerks, in close proximity to the easy-going, play-loving, sub-super capitalists, should provoke a friendly consideration that retarded the replacement of city workers by the machine in the high degree that the far-off (and, therefore, relatively impersonal) workers have been replaced by machinery.

The cityward concentration of mental activity also caused an influx of industrial managements segregating from physically decentralizing production, whose offices had formerly been located in the urban factories. These new industrial headquarters were equipped with much accounting machinery and occupied brand new buildings. This creation of new industrial headquarters, replacing dwindling business clerkage, did not offset the latter's *per capita* shrinkage due to the new machinery employed by industrial management. The incursion, however, did deceive the capitalist about the great business change. Seeing new offices renting, he was blinded to the general death of the warehouse city and commerce as he had known it.

Years ago real estate minded capitalists, with an eye to doubling their revenue, managed through political control to have enacted certain profitable legislation providing for a doubled city land requirement. These laws, known as Tenement and Housing Acts, made it illegal for people, wtih few exceptions, to live and work in the same shelter. They were passed with facility because of their seemingly benevolent aspect. It seemed reasonable, for instance, that the butcher should not sleep in contaminating proximity to his meats, and immoral that a business man or his stenographer should sleep at the "office." The sanitary "benefits" were, however, actually less important than the fact that from a profit viewpoint separate houses, or two shelters for every worker, one by day and one by night, would stimulate land crowding, thus increasing the intrinsic value of the land and also calling for doubled output of profitful building materials.

The sudden post-War exodus of physical industry from cities did not seriously affect the inland non-warehouse city, due to the fact that populations of the latter were relatively evenly apportioned to local industrial activities. Moreover, this proportioned and motorized populace was able to move in adjustment to the decentralizing process, resultantly integrating over the open spaces between centers, in many instances not far from the former inland center. Great coastal cities like New York, however, were seriously affected by the inland flight of industry. It left behind in these cities vast pools of undigested-by-industry immigrants—potentially helpless masses of people. There are still several million unemployed employables in New York City whose ½ million children (one out of every three children in N. Y. C.) are growing up under "relief."

The great modern business buildings were drained of their worker-population. Warehouses were deserted. The paradoxical picture developed of a horde of workless people crammed in hovels while business buildings remained empty. To the scientific minded, the exodus heralded the beginning of a new emergence. But Fincap, who was fast losing in the divorce action he was defending against his runaway bride, *industry*, (whose new complexities he was unable to fathom) continued dumbly at his desk, hoping to reap boom profits accruing from the post-War efficiency of *decentralizing physical* and *concentralizing mental* industry by building ever more gigantic commercial skyscrapers. He persisted—despite the fact that even the newest were rented with difficulty. As usual he way-over-milked a "good thing." Fincap, calculating potential profits, refused stubbornly and blindly to recognize the trend. Instead, he held empty space at "consistent," never-to-be-paid figures.

The mounting new speculative skyscraper-colossi increased the paradoxical picture between crowded sub-decency dwellings and empty, gleaming work shelters. The most ultra-modern buildings, efficiently heated from central steam plants (located at the river's edge, so that a through-the-streets haulage of coal would be obviated) and equipped with luxurious plumbing stood idly empty while beneath their giant shadows squalor increased in the congested hovels of a populace disenfranchised from work.

With an even keener eye-to-profit than that involved in the Tenement Laws, Fincap had, also, many years before inspired the enactment of other pseudo-benign legislation. Seemingly with the public's interest uppermost in mind, but with an underlying *motif* of assuring for himself a regular outlet for his not-too-frequent-for-detection overturn of debt (his prime revenue source), he manipulated the passage of laws specifying strictly the nature of investments that might be made by the enormous credit depositories of the populace, to-wit: insurance carriers, savings banks, and enormous trust companies and trusteed institutions in general: universities, hospitals, churches, *et cetera*.

The issues specified as legal-for-trust-fund included railroad bonds, shelter mortgages, so-called underlying equipment, city, state, government and utility bonds, in stipulated proportions of the total trusts. Although the lists of securities left by the will of a large finance capitalist rarely contained a single one of these bonds, nonetheless they were the stuff into which the people's, especially the widows' credit, was diverted.

Even if some of the money-custodians more recently have been otherwise inclined toward investment of funds in their custody, observing that widows of personal friends could make but a poor meal of foreclosed railway rails and rotted ties, the legal-for-trust-fund laws have continued to force the tremendous depositories of credit into the purchase of mortgages upon rail-roads or realty, *et cetera*, despite the evident fact that mortgages have been progressively dropping in intrinsic value with the acceleration of the industrial decentralization and obsolescence rate of mechanical-adequacy stages.

The Boards of Directors of great insurance companies, savings banks, and others—all representative of the capital-finance profit world—developed with passing years a hoary glamor in their pursuit of the lofty, smug GENTLEMEN'S business of producing "gilt edge" securities and directing "gilt edge" debt matters. They were careful not to spread the bond maturities over too short or too long a period, lest their vast turnover profit be either discovered or insufficiently exploited.

The most dignified of the elderly gentlemen serving as directors of the insurance companies, trust and savings banks, were engaged, also, in dividing the commission spoils amongst the various security-selling houses, and were assigned "duty" on the "boards" of great universities (the family-name-advertising gifts of funds to which have been enormous) and churches. The whole scheme of investment directors of large trust funds has been, of window-dressing necessity, an Old Man's Game. Elderly gentlemen can handle such matters with the utmost solemnity, being too worn out mentally to rationalize conscience-pricking problems. An exception, among the churches, has been the Roman Catholic Church. Its priesthood has served, and continues to serve, as its own board of investment directors without subservience to any state investment law, thereby constituting a marvelous source of indirect, imperceptible profit for politicians.

The legal set-up seemed so certainly-operative that those who plotted Fincap's advance attacks were glad to be relieved of the further tactical need of watching its operation—beyond seeing to it that as much of the property as was still unmortgaged became mortgaged, and that the sale of these mortgages to trust fund custodians would net them, in one way or another, at least 10% of the turnover. They were just sufficiently interested to be sure that none of the mortgages reached their own personal investment portfolios, and to see that their sons and relatives, club-mates and friends, were properly set up at a desk in one of the "bond departments" to snipe for their share of the boodle.

Indirect Effect of the War

Meanwhile, no pause occurred in the erection of ever more enormous business structures for which there was a continually decreasing tenancy, for two reasons: firstly, as already cited, the vain hope persisted that the industrial process would reverse itself, allowing high city tenancy to re-occur; and, secondly, because the legal-for-trust-funds legally designated quota in the mortgage field was having a hard time to find replacement mortgages amongst municipalities, railroads, farms, *et cetera*, that could legally be set up as certifiedly REFUNDING mortgages, a legal perquisite for any new "issue."

Railroads, mortgaged to the hilt, were no longer paying interest even on their extant mortgages; the decentralization from the cities of industry and warehousing was depleting the tax revenue of the cities to such an extent that they were rapidly becoming bankrupt; little-home mortgages, so long a stable investment, were going distinctly sour because home-owners (bound-to-locality occupants) were finding themselves less able than renting tenants (who were doubling-up) to move about in adjustment to the industrial decentralization, and, without wage earnings, they could not pay interest and amortization. Therefore, their mortgages bounced back merrily to trust funds.

Meantime the stream of popular exploitable credit mounted by deposit behind the great legal catch-basins of the trust-funders to flood and even spillway proportions. Tsk-tsk. Although "things" looked ever more sour to big business, the unquestioning "little" man continued to heed advertisements appealing to the thoughtful, good citizens who save and insure, and thus tide over depressions for selves and society. Guilelessly, little people went on popping their savings under the wickets of the life insurance depositories and of savings banks grotesquely named to appeal to the common man: "Immigrant," "Dry Dock," "Dime Savings," and "Bowery"!

"WHAT to do with the funds?" became a vexing problem for the silver tops. Ponderously, they decided that nothing could look more *respectably secure* than a conservative first mortgage on an Empire State or a Lincoln building—pretentious, mammoth structures in the Queen City, charmingly "rendered" on paper by "sterling" architects. So they signified their willingness to underwrite preposterous skyscraper buildings that had not the slightest possibility not only of total but even of paying occupancy, whereupon the proffered ultra-respectable gargantuan first mortgages became the nuclei of harum-scarum second and third mortgages, racketed off by mouth-watering builders, dealers in materials, politicians and lawyers. Any and all who could get "theirs" out of the building activity, promoted the sale of the second and third building money mortgages to stupid friends. The "guaranteed" mortgages "never a dollar lost to investor" type of business boomed anew.

The crowded dwelling *vs.* the empty, towering work-shelter paradox was ever amplified as more and more people became reduced to living in ever worse hovels, while monuments to racketeering shot up as thrilling but empty. The paradox was even more exquisitely exemplified in subscription drives concurrently running to raise funds from "all" "denominations" for the building of great cathedrals—non-dwelling monstrosities that cost multi-millions of dollars. The Cathedral of St. John the Divine in New York City, an "armory" large enough to sleep all the thousands who then slept on the open streets or in the subways, closed its doors to any such prosaic function as human shelter. New York's Trinity Church, owner of many empty multi-family dwellings, lifted not a finger to house the down-and-outs, although its congregation, be it admitted untutored in the man-arbitrated causes, dutifully shook their heads at the awful conditions.

It was not long before the non-tenancy and, therefore, the non-revenue of skyscrapers automatically "shook out" the third and second mortgage holders, representative of money investments at least equal if not double the value of the first mortgages that had been underwritten by the trust fund managers. Here was real-property "deflation" or Ford's amplification of dollarability dramatically active. A dollar could buy three times as much Empire State Building as before on a basis of the dollars still holding title to property.

At this juncture when it became evident that even the first mortgage interest and amortization could not be paid, Fincap and his revenue sinecures of the warehouse era, the cities, were in full financial rout. Banking failures multiplied. The little banks throughout the country, whose financial structures were replicas of the network thrown over New York and other Atlantic cities by Fincap, could not pry loose liquid capital by loan from their big brothers because the latter's liquid capital was itself rapidly "freezing." Hundreds of small banks failed daily.

The unemployment situation grew apace, due to the industrial flight and the increasing utilization of the inanimate machine. For awhile Fincap, automatically aligned against municipal, state or federal aid to the "stranded" (not for any moral reason), successfully bulldozed individuals, particularly the salaried saps of the low income group—under $2,000 *per annum*—to support the unemployed by "donations" from their meager wages. (Many corporations deducted "contributions" under duress of "firing," setting an able precedent for an ensuing underworld racket era.)

One reason for this Fincap "stand" is simple of detection. Others will be discussed later. Should there be set up the precedent of the state taking up the slack in employment, Fincap could not hold down labor's wage demands through the invocation of his unchallenged "demand-and-supply" formula and his "surplus-of-labor" doctrine. Moreover, if the precedent were set up, the industrial progression with its implication of an EVER-increasing human time disemployment, made it evident that state support would call for ever-increasing funds.

Fincap in no way pretended to himself that the federal, state and municipal governments would not have the support of popular credit were they to undertake efficient support of the industrially disenfranchised workers; or that popular support of the government's course would not be indicated by the people's high evaluation of its (the government's) legal tender for the re-purchase of its own promissory notes, issued for that purpose.

This popular accrediting of the government in taking over "relief" has been precisely demonstrated. Any recent appreciation in dollar purchasing value ("deflation" to the money broker) is in direct relationship to popular credit of the government's paper dollar. The constant over-purchase of any offering of government notes with diminishing interest rates in a financial market where little else has been saleable testifies to the truth of this statement. The immediate post-war 20% discount on government bonds changed to leading premiums. If it is pointed out by those eager to disparage this truth that recently there have been a number of well sold "old fashioned" private enterprise bond issues, examination will disclose that these represent simply wholesale legal-trump-ups to apply to the great trust-fund's legally enforced appetites which have had no recent amortizable fodder. Since government underwriting of mortgages·has, at last, made amortization budgeting possible in certain categories, the credit of these bond issues is fundamentally "federal" hence basically "popular." These bond issues are not, however, being purchased by individuals.

Why did Fincap, through his political job-machine racket-hold on government, resist the government's taking a hand in relief? Why did Fincap refuse, in face of the fact that private "charity" (a cheery little moral word inherited from the ancient days of complete and abject slavery) could not keep even minor pace with the vast requirement?

The reason is fundamental. Fincap was intuitively aware of the situation's being NOT AN EMERGENCY but an EMERGENCE OF A NEW ERA.

Fincap, in order to survive, strove not to allow people directly to accredit themselves through their government (themselves). Were they to succeed, Fincap could no longer keep his entrepreneuring position valid, this "position" being the "enforcement" of government's borrowing from him as the only "legal" means of establishing "liquid" government operating funds. By this "position" the process of "loaning" the "funds" to the people as unified in government and then selling the notes and bonds of the government back to the people, directly or indirectly through bank and insurance investments, entailed diversion of a constant cyclic 10% "take out" for his own "ingenuity" and "foresight."

Another vastly important reason for Fincap's opposition to government relief is to be found in the matter of specific account-ing *requirements* enacted into legal-for-trust-fund security laws. These called for a schedule of specific refunding of a municipal, state, federal or other security to be "attached" to the bonds, based on apparently predictable excesses of regular "revenues" of the borrower in excess of "expenditures." IF budgets are not balanced, no such schedule can be appended; therefore, no bond issue can be sold. This is the key to Fincap's wail for a "balanced budget."

There is no moral idealism provoking the cry, for Fincap has always winked pleasurably at government's acquisition of new debt which meant that eventually Fincap would have more debt to sell. Fincap, through political control, hitherto succeeded in periodic bolsterings of the tax schedules. Coincidentally, with much ballyhoo about the "government's getting out of business," he would draw up a plan of "retrenchment" of government activity mercilessly yet sanctimoniously "firing" thousands of government workers, thus theoretically providing a schedule of government expenditure less than the revenue from the jacked-up taxes. This "balance" legally implemented a fine new bond issue.

Of course, the municipal, state or federal government did not stay within these balanced budget figures. Neither did Fincap dream of its doing so. If it had, there would not be the need to borrow more and more. There was only and always the legal necessity of Fincap's controlling the debt amplification by "stages," that is, through the attainment of a theoretical monetary point of budget balance in order that debt might be legally sale-able. Ironically, as has now developed, the budget's unbalanced "condition" (which prohibits exploitation of the accounting sys-tem's nominated federal debt and which by random emergencies slips further and further from balance, despite "administration" attempts to heed the propaganda) has as a "joker" been saddled

on Fincap by the rules of his own original sanctimoniously con-
niving specifications of legal-for-trust-fund investments, through
legislative enactment.

This, then, is the explanation of the hue and cry regarding
budget-balancing. The current intention of such budget-balancing is simply that some 50 odd billions of accumulated federal
and state government's so-called "debt"—a debt not "called" by
the people who underwrite it and never to be "called" except by
revolution—may be turned-over with a neat five billion "take" by
Fincap. This would be "recovery" *de luxe*! It would be the
juiciest melon ever sighted by the "boys."

Prior to the "New Deal" Fincap disapproved, through his
politicians and press, the assumption by government of the maintainance of the industrially disenfranchised from work. Such
action would obviously have rendered it impossible to get the
government budget "balanced," at least for too long a time to
suit his watering mouth. Fincap's current reversed attitude toward relief underwriting will be considered at a point in the
book coincident with chronological order.

The vast majority of people have so long accepted the *slave*
outlook that they gobble up, with hearty cheers, the great press-
vomiting of the politicians controlled by Fincap, this discussion
of the affairs of Fincap always being in the latter's own "lofty"
vocabulary and outlook. The public has been slavishly receptive
to this chatter for many centuries merely because it did not have
the experience or the perspective to think in terms of the grand
*progression of the emancipation of man by man from animate
slavery, a progression pointing toward man's ultimate environment control by virtue of the "service" of his by-hand-and-mind
devised inanislaves.*

However, the day of potential fulfillment has arrived. It is but
faintly obscured under a veil—now a very thin veil of old words
and habitual ways kept alive by the press, radio and movies,
these three abstract monopolies being Fincap's last stronghold.

Unless people can speak clearly one to another they cannot

ascertain that they think alike or act in the mutual accord resultant upon their understanding of one another. So long as the press and radio impose on the public a 95% blanket of utterly meaningless chatter, through which the 5% voice of the people is discoverable only by persistent searching, just so long will Fincap be able to delay the moment of the mutual revelation of the people's understanding. Once apparent, this understanding is going immediately to articulate itself, through democratic perversity, in the emancipation of man from material servitude to his environment—the all-time teleologic goal.

26

Emergence Through Emergency

Despite materialist-chisellers' continual manipulations, life has been intuitively and unconsciously evolving its own emancipation along the route of chance-happenings. The chisellers' moments of highest apparent gain have always, and inevitably, been fraught with germs of another emergence stage through unforeseen emergency. These emergencies, with all their attendant travail, have been the "outs" for man. Paradoxically, potentially benefited man (the public) has usually been the most recalcitrant protester.

Let us recall and survey the workings of the EMERGENCY in New York just before the "New Deal" administration "came in" and declared a bank moratorium—just as Fincap was about to go down for the third and last time.

During Hoover's regime it had become evident to Fincap and his coterie of political servants in government that if the primary credit depository of the people—the insurance companies and savings banks—were to "go under" due to having been glutted by "practically" worthless "legal-for-trust-fund" mortgages, panic—REAL PANIC—would occur to a degree irresistibly precipitating SOCIAL REVOLUTION. Such a climax would not only have sacrificed Fincap's ability to sell the juicy, accumulated, unharvested three years' debt crop, but also Fincap's every "legal," constitution-interpretative monopoly and franchise, and the sequence chain of property "deeds" would have "gone by the board." Fincap would never again have been able to capture government control through politics because, with his unearned income shut off, he would have had no "wherewithal" with which to fee the politician whose job-machine would likewise be busted due to popularly accredited survival and jobs for all. In short, this would have been the end of Fincap whose original advantage was gained from horseback. Fincap's preoccupation "with the horses"—"sport of kings"—is religiously well founded.

To avoid utter panic and consequent revolution, the Fincap-tuned legislature of the Hoover administration "set up" what it called the RECONSTRUCTION FINANCE CORPORA-TION—a most suitable name, though the second word should be first. This new entity was supplied with an arbitrarily inaugurated capital of approximately 3 billion dollars, later extended to 6 billion. This advance of people's wealth to save Fincap was actually drawn from the people's credit of their own ability behavior. This "reconstruction" money was employed as a thawing fund, that is, to pay accrued interest, 12%, of debtors to the insurance and savings institutions so that it put 50 million into good standing again and allowed of refinancing generally without public awareness of the jeopardy of their depositories.

Yet, five years later, when a meager 4 billion was advanced by the government to protect itself (the people) against starvation in the midst of plenty, Fincap's still subservient press protested with a sanctimonious front page "cross head screeching" that was both awful and ludicrous. It was ludicrous in the light of the 1937 stock market "bust" paradoxically resulting from the same "New Deal" administration's announcement that it was going to *discontinue* underwriting survival and jobs, intending to force this function back through the old route of the states to the community "chest," that over-beaten, small-town-Tarzan's-bosom; and to the February 1938 20th page quarter column item that Congress had, by enactment, written off as "uncollectable" 2½ billions of R. F. C. loans to banks, railroads, municipalities, *et cetera*.

The '29-'31 panic averted, Fincap proceeded to shake down the numerical size of his *potential* bankruptcy by passing the bankruptcy along to individuals of the proletariat. This was done by foreclosing small mortgages on farms, homes and chattels on which interest was overdue. By "cracking down" on America's "home owners" and farmers during the last two years of the Hoover administration, Fincap accomplished an immediate reduction of 21 billions of potential "loss." Inasmuch as the 21 billions represented only a first mortgage equity figure, which was less than 50% of the appraised value of the property foreclosed upon, the home, farm and life-work investment loss to the small people was actually much nearer 50 billions—an amount twice that of the national debt of the time, and a 25 billion capital gain on paper for Fincap which he could resell to pay back the R. F. C.

Now, when the workers and people of a nation are taken for a buggy ride of 50 billion dollars simply because they made the mistake of accrediting Fincap's tenets of "good citizenship," they may be expected eventually, if not soon, to recapture that 50 billions, realizing that it was an accounting loss through legal fabrication enforcement and not a real all-people's loss, inasmuch as the houses and lands are still in existence. Moreover, they are not likely ever to forget the irreparable life loss and bitter unhappiness thrust upon them by Fincap.

An accounting system based on "debt" is so fallacial that it cannot take cognizance of true wealth, individual or popular, despite the common inclusion of the word debt in commonwealth matters. For instance, until an item of production has been utilized as collateral in one way or another, and, therefore, is set up in the debt structure it has no value. If a farmer on an island in Maine cuts down trees, laboriously planes them by hand and builds them into a house, he has actually converted energy into a work-and-use form product, conferring environmental control. A banker comes to the island and says, "There isn't any house there because it is not on the books." Nevertheless, the islander did cut down the trees, built the house and create wealth without borrowing from the debt system.

Such houses constructed on islands not only in Maine but throughout all lands, houses in which people live for generations and which are commonwealth in fact, would be said, in the fiscal accounting system extant between our government and the banking system, to have no value because no fixed credit was extended to the farmer to facilitate his fabrication of the dwelling. Similarly, the small roads that the Maine farmer-fisherman may have developed on his island are not officially accounted. The product is not appraised as an item of credit in the national economy, all of which is as preposterous as would be the statement by the president of the A.B.A. to a visiting Englishman sailing up N. Y. Bay that he and the "boys" loaned the money to build the New York City looming ahead, "boys" whose grand-dads were tailors and farmers and ministers. No, wealth does not come from money or from money manipulation.

The factor that Fincap brutally overlooks is that LIFE does account everything and must always balance. The electric polarity is consistently insistent. People will be glad not only to accredit themselves with an ever-increasing national "debt" limit of multi-billions but, in due course, will cut out the word "debt" altogether. They will suddenly AWAKE, no longer debt-bedamned, but DEBT-BEDAMNING (and coincidentally hydraulically damming sun-lifted water) to the realization that they possess in actuality though non-capitally accredited (in terms of an articulated, permanently-harnessed environment, in power-station harnessed water falls, and in roadways, production mechanisms, *et cetera*) a plant and structure in America for mutual interservice representing somewhere in the neighborhood of 500 billion current U. S. wage dollars. They may draw at will on this established-in-advance-credit without incurring debt, and, moreover, with adequate surplus to export to people elsewhere about the world who have scarcity of goods. ALL is theirs . . . "now, as in the beginning and forever shall be."

Reverting to Fincap's handling of the aversion of panic, his actions revealed that he was embarrassed, also, by other regulatory matters of his own early subversive contrivance. Suddenly he found the governmental accounting set up and its letter-following servants (whom he had thitherto encouraged) to be very much "in the way."

The government servants said (carrying out the letter of

Fincap's game), "In the name of the city, state and federal governments, we will have to foreclose the mortgages on certain giant buildings because the insurance companies and other holders of first mortgages, receiving no revenue from these buildings, are not paying the taxes due thereon, and taxes represent an *a priori* lien."

The civil servants, whether they liked it or not, were being forced to precipitate another panic angle. If the insurance companies had to foreclose their first mortgages, only themselves to be foreclosed upon for taxes owing the government, further cause for panic would inevitably be incited.

This was true not only figuratively but dramatically. People are much more impressed by the fate of one Empire State Building, simply due to its sensorial bigness appeal to their imagination, than by the fate of one million homes. Those responsible for affairs behind the scenes realized that the dramatic failure of the Empire State, *if recognized*, would be symbolic of "system"-failure to such an extent as possibly to stir the people to that ever-threatening awful revolt. So they spent enormous sums nightly lighting the eighty floors of the Empire State Building to make it SEEM occupied during the hours that rented buildings are illuminated, an obvious hoax to all who witnessed it knowingly night after night, but probably effective in relation to transient visitors who came, saw and returned to the "sticks" with the impression that the Empire State Building—Symbol of Financial Glory—was ablaze with light and activity.

More realistically, however, to avoid this dramatic detonator to panic, the city which, through tax failure, was unable to pay its interest to the insurance companies on its "legal-for-trust-fund" indebtedness, agreed tacitly not to foreclose upon the insurance companies on such buildings as the Empire State which had reverted to the Metropolitan Life in non-publicized but potential fact, provided the city's indebtedness to the state and federal government were also "given a ride" for the nonce. A hands-off agreement on a foreclosure merry-go-round was evolved, necessitating the New Deal's declaration of a general mortgage moratorium, underwritten by vast federal credit which, never forget, is the people's own credit. Thus the people, by "financial prerogative" itself, assumed potentiality of an at any time foreclosure position on all the "goods and chattels" of Fincap's debt structure football game. The accumulated recapture cost of this they will never be able to extract from the obsoleted structures of the by-Ford-evolution emasculated warehouse era.

Summarizing the primary results of the 1929-1932 emergence through emergency, we find:

The city went "into hock" to the central government in order to fund the municipal bond interest payments to insurance companies and savings banks, unpaid due to the depletion of taxes in the industrially evacuated city.

The insurance companies and savings banks were also factually, though not officially, "in hock" to the government through this indirect method of salvage.

The government through tax liens (non-foreclosing only to avoid panic) became the eventual proprietor of tremendous empty city skyscrapers.

The government was forced, due to the inadequacy of "charity," to become responsible for the feeding, housing and clothing of unemployed multitudes in addition to their policing, sanitation, hospitalization, penalization, and made-work occupation.

While there are eventualities of efficient integration of the "resultants" above listed, they have not yet happened and so discussion will be postponed until a later chapter (*Old Woman Who Lived in a Shoe*) dealing with trend extensions, to follow the chronological recitation of economic factors emergent in the twenty year post-War evolution. So multitudinous and overlapping have these events been that unless "picked" out carefully they are missed in the welter of murder, rape, prize fight, Charley MacCarthy, *et cetera*, gas fumes of paper and radio broadcast.

Focusing once more upon the Empire State Building as a clue to the social gains by inadvertence and evolution's certified accountancy we find that the Empire State's first seven years' rental averaged under 20% of full occupancy and "authoritative" claims are made today of 50% occupancy, but investigation would reveal that many of this 50% tenancy are "fill-ins" such as Al Smith's "Liberty League," and others.

Although a complete failure as a money-maker through rent, the Empire State Building is, nevertheless, an indirect social instrument. Its uppermost peak has become America's central television research laboratory due to the broad horizon available at that height. The short waves with which the television experiment are being conducted cannot be land focused beyond the sight-horizon. The building that was erected and preserved as a mighty gesture by the forces of exploitation to avert a panic, symbolically and paradoxically has become the *laboratory of one of the most socially EMANCIPATING of all the infantile scientific industries*—TELEVISION.

Television as a world-encompassing, non-opinion contaminated news-broadcasting agency, impossible to prohibit from the air, carrying such records as the movie-photographed "sinking of the Panay" will smash dictatorships as the hand of man smashes the mosquito. The overtone *motifs* of the universal social symphony, the exquisite notes of the "random element," are here detectable once more. Here is the "holy ghost," indeed.

27

Trick Balance Sheet

FEDERAL NATIONAL DEBT CHANGE 1928-1934 was an increase of 100% = 12.3 billion dollars.

FEDERAL INCOME 1928-1934:

Taxes on corporations and the rich declined from an annual 2.3 billion to .8 billion, a decrease of 43% for a total revenue of 4.9 billion.

Taxes on low incomes and upon user-consumer, same period, increased from annual rate 1.5 billion dollars to 2.3 billion dollars, an increase of 53% for total of 6.2 billion dollars.

TOTAL REVENUE, all sources, 1928-1934: 11.1 billion dollars.

FEDERAL DISBURSEMENTS 1928-1934:

TO direct and indirect pulmotoring of banks, insurance companies, "morgi-moras" (mortgage moratoriums) of property and debt structure, rich corporations and individuals: 11.9 billion dollars, 413% annual rate increase from 1928.

TO public works and relief, total 2.1 billion dollars, annual rate increase 152%.

TO *NEXT* war, total 3.1 billion dollars, 82% annual rate increase from 1928.

TO Federal Government's routine operation, total 3 billion dollars, annual rate decrease, 38%.

TO veterans, all previous wars, total 3.3 billion dollars. 27% annual rate decrease from 1928.

Recapitulation

TOTAL DISBURSEMENTS.............. 23.4 Billion Dollars
TOTAL INCOME........................ 11.1 Billion Dollars
_____
DEBT INCREASE END OF 1934...... 12.3 Billion Dollars

Note that pulmotoring and future war disbursements were

responsible for 15 billion dollars, over-accounting by 3 million for federal debt increase. Otherwise all relief, public works, regular government activity and long deferred compensation adjustment of human past-war imposts were carried on at 72% of the total income, which would have otherwise decreased the national debt.

Wages in the crisis 1928-1932 took a worse drop than unearned property income:

	(Billion Dollars)				
	1929	1930	1931	1932	% Drop
WAGES—all classes..................	53	49	41	32	40% Earned
Property and dividend income and interest	28	27	22	17	38% Unearned
TOTAL NATIONAL BUSINESS DIS-BURSEMENT...................	81	76	63	49	

From the above it is apparent that the disabled market condition was accelerated by federal manipulation of debt shift which, by inspection, derides the unearned-incomer's wails over supposed government confiscation. Remember, the golden-egg supply had ceased because of the death of the goose, i.e., the shelter industry.

Factually, shelter is (was and always will be) focally and volumetrically the largest industrial activity of mankind. Bogged down to its death by every financial and political exploitation possible, its super-vulnerability occasioned by tie to the land of its arterial roots, the "building business" death occasioned the dollar income decline, the "loss" accounting of which has been governmentally juggled in a maze of numerically staggering relief and recovery credit appropriations.

The national (or people's) debt, according to our legally imposed accounting system doubled 1928-1935, rising from 16 to 31 billions, a not surprising *per capita* synchronization considering that the populace almost doubled in the 40 years preceding 1935, and that debt *per capita* has never kept pace with population increase, that is to say, it shows an overall curve of shrinkage indicating a trend toward vanishment despite the latest trick impositions.

Trick Balance Sheet

The U. S. population's (man, woman and child) *per capita* debt was on March 1, 1938, exactly $290. To whom, as debtors, do we owe this $290? To our financial institutions, insurance companies, trust fund and bond holders, and to institutions in general: public and private.

At least $65 of this *per capita* debt was plunked upon us as an accounting "trick" in the 1928-1932 governmental "life saving" advances to the very institutions to whom we were in debt—a neat Peter-to-Paul trick. It was accomplished by advancing funds to the depository institutions by the indirection of loans to the investment revenue sources, i.e., banking institutions, railroads and mortgagors, which the Treasury subsequently, in ponderous and legally holy-ish manner, borrowed from the institutions to cover the advances, thus shifting the burden to every citizen. The bankruptcy of the old system was thereby shifted from banker "outlet" institutions to the people.

Approximately $30 of our unasked-for per-each debt increase since 1928 was pinned upon us as our individual subscription to the NEXT world war to which certainly very few of us would voluntarily subscribe.

The government was forced to take up the slack of unemployment caused directly by the dereliction of private credit finance in subscribing to the industrialization of new inventions particularly to the industrialization of shelter which is inherently mobile, non-exploitable and certain to bring about the acknowledged bankruptcy and annihilation of debt structure built up around static and now dead, land-wedded arts and crafts tailored buildings.

How could such accounting manipulation have occurred?

Because Fincap was making his money and increasing his capital out of the handling charges incident to the turnover of debt. But it looks as though this is to be his last "cash in." DEBT—DOUBT—FEAR—MONEY are necessitated by lack of credit, faith and understanding, these three being the colloidals of science and the coördination of industrial production, one for all and all for one—the inspiration of invention.

TRUE CREDIT and FEAR-MONEY are utterly incompatible. They were divorced by the World War, but the divorced husband's fear-money continued to aggravate "Dame" Credit until his sudden death in 1932. Although still mourned by some and despite the fact that his executors are still probating his will, we are nevertheless rid of the "old boy."

Just watch the important bankruptcies and judge for yourself.

28

Ecoballistics: Booms Boomerang

IT IS the intuitively-understood necessity pro-socially to adjust the legally-imposed debt manipulation that has been articulating itself in the "New Deal" administration's general attitude and which has been aptly press-cited by Fincap's publicity men as follows:

A fixed punitive policy toward industry (*"Industry" is the social mechanism behind which, as a "snatch hostage" Fincap is wont to shield himself,*—AUTHOR) with a series of Administration measures has so FRIGHTENED capital that it has proved impossible to finance most of the needed (central power station) construction. While money rates have been low (*referring to the preferential rates now accorded to the government,*—AUTHOR), the preponderance of the *industry* is unable to extricate itself, by refinancing, from the burden of *predepression* interest rates (*usuriously bequeathed by Fincap himself in his will,*—AUTHOR)—at a continual loss of hundreds of millions to consumers and common stockholders. All-important "equity money" for common stock, the necessary protective cushion to bonds and preferred stocks, has been frightened from the utility fields. It is being recognized at last that a policy of subsidized competition and strangulating regulation is in conflict with the policy of *recovery*.

In other words, on October 31, 1937, the "utilities" stepped into another offensive defense, attacking the "subsidized competition and strangulating regulation" of "punitive" Administration policies and announcing, through a Committee of Utility Executives, that they are ready to offer $3,600,000,000 in construction work, "provided present obstacles are removed." They failed to state that the 3½ billion dollars was not their own money but the bond-thirsty accrued legal-for-trust-fund popular deposits apportionable to utilities, through the employment of which

their holding company share-take would be Fincap rehabili-
tating.

This interesting announcement by U. S. "utilities" was made
in conjunction with their effectively propagandized emergency
announcement of the reconsideration by Congress of industry-
hampering taxes. At the same time, be it noted in contradistinction that the Tory Socialists of England passed a Socialization
of Coal Bill, admitting on behalf of Grandfather Fincap that basic
energy sources must be socialized in order to free from non-
paying monopoly-maintainance drag those operations the capital
investment of which for *manufacturing plant* is now larger than
the written off investment in monopolized *land* sources. Grand-
son Fincap in America probably had telephoned grandfather
that *hydraulic* power was the only out and suggested unballasting
the sinking H.M.S. Fincap by jettisoning *"coal."*

Of course, the phenomenon of taxation, which Fincap now
claims makes it impossible for him to go forward in industrial
growth, was originally self-devised for Fincap's own convenience. Taxation in the present accounting system was designed to
certify a balanced budget by indicating that governmental revenue would be in excess of government's expenditures, the
revenue being predicated upon a promissory schedule of future
refunding. These schedules of refunding are essential appendages
to the legal-for-trust-fund bond issue that the banking fraternity
craves.

The paradox that now develops is that Fincap, while hollering
for tax reductions that apply to his own activities in order to
save his increment, cannot cry for complete negation of taxation
because he would thereby cut off his own nose by breaking down
his bonding system with its recoup possibilities of 5 billion
"smackers." He will *inevitably* have to go back to his plea for a
general sales tax. This has worked quite well since its partial
inception and without undue hardship on the people. As an
eventuality of the 1937-38 crisis it will in all probability be
highly amplified to provide the revenue essential to budget balance. This will be large because it will have to take care of the

unemployment relief which was lopped off the budget scheme to allow a reduction in the excess profits tax. It was contemplated by political organizations that Fincap would be willing to take these taxes, but Fincap immediately cried, "I'm too hard up," and precipitated the state of mind of the 1937-38 depression.

An even more crucial paradox occurs at this point, for when the sales tax, which does work, is amplified and the population as a whole takes over the providing of the required governmental revenue, the populace will in *fact* be directly underwriting the government, which Fincap has hitherto claimed as his prerogative (insisting that by constitutional interpretation the government cannot spend money without first borrowing it from the banking system). In the old days, Fincap grumbled about bearing the burden of taxation and charity, but he knew that he was thereby maintaining his more lucrative prerogative as sole credit-source. The instant Fincap allows the population to become sole and direct underwriter of government he will precipitate by precedent the factual transfer of the credit-source to the people. The popular result will be the recognition that the government need never again borrow directly from the banking system, particularly since it has already been demonstrated that the Treasury can take care of its peak load requirements through note sale instead of through bond interpolation. Bonding gone and a broad sales tax in effect, the budget need never be balanced again. Fincap's prerogative will have been lost forever by his own manipulation.

When this has happened and the populace (government) has voted in favor of the socialization of unemployment and of medical service, *et cetera*, because paying the bills, it can thumb its nose at the money lenders in a merry farewell.

Inasmuch as fashions are *superstitious* symbology, and automobiles, from a scientific viewpoint, have changed only in visual fashion appeal in recent years, and inasmuch as the automobile industry led the way out of the last depression, its symbolic surface fashioning may be appraised as highly indicative of the superstitions of Fincap. No one item in the current superstitious depression could be of more significance than the fact that the Fincap-controlled section of the automobile producing industry (in contradistinction to what Ford offered the public in the fall of '37), at its usually highly dramatic annual automobile show (which Ford never enters) did not even offer a new fashion, thus superstitiously indicating that Fincap sees the end of exploitation, and that since dyes and tools for fashion-changing cost large sums, he is planning to ride out the momentum of the automobile industry's high production to get every penny he can out of the old dyes and then do a runaway. While the ostensible reason tendered by Fincap's publicity directors for this "stand pat" was the pile up of 2nd-hand cars, is almost as simple of interpretation as if Fincap frankly said, "I am pulling all the dollars possible out of the last surge forward, and am running for Bali and the South Seas."

There is no cause for wonder in the fact that the entrepreneur advertising agencies have begun the old story of, "I am not going to start with any expansion plan just now such as opening an office in Los Angeles," etc., etc., "because I sense a coming depression."

The downhill symbolical progression of 1937-38 is simply Fincap's intuitive and superstitious awareness of his own demise as industrial commerce entrepreneur through obscure bullion manipulation.

29

Speculation: Introducing the Mechanical Stock Exchange

A<small>LL</small> living mechanisms, that is, mechanisms commanded by the phantom captain (abstract life) are characterized by selective compositional growth organisms as distinguished from the erosive dissipations by all inanimate organizations. All living organisms have a SPECULATIVE trait. Living entities MUST SPECU-LATE TO GROW. Speculation is the first conscious stage of the teleological trial and error process.

A vine speculates with its tendril, geometrically spiralling it to find a point to which to cling. The insect speculates with its sensitive feelers. All speculations are trial leads for the detection of favorable survival conditions. Science calls speculation "assumption to be proven." Several speculations provide a progression trend for objective selection. At the point of imminent selection, teleologic rationalization occurs, objectivizing itself in a "doing" that will be proportionately adequate to the inclusiveness of the speculation.

Much contemporary "hue and cry" against the "speculator" has provoked a derogatory, special meaning for the word "speculate." This derogatory inference is born of a careless lack of search into the subject, for it is not speculation *per se* that is anathema to the sense of universal social fairness, but the employment by financial speculators of not only their own credit but of the credit of others who have no wish so to speculate their credit. They are able to do this simply because credit is abstract and intangible and, therefore, uncircumscribed by the strict legal and ethical protection accorded the tangible property of individuals. This is indeed paradoxical, for SPECULATION, CREDIT, IMAGINATION, INVENTION, *et cetera*, are exquisitely more unique to the individual than manipulatably acquirable physical properties. A nose may be completely altered by a surgeon, and land by a landscaper, but not so character. It is character alone that has developed the protective bulwark against the wolves, the sleet, the ravages of pestilence and all the forces of destruction. Why should society not nurture, cherish and protect these *prime* assets with far greater zeal than it furnishes to its secondary assets of physical time limited tangibility? It is then not speculation but misappropriation of speculation by peculators of the individuals abstract assets that is at the root of popular condemnation of financial speculation.

People have not only the right but the utter necessity, as living mechanisms, to speculate their OWN credit. When persons speculating their own credit speculate, for instance, that it will be safest for survival to place their accrued earned credit in a bank against an emergency, they assume that that credit will remain as an intrinsic entity in their chosen depository.

Some people's knowledge that it does not stay "deposited" in no way changes the fact, from the depositor's viewpoint, that the popularly-subscribed-to "banking" idea was developed under the specific notion that the deposit was to go no further than the vaults of the bank, wherein they had placed it in preference to hiding it under the mattress. Bankers have shrewdly promoted the continuance of this "illusion" by architectural devices, appealing to the eye as "securely vaulted," and other psychological means.

The bankers' plea that the deception is economically justified because a bank cannot be maintained without some earnings is "reasonable." So, also, is the thief's explanation that his family needed the loaf of bread. The bank, viewed as a private institution, does have necessity of earning "overhead" as contrasted to a federal depository such as the post office which, as an instrument of all people, needs no behind-the-scenes manipulation, being maintained by direct stamp revenue charge. This "reasonable" maintainance claim by the bank in no way justifies a continuance of the bankers' *pretense* that deposits go no further than the vault. Nor does it justify profits to bank underwriters, or a dozen $25,000 salaries within one such institution. Banks have actually speculated the credit of their depositors in, for instance, real estate, with regard to which the depositors themselves would not intuitively have wished to speculate. Banks, moreover, have loaned their depositors' credit "on call" to stock market speculators, and the credit has gone into stocks oft-times quite uncreditable to the original depositor. Definitely, this is not only speculating with another's credit but is nullification of it.

Stock markets are an essential mechanism to an industrial society, for it is essential that the relative credit popularity of an industrial undertaking be constantly articulated in order that useful industry may be abetted and non-efficient industry discredited. In no other way can the populace furnish the credit support required in tool-up cost prior to product revenue, which credit is so essential to the growth of vast industrial undertakings.

The discredit of stock market operations has been occasioned by the pooling operations of "privileged" characters speculating with vast loans of others' credit, either from banks or from their safe keeping trusteeships. This has allowed of manipulation, rigging, *et cetera*, bringing about arbitrarily false relative credit values of industrial issues non-indicative of the relative service, afforded and potential, of the industry involved.

As soon as speculation is confined to outright purchase and sale individually, without margin, the stock market will become a truly indicative graph of popular speculation as to the social welfare effectiveness and potentialities of all industries relative one to another.

It is parried immediately that popular purchases would be limited to units so small as to be utterly unfeasible if not impossible from the mechanical viewpoint of handling in stock exchanges. The usual units of popular speculation, it is argued, range from a "high" of two or three dollars on a race horse to a "low" of five cents in a slot machine. This mechanical limitation is true only so long as the stock exchange trading has to be done by the evidently limited human robot, the stock broker. What can we do about it?

Historically, "exchanges" have developed in the manner of all other monopolies. Merchants, specializing in specific products in season and having nothing to occupy them during out-of-season periods, began to anticipate or speculate regarding "futures," i.e., crops to be grown or produce in general, basing their speculation of *prices to obtain* when the "season" arrived upon factors of weather, population shifts, and so on, thus creating markets *in advance* that progressively corrected themselves in terms of the *in season* "spot market."

Likewise the money market, anticipating export, import and future industrial dividends and borrowing, developed an *anticipatory* activity among its traders, particularly the traders in shares of industrial activities, which latter have grown to such tool-up cost proportions as to call forth a widespread sharing of the tremendous investment required not only for equipment but for working capital.

Eventually those traders who controlled to a high degree the real estate, including the buildings, of the locality in which they traded, grouped together and agreed upon a monopoly by membership limitation, lest the trading be spread out so thinly as to preclude the high earning on the part of its members. While "curb" markets grew outside the "big board's" doors the latter held the reins through reliability, self imposed for survival efficiency, by control of the wired reporting system, and habit prestige.

The trading markets in *abstract futures*, *abstract shares*, and *abstract moneys* enabled industry and commerce to function smoothly, as far as liquidity of credit was concerned, despite seasonal intermittencies.

Inasmuch as it is perpetually NOW, the PAST is really only a mental extension backwards on a defined progression of experience which is extensible, in terms of experience, far beyond the limits of actual experience. In identical manner, the FUTURE is extensible in terms of a progression of actual *now* experiences into the ramifications of now existent phenomena. For instance, a New Yorker who has never been to the Argentine, finding cause to go there, can assume that there will be a specific hotel and specific people in the Argentine when he arrives there nine months HENCE, and the assumption will have an analytical reliability certainty of equal accuracy to his analysis of events of a political campaign nine months past. The degree of speculative certainty of analysis of past and future trends is teleologically predicated upon the degree of factor inclusion in the NOW observations.

Eddington says, "Science is simply the sincere attempt to set in order the facts of experience." Within the meaning of this tenet, speculative future prediction is equally valid to speculative historical interpretation. Neither past nor future speculation may be reliable if the ever NOW experiences are not inclusively set in order.

The constant setting down of scientific-world-experience-factors in analytical order for the guidance of market speculators has developed an high order of useful prediction-ability. It is only the excluding prejudice of special interest that permits (through the incompleteness involved in the extraction of special interest factors from the full array of ordered experience) the constantly recurrent improbable "street" predictions that give rise to the rather popular notion that accurate prediction is impossible. For example, a specialist in metal "stocks" who overlooks the fact that housing is predicated upon scientific sociological trends and dismisses the profusely available and concise data of these trends as mere political pish posh, obviously cannot visualize or realize the "future" of the role of metals in housing, and, therefore, cannot make other than erroneous predictions about metals futures.

Furthermore, the illusory prejudice of the fictional "property" viewpoint has made the predictions of predominantly property-ized "authorities" (property-ized both as to things and people) so unreliable as to have established the popular opinion that prediction *per se* is unscientific.

This popular notion consequently assigns reliable prediction to the category of mysticism insofar as it pertains to personal and social developments, but contrariwise, accepts as highly authentic and non-mystical the predictions made by so-called PURE scientists with regard to astronomical bodies' behavior for advance periods of hundreds of years. This general acceptance of pure science's reliability is, however, relatively new. Five hundred years ago such astronomical predictions would also have been popularly consigned to the category of pure mysticism.

The entry of the true scientific attitude into statistical recording market-establishments, super-rich in orderly but uncorrelated data due to "prejudiced" dumbness requirements, will, in the near future, through broad integration, provoke an astoundingly high order of reliable prediction ability. This will transpire as rapidly as property-loaded individuals are replaced as the dominant market speculators by a vast population of non-property-ized industrial co-workers whose leaders must, of necessity, be highly scientific.

As industry and commerce grew apace, the exchange monopolies became sources of tremendous revenue to their limited number of members. Memberships, appropriately called "seats," became saleable property of high value. When, however, the industrial era developed a popularly supported "market" in the late 1920's, the limited *human-mechanism-exchanges* proved utterly inadequate to the maintenance of a continuity of representative activity. In view of the exquisite importance of the "timing" of "shots," they failed completely as "true" representatives of buyers and sellers. Sales fell hours behind instructions.

The financial monopolist, ever fearful of machines though profiting in multi-billions thereby, has failed to recognize the extraordinary efficiency that could be invoked by mechanizing the whole speculative exchange activity. This can be readily done as of present, elsewhere-proven mechanical means.

Speculation: Introducing the Mechanical Stock Exchange

A *mechanical synthesis of pari mutuel* horse-racing machines, calculating machines, and averaging machines could easily be devised which would provide a continuous registry of the sum total of shares-for-sale and sum total of shares-required-for-purchase in any category, with a constant electrical integration of the coincidental *bid* and *asked* values and "sales," as well as a constant registration of the *spread* between required and offered, and *cumulative* volumes of transactions. Thus would be created a truly mechanical, non-doubtable and, therefore, POPULARLY ACCREDITABLE abstract industrial trend MARKET of inestimable value for industrial and governmental guidance and social progress.

As soon as shares are exchangeable mechanically, much of the popular discredit of the "broker's" ability or willingness to execute orders in the best manner possible will be dissipated.

The people will DARE again, as they did in '28 and '29, to speculate in industrial activity. This, for them, is a much more RATIONAL and FASCINATING form of speculation and one of greater inherent interest than their horse-racing and slot machine speculations to which they were forced back, first by manipulated losses and latterly by financial reform. In the "horses" and "slots" the possible chance of winning, which is scientifically stated as the "amplifying of speculative credit," is about 1 to 100 in proportion to the possible "amplifications" of their speculative credit of rationalizable industrial issues, granted the latter's relative value movements are mechanically insulated against false manipulation.

During the height of industrial speculation in the 20's, the people were enabled to participate in exchange activity through loans to them of other people's credit, known as "call money." Whereas they speculated basically with a small amount of their OWN credit, ultimately they were speculating with a large amount of OTHERS' credit, as high as 1/10 in "reputable" brokerage offices and 1/20 in multitudes of "questionable" houses. Naturally they lost quite consistently, due to the ability of those with vaster pools of others' credit to manipulate the market. Enormous "pool" buying and selling usually "wiped out" the small individual's OWN credit "margin" by virtue of this borrowed credit's false amplification of his original speculative INTENTION. That is, by using twenty "parts" of others' credit to his own one "part," he was unintentionally betting that the value of a share would amplify by twenty units; actually, he meant by only one unit. It was this false amplification of prediction that inflated the market to the 1929 "impossibility." Had popular man speculated solely with his own credit, he would still be custodian of his specific credit shares, regardless of the "relativity" fluctuation of the market.

Regarding the Exchange-members' protestations of impracticality—in the matter of the mechanical ability of the Exchange's handling of small-denomination-sales, or sub-fractional "odd lot" transactions, denominationally representative of the specific excess credit of the popular-average individual speculator, it may be stated that as soon as such a mechanical exchange is in operation its first function will be to eliminate the bottle-neck in the current mechanism, which is the human robot. The machine, being not only untiring but unlimited in its figure handling (an adding machine does not care whether it computes millions or tens), the "market" will be open 24 hours every day, everywhere in the world, and not only "odd" lots but minute fractional share-purchases, for example, 10¢ worth of U. S. Steel, will become possible of purchase as easily as would 10 thousand dollars worth.

Another objection that may be offered to the MECHANICAL EXCHANGE is that of the legal necessity of the actual *delivery* of shares involved in any transaction. This can be obviated, also, by the machine. It will be quite possible to place telegraphically connected "repeater" Stock Exchange Machines in every "United Cigar" or "Liggett's Drug" store anywhere in the world, each equipped with a means of revealing the spread and market of any issue and a means of executing any order (no matter how fractionally small), by purchase from the machine of a ticket imprinted with the quantity, price and share symbol of the issue being purchased. This ticket may represent: (1) an outright purchase to be held indefinitely, or (2) an addition to an accumulating quantity of fractions ultimately sufficient for the practical transfer on the books of the corporation of shares purchased, or (3) it may be turned in at any EXCHANGE MACHINE STORE immediately for cash gain or loss.

The "voting" right of shares on the basis of numerical holdings, necessitating "delivery registry" will, of course, have to be recalled. If every one dollar bill had one political vote we should have daily to register each and every dollar exchanged with the federal government. Preposterous! And the antithesis of the principle of democracy. Yet every single dollar bill is a share certificate in the industrial commonwealth. How will the directors be elected who in turn elect the administrative officers of the corporations? By ONE *vote* per capita by each stockholder, and by each worker for the corporation, of one year's *holding*, or *employment*, respectively. Mechanization of the Stock Exchange together with the cancellation of the arbitrary-by-legislation disproportional voting-right imposition on industrial shares bid fair to instrument the populace into a daily and hourly "vote of confidence" on all national-industrial problems.

30

24 Hour Year Round, World Wide Referendum Service:
True Credit Amplification

How will the Stock Exchange Machine be useful?

For one answer: as a means of support of pioneering ventures in scientific productions and services. None need be "afraid" with a Stock Exchange Machine to risk the $3 of his personal-credit-total that, prior to its institution, he was putting on the nose of *War Admiral* "across the board," in support of a specific manufacturer whose venture he deems to be socially useful, for instance, a manufacturer of radio tubes.

It must be remembered that when shares are bought "in the market" the money does not go to the industrial corporation involved; the shares are first sold by that corporation as an original issue to a direct buyer before they are exchangeable. Placing $3 behind XYZ radio tube, by betting on it in the Mechanical Stock Exchange, will not mean putting $3 in the hands of XYZ corporation. The eventuality will be that if Murphy's credit thought is shared by others so that a number of bets are placed on XYZ, the INDEX of share value of XYZ radio tubes will *amplify*—or *contract* as the case may be—*relative* to the index of the share value of *all* industrial issues. Thus relativity of *satisfaction credit* will be demonstrated in a most illuminating degree, "manipulation" being mechanically impossible.

This indirect credit will aid XYZ radio tubes because the industrial transaction "credit limit" of XYZ will be directly proportional to a true popular credit of its progress ability, new issues and amplifying "tool-ups" thereby being afforded through advertised sale.

The dollars involved will be those popularly earned through a direct interpolation of TIME ENERGY conversion rate equivalents. A man has but one life, with an average of 22,000 days and a "high" of 36,500. At the $1 BASERATE postulated in the "Dollarability" chapter he has a gross birthright capital of $47,085 time-dollars. He gives away many of these in mechanical service to others. How many days of control of his own time does he receive in return? How *much* of his environment can he control in his self-controlled days? These are the individual-time-control-dollars which are trying to break through the false-front of the legally set up gold or metallic base dollars, inherited from early days when a *lack* of *credit* in trading between people of unfamiliar tongues prevailed.

What is "CREDIT"?

The "credit" of the banker's language has been actually the converse of credit. Dollars made "liquid" for the borrower's use have involved intrinsic collateral values of 200% and more. If the liquefied capital was not amplified by the borrower in such a manner as to allow repayment of it to the bank, within a specified "time" the 200% was forfeited. This eventually involved, by the law of average, the constant transfer to Fincap of dollar dominance. This certainly is NOT "credit"; it is "credit's" antithesis: Shylock's pound of flesh, DEBIT, which is credit-contraction and is scientifically disynchronous with the expanding universe.

CREDIT is that abstract proclivity present in everyone to some degree, which man through experience of successful speculation accords the world populace in general as not only being able to "do" but "doing."

CREDIT, then, represents man's confirmed appraisal of general trends and the sum total of his KNOWLEDGE OF MAN'S ABILITY, through a succession of consummated speculations.

The socialized literacy that was recognized as potentially plenitudinous at the inception of the North American States provoked an entirely new plenitudinous category of *per capita* "credit." As a result today the total integrated U. S. credit is attracting world wide credit support, as super to any taxing requirement, and as adequate to accelerating industrial progress.

This growing, true credit of man's belief in other men's behavior pattern, and his readiness to speculate this credit in support of that behavior, was long the piratical monopolist's goal of exploitation. He was eminently successful in attaining that goal up to 1929. Then, in order to exploit popular credit to its utmost, he allowed true CREDIT to penetrate into his behind-the-scenes activities and thereby wrote his own death warrant. Popular credit, finding naught but a manipulation of truth behind the financial scene, immediately fell away from the manipulator— never again to be vulnerable.

It is evident that when the Mechanical Stock Exchange is in operation, abetted by televised world event inspection, a wide flux will occur in the amplification or deflation of the credit dollarability speculated by the individual relative to the "field." He may enter with a dollarability of three in the morning and come out with a dollarability of five in the evening, without having taken bread and butter from anybody's mouth, simply because he accredited what was popularly discernible as of the highest service potential to the public. This will benefit industry generally by making possible the maintainance of an open market in which industrial shares may be offered for original sale without recourse to falsehood and deception.

These conditions are developing with greater rapidity than is generally realized.

The Stock Exchange Machine is going to prove itself to be so delicate an indicator of popular sentiment at all times that it will replace in large measure the ballot box of politics. There will be no necessity of four year referendums to determine the sentiment of the people in relation to legislative progress, administration leadership, or the desirability of sit-down strikes as an effective means of worker welfaring.

Pure individual credit speculation, rendered non-exploitable through the Mechanical Stock Exchange, as criteria of popular expression, and an industrially reproduceable, fear-eliminating scientific shelter as the incubator of ever-amplifying credit and courage of speculation, are industrially potential (together with socialization of medics, precipitant through the dramatics of the potential syphilis purge) as the central objective trends currently fast expanding in the popular realization of science's great gift to man.

The Scientific Segregation of Scarcity and Plenitude

No matter how it is to come about, it is evident from a trend study on the basis of a synthesis of the mechanico-efficiency, philosophic and mathematical viewpoints that all categories of PRODUCE, PRODUCTS and SERVICES, attaining a *constant* production source and means potentially sufficient (with full "safety factor" allowance) to supply that product, produce, or service to all people on earth, must automatically become socialized.

To clarify: The air that we breathe is normally and to all intents and purposes socialized—because it is in such obvious *abundance*. However, in a case of a theater fire when air becomes a *scarcity* it is not only in a *competitively sought* category, but, exquisitely in a *mortally combative* category. Air, mechanically conditioned, is not socialized. Its use must be ordinarily paid for, even as a hidden overhead surcharge in movies, department stores, *et cetera*. Water supply is in many localities socialized because *plenitudinous*; in others, it is individually acquired by purchase because of its *scarcity*.

It is not merely the technical advance in the means of production or even the power to run the means of production or the plenitudinous of raw source that nurtures such potential socialization. Other important factors are world wide "availability-integration," through rapid and plenitudinous transportation means and the attainment of an almost negligible-in-cost instantaneous world inter-communication system to report and adjust "availability."

Up to the time of the outbreak of the World War there was a distinct scarcity of mechanical transportation and communication means relative to population. World export markets had not yet become glutted and the export outlet for the produce of any industrial country made possible price control in that country without abatement of production. It did not matter to the home producer that he "dumped" abroad his exported material at half the price of his home asking, because the home market was primarily so much larger that he could afford to dump his surplus at cost to maintain *semi-scarcity* domestic prices. For instance, the U. S. Steel Corporation did this in the Orient for years. More recently, producers of metals have been protecting their domestic "market" by exporting scrap to Europe and Asia, while reserving their "new" steel for domestic customers and taking from mines on high markets only. (Incidentally, there is no difference in metals refined from *scrap* and those refined from *ore*.)

With the advent of the World War, the great reaching out of the primary industrial nations for new foreign markets came to an inevitable impasse. The total of world population involvement had at last potentially been reached. By virtue of the scarcity and profit principle and because of production SURFEIT the victors in the fight for control of the foreign markets—a prime cause of the War, just as it is in the background of the now-being-agitated second world war—were unable to alter the fact that the world's production means had at last attained an ability not only of production but of *distribution* of "adequate" proportions in primary survival categories to all people. Inevitably EFFICIENCY, which controls evolution, will have to adjust men's affairs, whether through war or creative intellectual means, to this fact.

There was involved, in this world surfeiting, even more than the actually apparent numerical attainment of production means balancing potential consumption. Integration through transportation and communication brought about a strange revelation, namely, that the production means in the previously non-integrated geographical entities had been devised on a basis of "safety factor" production for all local needs in periods of potential high isolation. For example, every cold locality had by experience "planned" to endure long winter isolation. The whole commercial set-up was, therefore, prior to the World War based upon the warehousing or storage of surpluses for local isolation periods. When multi-amplified trackless transportation integrated these communities, a resulting total means of production and surplus of safety factor storage inventory was revealed equaling many times the potential integrated consumption on a mobilized short "time-lag" basis.

It is evident that artificial means such as tariffs, moratoriums, bonuses, discounts and plowings-under cannot long defer the full recognition of and adjustment to this attainment by man, striven for by every scientific thinker, and every unselfish person for multi-thousands, if not millions of years. To be sure, inefficient pile-up of surplus AFTER FULL DISTRIBUTION *is* a *problem*, but one of research only—cotton for wall sections of prefab houses, vegetable excesses for conversion to plastics, *et cetera*. One million of the billion given to Hopkins for his A.A.A. production limitation advanced to research would do the trick.

There are, then, two categories of production: one, the scarcity category, and the other the plenitudinous category.

In the scarcity category no artificial trading stimulus is required. It is necessary only that goods produced be adequately exposed for sale, at a selling price determined by specific adequacy in proportion to demand and supply. This applies to any new mechanical invention unit, to abstract services and to "what nots." It is the only true measure at present available for the determination of the adequacy of man's new inventions, products and services in relation to popular use ability.

Conversely to the status of these "scarcities," Mr. Clarence Francis, President of the General Foods Corporation, in a talk before the N. Y. Stock Exchange Institute, said with uncomprehending surprise and implied rebuke that stocks on the N. Y. Stock Exchange representing the food producing industry constitute but 3% of the market value of all company equities on the "Big Board."

"Yet," he pointed out, "this is our largest individual industry in the United States, employing more than one third of the country's total population. The annual value of the world's plant food is about five times greater than the yearly value of the world's mineral production. The American public spends considerably more for food than it does for automobiles."

Mr. Francis drew a further interesting word picture indicative of the proportion of the food to other industries: "A hen seen scratching in the front yard of a pig iron furnace in blast appears insignificant. Yet the annual farm value of chickens and their eggs is more than two and one half times as great as the yearly wholesale value of our pig iron output."

The fact that Mr. Francis finds so small a proportion of food producers' equities listed on the Big Board, in inverse proportion to the size of the food industry, is very important. *It makes clear that as any mammoth production category of man's essential "needs" approaches plenitudinous classification it also approaches relative socialization,* and, therefore, is no longer subject to individual speculation. *Individual speculation must be confined to the categories of scarcity production.*

A mechanical contrivance may be not only theoretically correct, but also mechanically highly efficient; but if it is an instrument that only a few people can technically operate despite its having a designed field of use in the popular retail category, it must be admitted that this particular machine is not popularly adequate and hence its functioning must remain in the scarcity category. Some other machine must be invented having a more timely relationship to man's intellectual control of the human mechanism before the mechanical service approaches the plenitude category and socialization. This is exemplified by the 40 year lag between the invention of the steam railroad and popular patronage, which required first the invention of the air brake, then shield tunneling, automatic coupling, dynamite, *et cetera,* before it became popular; in other words, popular confidence and use were withheld until contiguous inventions were brought about by supplementary individual ingenuity for which credit backing had first to be created. (See Charts.) The contiguous inventions to railroading are now so replete and have been so plentifully produced that the r.r. system is generally evolutionarily necessitous of socialization.

The Scientific Segregation of Scarcity and Plenitude

One hundred years after the invention of the first steam rail-road train, New York's vast subterranean railway system became socialized in actuality as a compound of a plenitude of individual inventions, power and credit speculations. The 5¢ fare is but a stamp tax overhead refund of a broad subsidy. It does not purchase a metered ride. One may ride a quarter of a mile or 100 miles for a nickel on the world's largest, safest and most intricate r.r. system, possibly the world's most superior engineering achievement to date. But the socialization of New York's subways did not come about either by revolutionary proletarian seizure or a voluntary vacating of the premises by capitalism. It came about through emergency compromises, bankruptcies and receiverships subsequent to potentially certified "plenitude." Despite legal accounting and the politico-financial maelstrom abstractly circling about the subway system of New York, ten million Murphys ride in the subway daily in innocence of the frustrating-to-Fincap confusion involved, as the system spreads constantly in smoothly and safely operated efficiency.

Neither of the political extremes of viewpoint has recognized in full (though it is now slowly creeping by inadvertence into their cosmos) the inevitable segregation by evolution of the scarcity and plenitude categories. Socialism, as theory, presumes a totality of plenitude; capitalism a totality of scarcity of all things. Wherever capitalism has found "plenty" it has sought, through legal means and political privilege, arbitrarily to manipulate the "plenty" down to "scarcity" so that demand and supply activity might be maintained.

Soviet Russia, representing socialism, STARTED in a condition of primary scarcity in all but a few agrarian categories. Nevertheless, Russia assumed an economic procedure based on a socialistic philosophy of plenty in the face of scarcity, which was as paradoxical as any capitalistic country's philosophy of scarcity in the face of plenty.

Obviously, scarcity has to be recognized. There must transpire, therefore, a scientific segregation between plenty and scarcity, and a scientific administration of the highly disturbing-to-society fluctuations of the borderline categories. In socialistic countries competition is already being allowed in the scarcity fields, and in capitalistic countries categories of plenty are now being willy nilly socialized with horrific *belly-aching*. It occurs in capitalistic realms in the guise of "emergency enactments": our old friend "Emergence Through Emergency."

In view of our present mechanization attainment, thinking or voicing a thought that assumes as attainable that which political parties call "recovery" is utterly puerile. The RECOVERY notion infers for the capitalist a RETURN, RETROGRESSION or ROLLING BACK of the years to a set of conditions that in some specific year were of special gratification to the individual speaker's outlook.

THERE IS NO GOING BACK. What is called "unemployment" is the borderline nomenclature for what will in due course be recognized as *socialization of leisure*, formerly an acquisition of distinct scarcity. With this socialization, "relief" funds will emerge as socialized "income" from the scientific investment of knowledge. So-called "unemployment" is here ultimately to stay and is going to increase geometrically except as, from time to time, it is contracted by the inception of some temporarily intense activity of replacement of old by new and more adequate mechanisms.

The last broad field of application of the industrial principle is in the realm of industrially reproduceable scientific shelter. This application will result in activity so tremendous as temporarily to take up all voluntary slack in unemployment, provided the latest emergent and popularly recognized efficient working hours and wage scales are progressively lessened in the first category and increased in the latter.

There is inherent in the new scientific repro-shelter industry such an advanced state of mechanization (delivery of houses by radio-controlled aircraft will be commonplace) that its accelerating ability will very quickly disemploy the worker so far as LONG hours of machine tending are involved. The breakdown in hours will not be along the line of forty, thirty or twenty hours a week, but will be on an annual service basis. Workers will go into their jobs on a periodic service arrangement. A work stint broken down into a few hours a week, calling for a worker's year-round anchorage in one locality, stewing and fussing aimlessly in order to render that short service, makes it impossible for the worker to decentralize efficiently and purposefully for play, rest and education which, attended to, would fit him for exquisite service ability, were he employed on a periodic basis. This will pay social extra-dividends. A magnificent start in this direction is outlined in the following (by Louis Stark) from the N. Y. *Times* of March 3, 1938:

An employe on a weekly wage, who refused to be dismissed, led Jay C. Hormel, Austin, Minn., packer, to work out a method of guaranteeing an annual wage based on the assumption that the employer's duty is to make every effort to keep men at work. Mr. Hormel described his plan today to the Senate Unemployment Committee.

When the demand for a new product declined precipitately, he felt impelled to drop some men, but one of them, who had given up a $9 weekly income from a peanut stand for $20 with the packer, said:

"You can't do this to me."

This set Mr. Hormel to studying the reasons behind the hourly wage, and in the end he retained his men, found other things for them to do, and added new products. He even went into housing, erecting thirty-four houses to keep his men occupied.

As a result of his experience, which began in a modest way with nineteen men in 1931, Mr. Hormel said that last year 2,373 out of nearly 4,000 employes were on an annual wage.

While "on paper" the books seemed to show that the plan had cost $300,000 a year, Mr. Hormel said that the money was still in the till as he had received the equivalent in better workmanship and savings in such items as electric light and water bills.

With the knowledge that they were secure for a year, the workmen had developed responsibility for his business. Not only that, he added, but the face of the small city had completely changed since the plan was undertaken. He said he could not explain it, but people seemed to buy more automobiles and more houses with the same amount of annual income.

Recently, Mr. Hormel said, the men, who had had an independent union, obtained a charter from the Committee for Industrial Organization. Senator Byrnes asked why his employes had joined the C. I. O. if they had been contented.

"Our people believe that if they have some strong union throughout the packing industry it would raise the level of the industry," was the reply. "They also feel that the union helps get petty grievances settled. The only difference between the C. I. O. and the independent union is now that we have to excuse four or five fellows once in a while to go to a convention."

Mr. Hormel explained that the work of his plant was budgeted on a forty-hour week basis through collective bargaining. If one kind of work disappeared, he said that men were transferred to the "extra gang" at the same rate of pay until the company developed some new product or some steady employment for them. If men must be dropped, they get one year's notice, but that is "theoretical" as none has been dismissed.

The trend of an annual wage plan is now politically on the horizon. In February, 1938, President Roosevelt cited the necessity of placing housing workers on an annual wage to permit their rendering intense service during peak seasons and avoid starvation through the balance of the year. This item may be the most important emergence of the current emergency. Any minimum-wage-maximum-hour legislation will be meaningless without an inclusion of the "year round" factor, and it is upon this factor of inclusion that Congress intuitively waits before voting enactment of the Wage Hour Bill.

When the industrialization of shelter has come into full swing the work of attending machines will have to be apportioned among all potential workers on some schedule such as that of annual manoeuvers of an Army Reserve Corps. Each worker will put in perhaps but two weeks' service a year at the machine. The rest of the year will be his own in which either to employ himself in providing advanced services at high return in the scarcity categories, by amusing or serving other men, or he may simply amuse or improve himself.

What has this to do with speculation?

Everything. It is speculation itself. The specific purpose for reciting the foregoing speculative prediction was to develop speculation as to whether Stock Exchange machines could play a part in a world where the tendency toward socialism implies, for the average thinker, utter socialization, and the mere mention of "Stock Exchange" is anathema to the socialist. The evident trend toward socialization of the plenitudes has awakened in many minds the fallacial notion of the impending socialization of *all* of man's activities in the not distant future.

Reviewing: *My contention is that socialization will occur only in the plenitude categories. In the scarcities, competition greater than ever will ensue.*

The sooner the capitalist and the communist realize that their respective "dreams" or methods of social welfaring, upon which each individual of both categories intemperately hangs his special undigested habits of resentment-reflex at any correction of direction, are not to be invalidated, but that, contrariwise, the valid phases of the "dreams" of both are automatically by evolution to be invoked and amplified, not as an "ist" or an "ism," but as a scientific segregation and recomposition of "a place for everything and everything in its place," the quicker shall we be able to incept popularly the thrilling pioneering of efficient mutual interservice. It will be thrilling because untainted with irrational compromise and "the taking of bread and butter out of the mouths of babes."

A trend in this direction is to be discovered within the field of education (e-duco: "lead out"), that tampered with but never abandoned field, which contains the embryonic means of ultimate man-emancipation throughout the vicissitudes of establishment of the world's industrial laboratory on the North American continent. The means is socialized literacy, which provides the key to abstraction, to science, to teleology, deep-rooted and subconsciously the MEETING PLACE of all ideals.

While Fincap snobbishly kept his hands off the public schools and universities in the U. S. his control of private universities for the sake of dumping his legal-for-trust-fund mortgages, as well as his fear-born necessity of controlling the ramifications of education and scientific development lest these articulate themselves in a manner disrupting to profit, militated against the procurement by private universities of the pulmotoring governmental aid in the same degree that it accrued to insurance companies and savings banks in the '32 crisis. Wherefore, the great universities, whose vast top-heavy endowments from self-advertising-Fincap were invested in bankrupt mortgages, became prime victims of the crash.

That these universities have not folded up is due to three factors: (1) the fact that their financial portfolios contained some of the securities the interest on which was advanced by the R.F.C. to save the popular depositors, which advance could not discriminate against other "holders"; (2) the rehabilitation of the mortgage situation by Federal Housing Act "pep"; and (3) the provision of liquid cash for their routine maintenance by subscription amongst the graduates of the universities to operate the primarily non-mortgaged university plants.

Since the '29 "fold up" of so many of Fincap's material monopolies, innumerable men in the scientific, technical and professional world dropped from the payroll of their former patron, have, as unworldly and embittered pawns, espoused the cause of Communism. The swelling of the ranks of Communism by these scientifically minded, university dropped or "laid off" people has recently changed the tenor of the Communist Party in America. Its self-deflating, original vituperance is fast disappearing under their thoughtful council. Communism is becoming for Americans a semi-digestible philosophy.

Before the high socialization of the plenitudinous essentials in America has been fully established, the Communist Party will have evolved into a body which has discarded its religious habit of non-thinking, blind "ideology" and conversely will be fully considerate of the utter necessity of a socialization-program's comprehension of an ever constant necessity of inclusion and refinement, and adaptability to change, which is, in effect, mathematic's ENERGY TIME manifest. Not until the Communist Party IS dominated by an awareness of the complete necessity of science's leadership of the popular cause (which latter in turn is the inspiration of all invention not by external command, but by inner longing necessitation) will it, Communism, be effectively articulate as a political philosophy and "cause" in America.

Pro-socially inspired science was the inventor of the machines which later evoked the Marxian trend observation and Marx's tactical regulations.

Man as "science" is causal; man as "politics" is resultant.

Communism as it first entered this country—that is, Communism as a political entity as differentiated from the spontaneously mushroomed communes of early New England—exaggerated and perverted the survival and growth problems of industrial man. The dialectics of Marxian Communism as interpreted in a peasant country, Russia, quite properly brought into prominence the illiterate agrarian manual worker as the (generally speaking) sole concern of the government. The illiterate agrarians represented 99% of the then non-industrialized Russian population.

In order to attain objectives in the "U.S." land of industrial pioneering leadership, Communists will have to abandon their agrarian era's revolutionary approach to serfdom when broaching the plea to scientists to join their ranks with conditional insistence that the scientist adopt their rules of progress, which are just second hand dogma of science's ORIGINAL thought.

Science has no rules of personal conduct. Science articulates the first means of progress. Paradoxical to its ego, Communism will have to join the scientist to be successful. It futilely urges science to limit itself "down" to joining communism. A true scientist joins naught but universal mechanics.

In Russia, where the establishment of socialism at the outset disenfranchised the scientist and philosopher due to fear of the perverted outlook of professors long patronized by the Czarist bully, the original attitude toward the scientist and his pertinence to social survival and progress has now been completely reversed. In Russia today the scientist, inventor and mechanical pioneers are given first consideration. They are the nuclei of popular credit maintainance. They receive twice as long vacations as manual workers and are afforded access to mechanisms and data that are withheld from those whose activity is confined to the minimum manual social stint.

The political agents of Russian Communism, not understanding the new land of high industrialization (for the nonce America) or the underlying forces at play, converted to their political cause in their first contact only escapist-ineffectuals who, nondigested by American industry, were stagnating in the immigration pools of large American cities. Proselytizing by this type of individual resulted only in the romantic and dramatic enrollment "in the cause" of a relatively small number of disgruntled, unemployed manual laborers and pathological "Bohemians." The latter, assigned to canvas the "white collars" found that their "clever" and vituperative prattling called forth no sympathetic consideration among those conversant with American ways and world trends. The proselytizers did, of course, win favor with many equity-loving though relatively ineffectual intellectuals, dilettante or otherwise.

Sum-totally the intellectual uplift involved in the educational "shot in the arm" of an Americanizing-industrializing "Communism" in the land of its own first spontaneous experiment, together with the emergency necessities of deranged Fincap's progeny to think for survival's sake, coupled also with the main body-politics' horror and disgust over Naziism, will suddenly let in the light by segregation of the clouds into the simple *plenitude* and *scarcity* categories.

32

Universal Language

B Y "IDEAL" is meant the latest sensation of refinement towards perfection along any one time line, and by "standard" the group ideal, the "standard" being graphed by the most encompassing sphere of our awareness terminating the conscious exterior limits of all our radionic time lines of *interests* and *experiences*.

The history of straight line measure and of graphing constitutes an example of the inevitable progression in scientific satisfactions of standards, by design evolution predicated upon the specific WEIGHT-STRENGTH-ECONOMY-FACTORS instrumented sequentially by solutions respectively in compression<tension<abstraction.

The first linear measurements were made by man in feet, compressively walking. Then man made a yardstick or pacestick of three feet with which he could draw approximately straight lines. Beyond this measure, in his ever insistent physical decentralization requirement, it was relatively impractical to draw straight lines with compression sticks, although "rods" were tried. Wherefore, string tension lines were introduced as seen in building foundation layouts, or for brick and shingle lines, *et cetera*.

Sea soundings greater than *compressive* oar-handle depth (as ships were increased in size and depth and traveled further) called for *tension* lead-lines forwardly "heaved," while the boat was in motion. Soundings were measured in fathom units, a fathom being the average span of the extended arms of man, approximately six feet, or twice the length of the compressively foot-paced yard. However, catinary sag and wind deflection curvature rendered the tension means of line-drawing impractical over large earth-surface distances. In the latter field, the surveyor's telescope, an abstract sight line, was evolved. In navigation a vibration echo system was instituted for soundings, an *abstract* vertical line of measurement.

The error present in the use of tension line drawing was illustrated in the building of a mile long wind tunnel at Langley Field, Virginia, in 1932-33. In the construction of this, the longest wind tunnel in the world, through old craft habits of the contractors, spirit levels and tension lines were used to determine foundation lines. When finished a marked curvature, corresponding to the curvature of the earth's surface, was found to characterize the base, constituting so great an error even in a mile as to have invalidated the wind tunnel's scientific effectiveness if it had been superimposed upon this deformed base. So the whole job had to be done over again with surveyor's instruments.

The surveying instrument, also, has its limitations. For instance, it cannot be used to measure and describe straight lines beyond the horizon in a single operation. So the radio direction finder was developed to provide a means of measurement and line determination, through cross bearings of lines of intersecting directions to or from two or more broadcasting stations, limitless and one thousand times more accurate than the surveying instrument employed over long distances.

Each of these successive steps in measuring and line determination ability represents a progressive amplification of space-time saving and precision ability of geometric proportion. It is to be noted, moreover, that the ratio of specific weight of the measuring means to measuring ability has constantly decreased.

This history of measurement exemplifies the trend progression factor which I have entitled EPHEMERALIZATION. This progression, evoluting from compression<tension<visual<abstract-electrical, is typical of all evolutionary trends: from might makes right to right makes might, to technology, to science, and to pure mathematics, the latter being contactable only through mind-functioning.

Another demonstration of the trend toward ephemeralization is apparent in the fact that the sewing machine of this year weighs one half the sewing machine's weight of yesterday and yet has greater rate, precision and versatility ability. This is true, also, of calculating machines. But, more exciting, dramatically, to popular conception, is the history of the key which has constantly diminished from the great implement of the early turnkey (a special job in itself) down through the more able and ever smaller units until finally we have the photo-electric cell or ephemeralization of the key itself, a transition into a pure scientific abstraction of energy control. The key to trend comprehension is progressive ephemeralization. This is a practical key which may be applied to market speculation if coördinated with pertinent contiguous factors.

The implication of recognition of *real* values in an ever more ephemeral order is a happy one for all who deal in thought and many of whom have been branded, through all past history, with titles of inconsequentiality such as "professor."

The highest values must inferentially be apportioned to the abstractions, and it is paradoxical that the legal property mechanism has only effectually protected the utterly physical. The true realist can point out, in view of the ephemeralization trend, the abstract quality of realities of the great revolution of today which are inherent in the dominance of mind over matter values and activities.

Even on a much lower level of rationalization, an intuitive awareness of the ephemeralization trend reveals itself in the "flapper's" flippant evaluation of the purely physical, which older and former generations valued so highly. Some call this the "raspberry" revolution. The court's jester was often its greatest sage.

In the matter of units of measure, science in due course evolved the metric system, which is a decimal system of potential (though sometimes devious) correlated integration with scientific measurement in all fields. It was designed to clear up the misunderstandings universally developed through oddities in humpty-dumpty measuring units—hands, stones, feet, rods, grains, *et cetera*, thus through abstraction to make possible world-widely understandable decimal and electrical calculation in the development of all scientific problems. (Some scientists think a decimal system of twelve instead of ten would be more efficient.)

The metric system evolved by the French was adopted by the the radio world at the latter's birth. So universally practicable was this abstract measurement language that radio's world-girdling, national-boundary-eliminating integration was undoubtedly sped by many years by the metric system employment. The metric system, despite certain limitations only recently evident, has penetrated into all behind-the-scenes mechanical and electrical worlds.

Why has the metric system not been universally adopted in all of man's important activities? Mainly because, prior to 1929, building (our largest single industrial activity from a sheer weight and volume of end-product viewpoint) was an arts and crafts tailoring trade developed out of a "traditional" evolution of apprenticeships and guilds, the early centrals of labor union strength. Its basic trades, masonry, carpentry and metal working were developed by apprenticeship from father to son. Stubbornly unscientific, each generation continued to talk FEET and humpty-dumpty minimum TOLERANCES of error in terms of inches. These "tolerances" in building error are still adjusted haphazardly by the mason or the carpenter's "joining" skill and are called "fudging" in trade *patois*.

This very gross tolerance, in all senses of the word, is less true of the steel "skeleton" building, which has surreptitiously spirochaeted old architecture. But engineering calculators in the steel plants still have to interpolate from the architect's humpty-dumpty ATHLETE'S FOOT measurements into metric system in order to perform industrial establishment calculations in "metric" only subsequently to reconvert them into "feet" of finished product so that they may be handled by the field assembly crafts.

Throughout the building trades we find compromise adjustments to science-abandoned feet, and to the "a pint's a pound the world around" jargon of "rule of thumb" standards.

Only when scientifically evolved and industrially reproduced shelter gets into full swing will the metric system be practically and popularly adopted for all measuring purposes by the new life growing up in the new compromise-eliminating shelters. So long as the shelters harboring new life continue to be romantic compromises (we do not war against harmonic growth), just so long will that new life be subject to a prejudice of confusion and the inability to talk or comprehend universal languages.

33

Ephemeralization

THE very character of simple arithmetic of mathematics indicates that all progressions are from material to abstract, by which we mean intangibility, non-sensoriality, EPHEMERALIZATION.

Starting with 1, man developed first 2, then 3, then 4, *et cetera,* all parts of 1. This division of 1 evolves a progression of a particle diminution which, although it may never become 0, as particles, is none the less toward 0.

The progression in the art of measuring has been pointed out as evolving from the physical foot rule to radio cross beams, the latter being far more able, as an instrument of abstract measure, than the earlier developed surveyor's unit of measure. There is, in reality, a distinct difference between the two in that the surveyor's operation involves sensoriality throughout its dimensions, whereas the radio cross-bearing measurement implies an operation of measuring in a non-sensorial band or octave.

Up to the time of the World War major industry worked practically only in four sensorial or material bands, and man is still sensorially aware only in four. Industrial research is now working in 70 bands of energy radiation, that is, on a 17 to 1 basis of industrial guidance in bands that can be contacted *only* through mental activity *vs.* sensorial experience. This is proof-positive of a mind-over-matter dominance and frees mind-over-matter dominance from a purely "mystical" or "literary" connotation into a bread-and-butter economic significance.

At either end of the radio process of measure there is a mathematical STEP DOWN or STEP UP, INTO or OUT OF the non-sensorial band, FROM or TO the sensorial band of awareness. These steps up and steps down have become possible through the scientific pursuit of a purely mathematical path which,

SPECULATION indicated, MIGHT provide a non-sensorial path. When explored this path proved the reliability of mathematical speculation, and its translatable truth in reality, a noncompromisable reality far more actual than subject-to-illusion, direct sensorial means.

Radio measurement is teleologic measurement, for sensorial ends are jointed by an abstract means ⋈ . The TEL in teleology is the TEL of in-TEL-ligent, TEL-epathy, American TEL. & TEL., TEL-evision and TEL-escope, or "TELL what you saw, or "It TELLS" (i.e., it COUNTS, it mathematically rationalizes to advantage, a TELLER, an interpolator and COUNTER-OUTER of abstractly accounted credit-in figures on the books into units of sensorial specie. (Something to show for speculation.)

A measuring method more abstract than the radio crossbearing measurement, the surveyor's visual line measuring, or the humpty-dumpty foot rule measure, is unquestionably the astronomer's measurement of distances to heavenly bodies, through far-pentration to non-sensorial octaves by means of mathematics, currently running into measurements as great, to date, as 2,700 billion billion miles (a mere fraction of the measurements of tomorrow).

This is as true of the microcosm as of the macrocosm. In the microcosm weights and measurements must be made in minute fractions beyond the current sensorial (5000 diameter) amplification of the most able microscope. Purely mathematical and abstract calculations beyond the sensorial in the microcosm are carried out in terms of atomic weights and electrical characteristics of the elements. There is also a time rate universe which we might call the chronocosm in which abstract calculations must lead us when venturing beyond the sensorially apprehended fastest and slowest. Old religion's "the quick and the dead" quite reasonably assigns to the dead all sensorially measurable speed.

As one of the most thrilling examples of such calculation and its prognosticating ability, one may cite Dmitri Mendelejeff's demonstration (1868-1870) in this abstract field of measurement in the microcosm. At the time of Mendelejeff's entry into the electro-chemical world basic chemical elements were known empirically to exist. Certain of the mathematics of the empirically known elements' electrical, weight, and activity properties had been determined. Mendelejeff ramified a complete mathematically inferential universe based on the detected properties of the 71 elements that had been discovered, and ascertained mathematically that there would be discovered 21 additional elements in the universe the characteristics of which would be not single but multiple, and would thus provide a certainty of identity by "cross fix." He described accurately the multifold atomic characteristics of the as yet undiscovered elements and stated that their existence was necessary to "satisfaction" of mathematical periodic-progression and a mathematically ramified and balanced cosmic symphony. Bach's point-counterpoint mathematical ramification of music is the harmoniously sensorial counterpart of Mendelejeff's abstract exploration; interestingly the octave period is common to both.

Mendelejeff prognosticated a total of 92 elements and a mysterious 93rd to cover the infinite factor of error—the "random element." Mendelejeff prepared a chart which he called the "periodic chart of the atoms." It was somewhat similar in appearance to our every day of the month calendar, that is, with numbers in rows and with columns 1 to 93. The columns and lengths of line were, however, unequal in numbers of squares. The further to the left and the higher on the chart, the more "active" the element. Mendelejeff inserted all the mathematical descriptions of the undiscovered elements. One by one over a period of 70 years science has discovered them and has found them to have precisely each and every characteristic prognosticated by Mendelejeff. He did not include their electrical properties of *electron* and *proton* and *neutron* arrangement for the latter was not as yet discovered. Their subsequent discovery and effect of changes upon his chart were substantially slight.

A popular understanding of this truly miraculous penetration by Mendelejeff from the sensorial into the abstract and return should certify industry's unfaltering and ceaseless subscription to its research departments' activities whose current establishments (approximately 5000 in the U. S. alone) are constantly threatened with extinction through impulses of false "practical" economy. (Incidentally Fincap might be cautioned against the undue discount of the Russian mind.)

Another thrilling EPHEMERALIZATION has been the development of the treatment of syphilis. From complete *failure*, syphilis therapy has progressed through meager but scientifically promising stages of complicated malarial infection compounded with 606 (neosalvarsan) to approximately certain success in simple electrical energy control, "sandwiching" 606, a chemical energy constituent, with electrically induced special temperature, all emulating mathematically the essence of circuitous and dangerous empirical trail blazing. The dramatic lifelong tenuous and ultimately successful pursuit of this "miracle" by Wagner-Juareg is inspirational. The ephemeralization in this case was neither of space nor weight but thermal, i.e., a TIME-ENERGY progression of the "chronergeticosm."

It is of more than casual interest to note that every one of the ephemeralization trends, whether in measuring or medicine, eventually hits the electrical stage wherein Einstein's formula, with "E" for energy, which can stand also for electricity, becomes the most simple symbol of the unity toward which the relative progression on the other side of the equation (mass) must evolute.

A corollary to the ephemeralizing-toward-pure-energy progression that is taking place throughout all science, and, ensuingly, throughout industry—which simply translates science into bread and butter for people—is that the more abstract the means of accomplishment the more *specific* the results:

> *Efficiency = doing more with less.*
> ∴EFFICIENCY EPHEMERALIZES.

34

Science and Industry "Take Off" as the Boys "Get Down" to Business

It is evident that those industrial activities which we explore CONSCIOUSLY and rationalize ABSTRACTLY, rather than follow blindly through chance emergence, will automatically increase not only their specific satisfactions for popular man but, also, the scope of their activity. So doing, they must inevitably become ever more powerful in comparison to groping notion-and-whim conducted predatory businesses.

Exploiters who are dominantly materialistic-minded and who grant naught to right but espouse might as a means of progress will find in this truth cause for reflection of little comfort. Both the dinosaur and the giant mammalian mastodon have fallen by the wayside. Might made little right for them, and in any great swamp today more mosquitoes—tiny flying machines—are in circulation than there are men on earth. It's the microbes that would get us if our fate were confined to the dictate of Fincap. The further up the type scale we go in the size of integral living entities, the scarcer the individual becomes. On the other hand, numbers increase as we go down the scale in size of living entities. The scale into ephemerally small is exactly like the scale of 1 into 2; 2 into 3; 3 into 4, and so on.

By dint of fear and emergency "indirection" rather than by rationalized consideration of the ephemeralization trend, Fincap has been forced to retire into highly abstract monopolies as his last stronghold. By "dint of fear" is a scientific and not just an emotional actuality. There have been scientific invention *exceptions* that were patronized directly and immediately by Fincap, but they have been obviously fear-motivated patronages. To wit: the immediate availability of huge "Foundation" sums for research and invention in the medical world, whose end-results are constantly applicable to the frailties and diseases of the aging capitalists who cannot buy health at any price in their own exploitation markets, and whose fear of death or mortal or even "potency" loss to self is wonderfully dominant over the pro-social longings, under the banner of which they underwrite "Foundations." Let any proletarian seek the latest research aid in medicine and this is soon evident.

It is appropriate here to remark that the surgical and medical boys through their "frats," under guise of "protecting" the public against inferior service and exploitation, recently stated that they were unswervingly *against* the socialization of medical care even in the most common categories. Suddenly and revealingly they have reversed their policy and ostensibly "endorse" planned medical "care" under the leadership of state and county medical societies. They even offer "to act specifically as a clearing house in the initiation, development and functioning of what may well evolve into a comprehensive system of medical care for all the people according to the American plan of medical practice," the "American plan" being, of course, the joker—that of "scarcity" price demands. Traditional practice is still determined to smoke-screen, by such specious, fly in the ointment statements, the significance of the offensive recently launched by 430 highest-type, widely accredited "rebel physicians" in a publicly announced thesis that "medical care is the prerogative of the Federal Government." The business-doctor not only attacks the "rebels" but directs his fire against those funds and foundations, such as the Milbank Fund, that have dared to propose more governmental interest in medicine and against those Federal agencies which have listened interestedly to the proposals of the "rebels."

What is the method of functioning of the Foundations *approved* by Fincap and his "Doc"? If Mr. Link or Mr. Pink, for instance, is prevailed upon to make a donation to a medical foundation of the kind approved by the "boys," he is in a better position to be granted an exploiting franchise by the "committee" in control of patents, thus exploiting, directly under hypocritical benevolence, man's physical vulnerability.

On the front page of the N. Y. Sunday *Times*, February 28, '38, in columns 1 and 2 there appeared two extraordinarily pertinent articles:

Column 1: "TAX CUT SENTIMENT TO HELP BUSINESS RISES IN SENATE"—enough said.

Column 2: "WIDER HEALTH AID FOR NATION URGED. THE COST OF ILLNESS AND PREMATURE DEATHS IS ESTIMATED AT $10,000,000,000 ANNUALLY," a report by the Technical Committee for Medical Care of the U. S. Public Health Service. Consider these items:

Mortality of mothers during child birth:	½ to ⅔ *avoidable.*
Mortality of infants during second to twelfth month of life:	½ *avoidable.*
Appropriate treatment of children with rheumatic heart disease:	*will restore ⅔ to normal life.*
Penumonia typing and sera *effective* if applied:	44 *states have no pneumonia control program.*
Mortality of tuberculosis can be reduced:	50% *by health supervision of workers in occupations predisposing to disease.*
Disability from malaria:	*excessive in the rural south.*
New cases of syphilis annually:	518,000. *Awful toll reducible by 95% under program of control.*

The Committee declared that:

As a nation we are doing vastly less to prevent suffering and to conserve health and vitality than we know how to do through tried and tested methods. . . . Sanitary advance owes much to epidemics or threats of their approach, to outbreaks of contagious disease among school children, to floods and other disasters of the past; *but we cannot permit the future of health services to continue to rest with the accidents of history.* The systematic warfare against disease on a broad front is long overdue.

More than 1,100,000 births are occurring in families which

are on relief or have total incomes including home produce on farms of less than $1000 a year.

The poor of our large cities experience sickness and mortality rates as high today as were the gross rates of fifty years ago.

Why not be even "mechanistically" intelligent (to say naught of the abstract, mystic and harmonic riches to accrue) and cut the gross costs of the body politic thus reducing "unseen" expenditures and ∴ automatically reducing necessary taxation income to government for inefficiency-outgo. The "practical" man's way of paring expenses has too long dominated politics.

Granting that there is certain logic in the saying that a "stitch in time saves nine," or "an ounce of prevention is better than a pound of cure," we may discover that if there were any pro-social integrity in the guiding philosophy of the Rockefeller Foundation to advance the well being of man, it would surely long ago have underwritten scientific re-pro-shelter. The Foundation's trustees and executives have been legally helpless to become actively interested in such development because the "deed of trust" ("deed" is first cousin to "dead") specifies *curative* medicine, not mechanically aseptic prevention. They are financed to look for a filterable virus, but have no wherewithal to place the filter at the entrance portal of the home.

There are, of course, certain virtues in "individualization" in the advance research field and always will be. It is self-evidently impossible to consider the overnight socialization of an antidote which, although found by test to be effective, lacks a practical means of production. Granted, for instance, the theoretical possibility that Rockefeller Institute's cancer researchers may have developed a serum and procedure with every indication of effectively curing cancer, and that the "serum" evolved is the result of a long series of apparently accidental biological transactions complicated to such a degree that it is impossible to obtain it in more than intermittent and minute quantities, it would surely be socially catastrophic for the Rockefeller Institute to announce its success in curing one or several cases of cancer. The myriad of victims of cancer would futilely inundate the premises to the devastating detriment of progress toward the ultimate broad victory. Long years of pioneering and individual sacrifice would still be required for the development of adequate quantities of such a product. Might represented by unlimited funds and the mightiest of armies could be of no avail in the acceleration of such an event.

IF (cliched "the biggest word in the language" because it cannot be hurdled) Fincap *had* accredited the inventions and processes to be utilized in vital abstract monopolies (radio-aviation, *et cetera*) not only at the time of their first demonstration (which he did not) but more pertinently at the time of the rational citation of the various inventors of their earnestly proposed developments, *then it could be said truthfully* that Fincap was motivated by longing in so doing because longing wishes to include for another or others ever more embracing and refining harmonious means and processes. However, this has never happened, for whenever the inventors of these instruments and processes have invited Fincap's backing (by Fincap we mean the formal banking world, not foresighted exceptional individuals), they failed utterly to win such support at the crucial time of invention.

Fincap was and is *not* longing-inspired. He entered the fields of aeronautics, radio, advance medicine and publishing (the first two highly abstract, the latter relatively so) only after hundreds of men had given their lives for the practical establishment in the popular mind of "credit" in the performance of these mechanisms and their use processes. When Fincap did invest, finally, in these activities, he did so with his usual scheming, law-evolved, bully-imposed legislative franchise monopoly "set up."

Prior to Fincap's advance into such monopoly of the abstract fields in America, he continued to weave, fearfully and cunningly, about these "fields" lines of legal argument anent "constitutional interpretation" and, in England, about "precedent," with oft-repeated references to the "spirit" of the "people," *et cetera.* Under the cloak of slippery hoodwinking and only when the new pastures had been walled off by his lawyer-raiding army, Fincap mounted his abstract-legalized-monopoly steed and ventured timidly, but quite safely, into the new grazing fields. Once inside, Fincap was reluctant for a time to ride about because he was afraid he might break off his steed's dummy legs. These ridiculous abstract-monopoly steeds, guided by frightened (because abstract-blind) poltroonish riders who quivered inside their chrome-nickel-steel armor, nibbled around front lawns, and fearfully and jealously listened to the browse-wandering of other Fincaps' steeds in the same fields. But Old Man "Evolution" has no time for such mummery.

Wild, winged horses are constantly being born outside the walls to be ridden bare back by a roving band of pioneering minds. Eventually this herd will agglomerate into so large a mobile horde as successfully to stampede the monopoly plain, as have mobile hordes through all times. The legs of the wild horses are not fictional and created to fool the riders into believing they are legs. They are "the real thing."

Prior to the World War, many individuals broke their necks in aeroplanes and thousands of boys for years spent their allowances in evolutions of the primitive wireless. These experimentors (or "nuts") received no support from Fincap, that is, not directly. Indirectly the "wireless" and "roadless" received developmental backing through military departments of government which, in time of peace, will fear-accord vast sums for the development of the scientifically indicated defensive appurtenances of a theoretical and always potential "NEXT" war.

Radio, particularly for naval communications, and aeroplanes for both navy and army tactics had been developed to primary workability in the pre-1914 period. Fincap, however, from a direct profitable peace time employment viewpoint, laughingly dismissed them as mechanisms of a remote future—say, some thousand to five thousand years hence. H. G. Wells's "War in the Air" was viewed as an "Uncle Lubin" visiting the moon. Fincap was utterly blind to the industrial significance of these two activities for he was still interested solely in TANGIBLE monopolies and the TANGIBLE linkage of monopolies. He could conceive of no way to monopolize wire-less and track-less communication and transportation. Moreover, these were dangerous activities to develop. They MIGHT prove to be the means of people's escape from the web of tangible monopoly.

Eventually, however, fear necessitated Fincap's recognition and support of the Navy and Army's defensive inclusion of wireless and aeronautics. The monopolists for all time had been articulating this fear in the theory of necessity to sovereign governments of military weapons as a constant safety factor, not only for the protection of their skins but, also, as an assured outlet for certain products in peace as well as in war, at gratifyingly high profits. Even as military exploitation possibilities, however ephemeral, aeronautics and radio could not be conceived of by them as involving any "tonnage" of raws.

As a result of the behind the scenes battles between individual inventors ambitious of usurping the military defense patronage of wireless and aeronautics prior to the War, unique and divergent design developments occurred respectively within each of the sovereign entity camps. When the World War threw these mechanisms into an almost universal competition and mortal combat, their human operatives appraised and integrated, with an alacrity born of mortal necessity, the individual unique developments, not only in all of the allied camps but in the enemy camps as well, through the capture of enemy mechanisms. Thus an accelerated and integrated progression of aeronautical and wireless development occurred.

The great armies of scientifically minded young people who had longed for this-and-that new accessory of their radio and aeronautic mechanisms without hope of being able to afford it, and in the terms of the operation of which they dreamed without hope of gratification, were immediately and suddenly empowered by war credits to "shoot the works."

Struggling designers, builders and fliers of the early planes became men of marked importance backed both with the best of media, and almost unlimited credit. In the army and navy, those assigned to aeronautical duty, whether in the fighting zone or not, were paid double the amount paid others of their specific rank. A special enlisted-man rating was evolved in the U. S. N. for aeronautical mechanics. This rating was "Chief Special Mechanic" and called for more dollars than were paid to the ground officers immediately in command of these mechanics. However, this is not surprising; they were worth a hundredfold this bonus.

Special ratings were evolved, also, for the mechanical developers of radio in the navy. As the immediate hazard to life, so dramatically inherent in aeronautics and submarine service, was not apparent in the radio field, the radio *operators* received no bonus in excess of that given for service in war zones to those of any rate or rank. Consequently, no man of radio *developmental* ability could be induced into the "service" except by draft, and by the time the drafting idea matured those distinguished by their developmental ability in the art of radio communication had already become employed as "exempt" civilian technicians in the army and navy departments.

At the beginning of the War in 1914, and, indeed, in 1917 when the United States entered the arena, radio was still in the infancy age of distance-limited "spark" sets. It was the long distance, gargantuan high seas troop and supply transportation, opposed tactically by the all-seas passaging submarines, that invoked the necessity of radio communication "extraordinary."

Important distance refinement occurred with the inception of "arc" sets. First accomplished experimentally in 1901 it became economic to telegraph across the Atlantic. "Arc" was employed, however, primarily in large land stations such as at Arlington, Washington, D. C., Bar Harbor, and aboard first class men o' war and large transports. Smaller craft, destroyers, *et cetera*, continued to work on the old spark sets. The operators were nicknamed "Sparks."

Although radio telephony had been invented prior to 1917 (1902) and experimental-stage-mechanisms had been placed aboard battleships, destroyers and ships down to submarine size for use in close fleet formation manoeuvers, anticipatory to major naval engagements such as occurred between Germany and England at Jutland, these experimental devices were so poor that throughout the next two years (until the Armistice) they were retained merely as mural decorations in conning towers of ships. When they did work, their usefulness was limited to horizon distances, for which visual communication, systems of blinker, wig-wag and semaphore were more useful and familiar.

Meanwhile, civilian experts like Dr. Lee De Forest continued their efforts in the development of their arts. Dr. De Forest succeeded in devising a radio set so light and able that it could be used in an aeroplane for communicating with others on land and sea. By the end of 1917 he actually succeeded in establishing communication by voice between an aeroplane and a vessel. His important tube invention, isolating regenerative elements in vacuum, foretold the opening of a new era in communication, all radio work thitherto having been exposed to the vagaries of the chemical chaos of environmental gases.

When the Armistice was declared, President Wilson, professor-idealist, decided to attend the peace conference in an endeavor to establish a League of Nations that would prevent recurrence of world-warring. The intimate picture of the behind-the-scenes mechanics of world-warring, necessarily revealed to the President of the United States, must have been God-awful. The S/S *George Washington*, a by-America-seized German ship converted into a troop transport, was selected as the ship for the Presidential passage to the peace conference. Congress granted a special appropriation to the Navy Department for equipping this transport in the most able manner for the presidential-entourage crossing.

Wilson's administrative activities, which had amplified an hundredfold over those of any previous President, involved a constant necessity of most able communication. Therefore, all necessary funds were available to radio experts to evolve for the

The Boys "Get Down" to Business

George Washington the most extraordinary radio equipment that had ever been put into marine use.

Radio telephony, which theretofore had been used only in the spark field, was extended to the long distance and high powered arc field. Thrilling new distance operations occurred in the radio shack atop the ship. In the few months between the President's first trip to Europe and his second trip, arc telephony was so improved that by the time of the second trip human voices conversed across the Atlantic (from Brest Harbor to Arlington) for the first time in history.

War ended, Fincap became very busy recapturing, through his legally established power-over-government, his "inalienable divine property rights" which had, for efficiency, gone under government control for the "duration" of the War.

The widely convincing, peace-time clamoring of business bullies in the press that a free business reign is far more efficient than so-called government "bureaucracy" is quickly forgotten by the business man when the emergency of war arises. During war, however, not only the efficiency but the mortally-inevitable only-possible-chance-of survival is seen, with the brilliant clarity of lightning, to inhere in complete governmental mandate over all of man's activities. It is simple: Men freed of money-accounted cost and initiative-crushing by Fincap and his chiselling cohorts, coöperate efficiently in war for survival purposes.

The railroad slump caused specifically by the automobile and truck mileage ascendency which outdistanced the r. r. in 1918 thereafter to take away the profitable bulk of transportation, occurring by *coincidence* in the same year that the r. r. were turned back by the government to Fincap, was seized upon by the latter as his outstanding argument—"proof positive" that the government is woefully inefficient as a manager of industry. While Fincap's conclusion may be right in certain categories his trump card as played was a joke.

During the War, open-hearted tolerance and consideration of others became universally possible in home fields because people, "great" or unknown, rich and poor, and with all manner of habitual special interests, were freed, for the nonce, from business's "class" requirements and activities. Business's greater preoccupation was in vast war profits, whose frequency precluded time for "penny pinching," whereas the preceding era of peace business, in its activity in the HOME field, imposed on the populace the necessity of a YOU or ME survival, egocentricity, and intolerance. The open-hearted, open-minded inclusion of the welfare of even the most remote stranger, which became rampant and harmoniously active during the War, persisted in festivals of reunion and in memorials-of-individuals and common grief during the whole of two years after the Armistice, that is, so long as the homing movement of integration lasted. Today, excepting an annual mass Legionnaire or other convention, it is all but forgotten. The dreary existence of disabled veterans in "HOMES" is nauseating.

While the reunion was going on Fincap had ample opportunity —that is, he was free of penetrating public scrutiny—to carry out the legal capture or recapture of every possible profitable mechanism, method, process and organization developed by the War.

Great abstract services like transportation, communication and information diffusion, coördinated during the War under strict governmental supervision, were withdrawn from that control, not as the simple specific plant, structure or system originally taken over by the government, but as tremendously advanced, efficient mechanisms, in many cases completely re-instrumented. Ships were turned back to original or new owners with completely new power and communication mechanisms, *et cetera*. In each major category, however, the directionary control had gone scientific by abstract-mind interpolation.

The rugged individuals in their chrome-nickel-steel armor, on stuffed horses, set about "audaciously" once more to carry the "banner of progress." Finding, however, that their War baptized monopoly babies had grown up somewhat and had gone abstract, "fixing" nitrogen from the air, *et cetera*, they had need to employ "trouble shooters," semi-technical liaison men between themselves and the scientific leadership intent on progressive deflating of the latter.

Their idea was to get people and industry *down to business*.

Those that they brought down died of the shots or had their wings clipped never to fly again but the main flight soared away unscathed. Tantalized by the flying and counseled by the trouble shooters, business decided to revamp its tactics of capture.

35

Flimsy Fabric of the Abstract Monopolies

In 1918-1919 a fine point of legal statecraft arose.

Long, long before the World War Fincap developed his by-legislation-granted track-and-wire franchises, and evolved from these certain monopolies of transportation and communication despite efficiency's having demonstrated, in older and more integrated foreign countries, the necessity of socialization or governmental control of inter-locality communication facilities, including transportation, which is a "face-to-face" form of communication articulation.

The franchises in America were obtained originally from sovereign federal government, sovereign states and sovereign cities by virtue of the size of the operations to be incepted. Between cities in the United States, the wide open land expanse dwarfed the proportions of such inter-unit operations in Europe where smaller scale services were often underwritten and maintained by the government.

These operations in America necessitated a vast capital expenditure. The debt-accounting system, imposed on the American Government by feudal Fincap, allowed of no legal way in which the government might provide the funds for underwriting such vast transport and communication instrumentings. Government could pioneer "legally" only in the mechanics of war. So Fincap insisted that unless he were accorded PERMANENT franchises, by legislative enactment, he would not "PUT UP" the capital to inaugurate these popularly acknowledged to be desirable mechanisms. Of course, Fincap never sought mail franchises, because on a complete national scale they would have been too costly to maintain, although he did procure subsidies for carrying mail over his franchise routes set up between points where traffic was voluminous enough for profit.

The fine legal point that loomed at the end of the War was: How could the wireless and trackless radio and aeroplane services be CAPTURED by Fincap within the frame of legal advantage? Answer: Through "precedent interpretation" of constitutional rights. Fincap awoke suddenly to the fact that these pre-War derided services were not only important and imminent industrial services, but that they were essential of capture to protect his wired, tracked and, therefore, comparatively highly limited monopolies.

The earliest precedent, in demonstration of Fincap's "right" to interpret the volition of the United States people, occurred in his dominance over the enactment of the Constitution itself. This was a post-Revolutionary War interpretative document of a pre-War Declaration of Independence on the part of the people. Its writing occurred to a high degree under circumstances of popular unawareness, i.e., while the populace was preoccupied with a post-Revolutionary family rehabilitation and reunion similar to and necessarily of longer duration than our own generation's post-World War readjustment. True, it was written by representatives of all the states assembled in constitutional convention, but these were primarily butter-and-egg men who haggled almost to the point of agreement failure over their special interests. The recent "little businesses" Washington conferences is reminiscent of the original Constitutional Convention. The big brains finally carried off the victory with various important loopholes for Fincap. The Constitutional hagglings took weeks and months for news-broadcasting. There was no Tel. & Tel. Stage coach travel was arduous and letters and word of mouth tales were vague, wherefore public reaction to the "fine points" was virtually impossible.

At the conclusion of the World War, radio had a limited set of wave length octaves, in the terms of the radio instrument's then-current limitations. Despite the fact that these wave bands were, in theory, globe encircling and, therefore, non-characterized by national sovereign borderlines and non-subject to titular franchise grant by the constitution of any one sovereign state, the bands, nonetheless, became the objective of legal capture by Fincap's lawyer-slaves.

During the War, as a matter of expediency in non-confusion of broadcasting stations, afloat or on land, special wave-bands were assigned to respective allied nations. These "bands" were subdivided within the nations for specific operations. Although radio receiving sets could be tuned in on any wave length, broadcasting equipment was designed for elective operation within a specific wave length band.

The legal representatives of Fincap found it expedient first for "sovereign nations" to agree to a division among themselves of all of the available bands. The joker in evolution's unbeatable pack of cards lay in the fact that the up to then discovered span of bands was conceived of by the non-scientific legal fraternity as constituting the full expanse of ever-to-be-discovered radio "bands."

England and other nations, much closer by actual experience to the horrors and bloody chaos of the War than was the United States, maintained a socialized government operation of services and a more generally tolerant attitude for a much longer period after the War than did America. England and some of the other nations, internally fraternalized through the social momentum of the World War, legislatively adduced that radio was a SOCIAL property and, as such, should be managed by the post office or communications branch of the government.

Contrariwise, Fincap's lawyers and law-passers in America adduced as factual precedent that since the communication system was, prior to the War, a private franchise property and monopoly and since the NEW means of communication was simply a subdivision of communication, it must, by divine right, be regarded as an appurtenance of Fincap's repossessed property. To avoid over-publicity, Fincap conceded a few bands of operation to the Federal Government for statecraft and military purposes, while retaining for himself the majority of the bands (including the central bands) of most facile-to-instrument-ability use.

For the first few years, Fincap had little means of exploiting his new property other than in wireless communication between shore and ship and between countries which he had not linked up by commercial cables.

Meanwhile, another phase of the problem developed, necessitating Fincap's legal scrutiny of the most attentive kind. This related to the mechanics of exploitation of the hitherto unthought-of popular broadcast and reception, essential to the profitable utilization of the world-encircling waveband properties. The capture of these bands had been originally viewed only as constituting a defense structure tactically of great use in preventing upstart intrusion into the potential enjoyment of high profit from their wired franchises of earlier piratical seizure.

36

Throwing in the Patented Sponge

As soon as one considers the economics of highly scientific and abstract instruments, such as radio sending and receiving apparatus, another extraordinary monopoly, sustainable by legal fabrication, becomes apparent. This monopoly, most popularly and unwittingly supported, confers a control-and-retardment-of-progress ability and is inherent in our "constitutionally" supported PATENT law.

Patents originally represented gestures of "largesse" on the part of sovereigns, monarchs, dukes, or lesser feudal masters, to members of their court or tenantry. They were designed to encourage thoughtful pioneering, the results of which might obviously be productive of greater wealth both to the feudal leaders and indirectly to their hosts of followers and subjects.

The title "Court architect," "Court painter," "dancer" or "astrologer," carried with it certain patronage privileges and funds. Although utterly arbitrary in amount, as pleased the monarch's mood, such grants supposedly enabled the "loyal" FOLLOWER profitably to exercise his specific ability.

When emissaries of a monarch had cause to go far afield, as in exploration for the capture of foreign lands to enrich the empire, they were given, also, "letters patent" citing them as temporary emissaries of the sovereign in their particular field of activity.

When the democratic idea broke loose in Europe, as a result of the partial emancipation of man by his artist-and-scientist devised mechanisms, the popular representatives of that time, thinking by habit in terms of feudal structure and laboring under the problem of transferring privilege of sovereignty to the populace, deemed it a wise and just act to embody the "letters patent" idea in their democratic constitutions.

Throwing in the Patented Sponge

The intent behind the democratic governments' granting of patents to individuals was that such licensed persons might, through a temporary monopoly of profit, be compensated for their initiative and extra-time occupation in the invention and devisement of socially useful mechanisms and processes, inasmuch as abstract entities did not come under the traditional "real" property protection. It was also considered that the giving of time to an inventor to earn an encouraging excess of profit would encourage others to similar pro-social activities, thus enriching the national capital for favorable international trade balance.

The patent monopolies were of variable duration, let us say, 1 to 30 years, but all were SPECIFICALLY limited-by-time monopolies, whereas the royal patents were often given for "life."

The necessity of invention growth was highly apparent to the budding democracies, for had not invention itself forwarded man to the possibility of emergent DEMOCRACY? (It is not inappropriate to note that Bernard Shaw was able to remark centuries after the first illusory *notion* by man that he had established a democracy, "There is nothing the matter with democracy except that it has never *really* been tried."

Paradoxically to the original democratic patent concept, today the licensed invention monopoly is no longer useful to the individual citizen in terms of its design and incorporation in democracy. It is in fact not only non-operative as designed, but is definitely a boomerang to democracy. The explanation is simple.

Few and far between were the inventions on which patents were granted in the early days of any of the, as Shavian appraised, quasi-democracies. When the U. S. devised her democratic principles in the writing of the Constitution, she incorporated also the patent-to-the-individual feature. At first the patents granted throughout many years could be counted on the fingers of two hands. Then, as industrial growth developed into a highly mechanical state, patents became more numerously applied for until, suddenly, the applications attained immense proportions. (See patent curve on Charts.) More than two million have been granted in the United States alone to date, a figure bemusingly to be compared with the relatively meager 700 items of basic scientific achievement during the whole period of history.

Inasmuch as the patent idea was designed to be of use to the unfunded individual who gave his time to pro-social thought, the license fee was relatively insignificant in all countries, being solely accounted as a handling charge. In America $20 supposedly gives the inventor full and free privilege of dictation of his "royalty" therefrom.

As evolution developed the scheme, patents were applied for to cover a multitude of utterly useless devices. In fact, the vast majority granted in all countries have been unadaptable either to industrial or consumer use, or have been so untimely as to have exhausted their privilege periods prior to use.

The patent files are glutted with relative nonsense. There is a type of citizen, for example, who fanatically enjoys legal "privilege," whether or not the enjoyment be useful to himself or others. He represents one of the many kinds of patent-file stuffers. Another type is the "Rube Goldberg," the with-self-chess-playing mechanical humorist, or crank.

At present the files are so extraordinarily complex and the items so multitudinous that a veritable army of governmental servants is required to attend them and sort them into some order of distinguishable categories to which reference may be made when corresponding with patent applicants for purposes of examiner citation of "prior art" disclosure. This complexity makes it inevitable that the human-equation involved in government servants relative to carelessness or mechanical limitations should occasion the granting of multitudes of "probably" invalid patent claims.

Furthermore, search within the files of all the many countries that subscribe to the international patent convention frequently reveals foreign inventions which are of current precise *necessity* of consideration by domestic applicants, even as these same foreign claims were formerly of inconsequential inclusion at the inception of patent granting. This change is due to the close integration of nations by accelerated modern communication and transportation. Such an international inspection usually reveals quantities of citable prior-art disclosures proving non-domestic invention.

Court-decisions-precedent in the matter of patent litigation inevitably developed a necessity of intricate and popularly obscure legal foresight by the applicant in the matter of the specific language of validity of his claims in anticipation of the claims of potentially contesting patentees.

The little inventor may prosecute his own claim upon the patent office for a cost within the minimum limit stipulated by law. However, even though he be granted a patent claim or claims (which is relatively unlikely), it will represent much time and expense for searches, *et cetera*, and then, although the patent may be granted relative to a basic invention its validity in litigation, due to lack of legal experience and astuteness of wording, is questionable on a probability basis of 1000 to 1 "against."

This being so evident, an army of shyster patent lawyers has mushroomed up who can easily convince *quasi* inventors that their services are essential in the matter of application for patent. These chiseling entrepreneurs know the tricks of patent soliciting well enough to be able to assure the granting of a patent by the government of even the most questionable claims. Their ability to produce a piece of paper pleases the vanity of the applicant and provides him with a vague notion of some potential profit. There is a better chance that such inventors will discover diamond mines in their cellars.

To sustain a patent claim in the courts today, where an apparently obvious infringement provokes an injunction suit by the holder of the patent, necessitates, if the apparent profit involved is worth prosecution, the availability of literally millions of dollars since legal finesse and appeal-decision precedent are so illusive in this highly abstract field.

Patent litigation is so expensive and long drawn out that large industries, despite piratical tendencies in the directorships of many, no longer resort to patents as an OFFENSIVE means of attainment of profit, having often spent millions of dollars to prosecute a claim yielding a gross return of only a few hundred thousand, or even a $1 "moral victory."

Conversely, the tremendous cost of "tooling up" in an industrial establishment for a new and highly intricate mechanism or the production of highly intricate mechanical products represents a vulnerability to patent suit which may necessitate defensive action in litigation or costly injunction stoppage, also running into millions of dollars, together with a depletion of profit from the original operation, even though the patent title be successfully defended. To avoid possibility of deprivation of profit, most large industrial organizations whose production involves high mechanical intricacy, have developed able and large patent departments whose function it is to make world wide intensive search of patents that may in any way be uncovered by competitors to be used against them for their enweakening as a competitor, rather than for profit.

PATENTS, then, have become DEFENSE mechanisms "in extraordinary," and practically every big industrial outfit has agglomerated a vast array of protective patent titles.

Incidentally Henry Ford, though holder of a few patents on his "own inventions," as protagonist of the SERVICE principle and not being fear-motivated or competitive in intent, discerned that, offensively or defensively, a policy of wholesale patent activity inclusion in his operations would incur a vast credit appropriation reserve. In his judgment this could be better utilized in keeping so far ahead of competing organizations as to make it possible for him to pay off claimants daring to sue him, even under gigantic figures of judgment. He computed that this patent disregard would entail less overall expense than if he were to arm himself with a patent department and an array of trouble inviting patent titles.

The great patent departments of the General Electric, Bell Telephone, Radio Corporation and other companies are finding that, despite their enabling efficiency through specialization and relatively unlimited funding, it costs an average of $1800 to procure a patent claim that has any possible chance of litigation sustenance.

The small inventor who has non-available to him the ramifications of the "company patent office," finds however, that there are available to him at high fee a few truly able private solicitors who have proven their ability to obtain valid patents and to sustain them in litigation through years of familiarity with the delicately abstract nuances of the art. It is said, and probably truly, that the language of patent soliciting represents the most scientific and selectively profound employment of words. Through these few able private solicitors the small inventor, as an individual, *may* obtain what *may* be a valid and sustainable patent at an average cost of about $5000 per patent for the U. S. only. This has, it is true, a certain short-lived (approximately one year) "binder" advantage through the internationally accepted covenants of the Berne patent convention. Nevertheless, in view of the fact that inventions become progressively universal in application as well as in view of the close integration of industrial countries, the patentee, to make his patent of sufficient value to be saleable to one of the large industrial corporations who progressively operate internationally (without which sale there is slight hope of obtaining profitable production of the patented product or process) the patentee must, of necessity, procure patents in all pertinent foreign countries. This involves a probable additional expense averaging $5000, plus high annual foreign "maintainance" fees, for which latter he should have a reserve of $5000.

So far, the individual inventor must have available $15,000 for the procurement of potentially valid "letters patent." Next comes the possibility that, after issuance to him of the paper, what is known as an "interference" suit may occur, arising from the fact that a relatively identical patent application was concurrently in process of review by the "examiner." It takes approximately two years to process the solicitation of a patent prior to its issue, which, in the case of unwitting multiple application (a common occurrence), calls for what is known as an "interference" suit which is conducted by the judges of the patent office. This form of suit is not to be confused with suits instigated at the behest of a patent holder over apparent infringement *subsequent* to the issuance of a patent. If not successfully defended, "interference" cancels the issue of the patent itself.

It becomes apparent that although a patent applicant may have expended $15,000 in the solicitation of a probably valid patent, he may be saddled with high litigation cost mandatorially. So he must set aside a protective fund to cover this contingency. This should be another $5,000. Sum totally, then, a minimum of $20,000 is required for an individual citizen as contrasted with a corporation servant to obtain what MAY be a potentially profitable patent of an originally true invention, which latter status can be determined only by subsequent litigation running into *x* dollars, not infrequently of seven figures.

The rationalization that evolves invention is primarily born of the experience of attenuated necessity. There is one chance in ten million that an inventor will have, in his own right, the financial means to procure a "true" patent for his invention.

There are, of course, freak exceptions to this as to all generalities.

In view of the foregoing facts it may be judiciously stated that the original intention of democracy in incorporating the patent privilege in its constitution for the abetment of pro-socially thinking artist-scientists of the proletariat is no longer operative or democratically valid. It is further to be seen that Ford's attitude toward patents is popularly just. Serving the public to the best of his ability, without subscription to the propriety of patents, he is not riding ruthlessly and piratically over the *operative* rights of individuals.

The 17 year temporary monopoly granted a patentee was of supposedly long comparative duration to the earning ability of an invention at the time of the inception of the patent law and of necessity as the industrial "lag" was then so long. One would certainly earn and obtain his reward within and throughout all 17 years. Today in industry—as demonstrated by the automobile section which dominates it—a patent is voluntarily held "exclusively" by the licensed manufacturer for two years only. After this time he passes it along to the entire industry because acceleration of technique is so great that a patent is worthless exclusively for a longer period.

An illuminating rationalization of the patent morass indicates that Fincap himself, its sole (and at that, "questionable") beneficiary, may soon sue for its nullification. The current development of multitudinous synthetic substances necessitated by sovereign "nationalism" is currently cited by big business men as promising the death of that portion of capitalism which is based on the old time raw material source monopolies.

Artificial rubber, artificial rayon, artificial cotton and wool, and artificial gasoline were characterized recently by Arthur Brash, Fincap economist, "as malinventions which will produce a destruction of capital such as has never been witnessed before. These substitutes cannot be produced as yet on an economical basis, but the dark side of the picture is that they will compete in the near future with the natural products."

The cataclysmic abrogation of international contracts now evidenced throughout the world, coupled with the increasing time space proximity of countries, also foretells a complete invalidation of local patent privilege enjoyment.

The vast monopolies built upon patent pool agglomerations can only serve to retard progress for man in the realization of what might often be most timely mechanical invention extensions for him, the arbitrary withholdment of which are within the power of the abstract patent monopolist. The latter may, and in fact does, continuously pigeon-hole invention in order to reap protracted profit from an inferior and otherwise-obsolete mechanism.

As popular attention becomes directed to this fact, popular indignation may be increasingly provoked, which in time must bring about constitutional amendment retracting the whole structure of patent monopoly.

What happens to the inventor?

When large corporations can save vast sums now being expended in patent prosecution and stop wasting the time of the men in their research departments who must review and aid in the prosecution of patents to the exclusion of progressive work, industries will not only be able to afford taking on valid inventors at an adequate salary return, to invent relative to the production problems of the specific industry involved, but will be forced by the "free for all" competition let loose by patent repeal to pay inventors retainer fees in excess of any previously dreamed-of royalties—IDEAS will be at the greatest economic premium.

Continuing the discussion of the post-War development of the abstract monopolies in which patents have played a major part, we find that, after entrenching himself behind the allowance of his titular claim to the then dominant long wave bands, Fincap extended his wireless franchise piratical grab to an appraisal of the mechanisms of broadcast and reception. With tremendous financial means available through his "control" of wave bands and his "protection" of the obsoleting physical monopolies, Fincap set about to acquire PATENT control of all the centrally important radio mechanisms, processes, and circuits, as well as of the mechanisms for the production of these end objects.

Whatever he could not acquire by purchase, he litigated to obtain. Multi-millions were spent in the fray. Little inventors fell by the wayside. Bigger and stronger patent holders, able to fight for awhile, also finally fell or sold out. With the mechanisms under his complete control and with an army of patent attorneys and scientific researchers, Fincap evolved an impregnable front designed to steam-roller any mushrooming of ideas in the radio field.

At this point the radio monopolists were willing to incept broadcasting for domestic consumption.

With the intention of reaping high revenue from the sale of receiving instruments, Fincap carefully placed on the market instruments in various stages of compromised adequacy. He could completely control the obsolescence rate and provoke a progression of conspicuous waste, by discard, through advertising the rapidly-obsoleting reception mechanisms. Amateur set-making, which could not dare mass-reproduction sale for fear of infringement, nevertheless grew apace as individual handicraft and was unchallenged because it served to aid in the obsolescence exploitation scheme.

Fincap was appalled at the power of the radio to penetrate into every home instantaneously, making it (if it were not for his apparently iron-bound monopolization of the phenomenon) a means of political control that could overnight provoke a popular awareness of Fincap's untenable abstract monopolies and possibly general revolt from Fincap.

Seeking to establish a use precedent that would obviate such an eventuality, Fincap endeavored to limit the use of the broadcast to entertainment purposes only, or innocuous *quasi*-educational blurbs, or political harangues of a sort useful to his own ends; and last, but not least, for a machine gun fire of advertising interspersing any possibly entertaining program in a manner nauseating to decency and equity that, through exaggeration of every dumbbell proclivity of the populace, has abetted to some extent the sale of his profit-enslaved products.

Advertising revenue was not originally contemplated at the time of incorporation of "N.B.C.," the total issue of stock of which is owned by Radio Corporation. "N.B.C." was devised as an instrument to limit possible liability in lawsuits arising out of broadcasts, *et cetera*. Salaries were not contemplated for entertainers. It was thought that amateurs and even professionals would consider the publicity involved sufficiently advantageous to themselves to broadcast without compensation. It is a matter of record that it was a complete surprise to Radio Corporation that "N.B.C.'s" revenue became the vastly dominant earning item of its portfolio, despite astronomical fees to entertainers precipitated through competitive advertising which profitably footed the bill of the mass trespassing license.

The national emergency of '32 further called into obvious necessitous use broadcasting as a means of popular reforming from panic trend. Hence political messages were temporarily countenanced. The government, in its reform movement, increased its power of censorship over the radio under emergency precedent, and the administration was given the use of the air that it had previously relinquished to Fincap.

Without waiting for the public's eventual revolt from Fincap's usurpation of the for-the-public-designed-by-artists-and-inventors radio mechanism, the young amateur radio-inventing world discovered an "out."

The "amateurs" penetrated very rapidly into the practically unlimited short wave bands not included in the original "franchise" and which had been by precedent governmentally conceded, through inconsequentiality, as "open" to amateurs. This super-short-wave usage by "amateurs" progressively necessitated more minute and exquisite means both of reception and sending. There developed an imminent need by amateurs of an inter-communicating system requiring minor and domestically available power, such as the Ford motor or "domestic current," in contradistinction to the costly high powered long wave transmission means available only to interlocking-directorate-Fincap. Through this abstract and behind the scenes network, the young amateur radio populace soon became integrated in its knowledge and mutual understanding of its progress problem, which involved the potentials of eventual disenfranchisement of Fincap from these last abstract strongholds, of which radio is a typical example and which include aeronautics, the press, telephone, electric manufacture, medicine, movies, and TELEVISION.

Television, feared in its potentialities by Fincap, as he has rarely feared a "new" is at present being specifically funded for development through monopolized cable distribution, but an "out" will as always soon occur.

A monopolistic integration between the Fincap-controlled press and the radio monopoly was arranged in the early days which restricted the broadcasting of news to such "news" as was at least 24 hours old. However, a minor independent system, employing at first a small non-monopoly-controlled broadcasting station, supplied by world-wide short wave amateur operators, started a news reporting system which was so eagerly listened to by the public that the big monopoly "family" had to break its rule and follow suit in self-defense.

And so it goes.

37

Scrap—Coup d'Etat of the Random Element

Inherent in the new industrial principle, developed most clearly since the War, is the periodic replacement of old forms by new forms. In no more dramatic way does old economics demonstrate its inadaptability to new industry than in the used-car problem of the automobile businessers—*what to do about the old cars?* Amplify this problem, relative to all activity, and one can understand why politics and business throw up their hands and liquidate "used" product through war's destruction.

Ford, recognizing this liquidation-of-old-product problem, set about economically to salvage scrap from old cars, just as telephone companies, unhindered by consideration of second-hand telephone purchase by consumer-users, and railroad companies who had sold transportation service rather than railway cars, found it of high economic advantage periodically to scrap obsolete equipment and refine it into basic materials for refabrication in new-use-forms as INSTRUMENTS of their ABSTRACT "END-PRODUCT," i.e., WIDER and MORE EFFICIENT SERVICE.

In 1927, Ford went so far as to propose RENTING his Lincoln cars rather than to sell them. This was a mistake, for the Lincoln cars went to the cash-paying minority—the property-vain class. He would have done better with Fords. This was also premature. But in effect Fords are today rented transportation service since they are generally "purchased on TIME" and are turned in for another time-purchased new product at about the end of the first contract. Lincolns are for the most part "sold" outright.

There is now a consumer tendency toward this "turning-in" of a contract "purchased" house evidencing itself in greater

New York, wherein the small down-payment buyer abandons the house for an improved model, but has to go through a legal mess because of which realtors also suffer high depreciation value through loss of the new house premuim. This is but one more item of the inevitable trend towards economic "abstraction": "USE *vs.* OWNERSHIP."

It is at last obvious that the recirculation of basic materials, first "noticed" in 1909, through the scrap developed in industrial obsolescence of out-moded products is tending toward greater importance by actual tonnage than the production of NEW raw material, which latter will become progressively of smaller percentage, and simply supplementary to the recirculating scrap materials:—the quantities of new materials mined to be determined by population growth and industrial decentralization beyond the borders of the current leading industrial countries into the lands of high population and current low industrial standards (the Orient, India and Russia representing three quarters of the world's population) as well as by the final factor of replacement of shrinkage by actual loss in pins, shipwrecks, *et cetera*. Only 15% of all copper ever produced in the world has been lost. The remainder—27 million tons—*is all in use.* In 1933 the U. S. consumed for the first time more recirculated copper than new. The U. S., which has virtually no tin ore source, is the largest tin user in the world and has an accumulated "in-use" ore body of 2,000,000 tons which it recirculates at a rate of 25,000 tons annually, supplemented by 67,500 tons (the last ten years' average) annual import of "new" and "old," and has now placed an embargo on the export of tin scrap, hitherto a large business—a *mobile* "mine" above grade.

Most interesting of all this recirculation phenomenon is the fact that in the U. S. 256,000,000 tons of steel *scrap*, equal in every way to *new* when refined, were consumed in the decade 1925 to 1935, whereas only 200,000,000 tons of new ore, as both iron and steel, were being consumed.

The steel, copper, nickel, and aluminum producers, *et al.*, in order to survive by direct economic validity will have to inaugurate regular repurchase of obsolete industrial products, such as automobiles, buildings, railroad equipment, ships, *et cetera*, directly from those industries, rather than wait for the junking and bankruptcy breakdown in these non-self-liquidating industries; this will be done upon the basis of the quantities of material known accurately to exist in them, extractable at a KNOWN cost, just as they would purchase below grade surmise-quantity ore properties. The basic producers are better equipped at present, and MAY persist, if they have enough foresight (questionable) in remaining so, to refine this so-called "secondary" material.

Prior to the World War basic metals producers carried their product from the ore stage only through to elementary forms: ingots, bars, sheets, tubes, wire, *et cetera,* which in most cases had to be further refashioned to *end* or *intermediate* product stages by a fabricating industry. The latter, after the war, suffered high mortality due to the complicated and expensive state to which mechanics had developed as a result of the war speed-up, and the lack of ability of the fabricators to purchase competitively essential equipment. This mortality forced the well-funded basic metals producers reluctantly to fill the gap in order to sell basic product to the end-product and service industries.

Also before the War, mine "owning," large or small, was potentially profitable. Today, owners of small mines of common ores unless absorbed by one of the larger "fabricating" corporations have no marketing or earning outlet.

The last two decades have witnessed so large an investment by the basic producers in fabricating equipment that it is now equally as great an investment as that of the mines long ago "written off." Whereas a mine costs little when idle and may increase in value, and is virtually "money in the bank," the converse is true of fabricating equipment which has high overhead in proportion to rapid obsolescence. For this reason the more rapidly metals are run through the fabricating equipment, the lower will be the unit cost and the higher the profit. Fabricating equipment takes no cognizance of the origin of metals, granting equality of product, and, therefore, high recirculation of "old scrap" is quite as profitable as circulation of the "new." *This creates the paradox of putting the new metals basic suppliers into the business of promoting what they had hitherto considered as their prime competitor—scrap.*

THE BASIC METALS MONOPOLY, BACKBONE OF CONSERVATIVE FINANCE, IS BEING DRIVEN WILLY-NILLY INTO A POSITION OF FAVORING AND ACCELERATING "CHANGE" IN ORDER TO "MINE" SCRAP BY OBSOLESCENCE OF OCCUPATION TO MAKE PAY THAT VAST INVESTMENT IN EQUIPMENT WHICH IT HAD TO MAKE AND MUST CONTINUALLY RENEW IN ORDER TO JUSTIFY ITS ORIGINAL MONOPOLY AND ITS "CASH IN THE BANK" RESERVES.

Originally basic metal monopoly was for minimum end-product change as it was desired that the product stay *put* so that it could, through production schedule, control scarcity and ∴ demand high profit. Now conservative monopoly is favoring change and must patronize science to obtain it and man is thus coming into that inheritance from science which conservative capital has fought to keep from him.

This phenomenon explains the new political term in England, "Radical Tory." In England the ratio of mine to fabrication is even wider and England leads in recirculation, scrapping her *Mauretania* and buying our *Leviathan* with its high nickel content, steel, *et cetera*, for conversion of the same metal into higher use-form and earning ability—a mechanical reincarnation progression of doing more, if not with less, at least with the same.

The basic materials producers must come to the realization that they are irrevocably interlocked in their interests, one with the other, rather than opposed, due to the constantly increasing inter-alloying of their products by the use-industries. There are more than 10,000 alloyed metals in current industrial use. They are multiplying constantly, developed most conspicuously by the automobile and the aeroplane. There were but a handful of alloys before the World War. This fact constantly belittles the basic producers' "sales" efforts to impose non-functional substitution of their respective pure products for the pure products of other basic producers: copper instead of nickel, *et cetera*. Nickel made an all-time high in 1935, but primarily in alloyed form. Both copper and steel tonnage was vastly increased by sales developed directly by the nickel people. For instance, "Monel," an International Nickel Company product, is 70% nickel and 30% copper. A prominent engineer, H. W. Gillete, Chief Technical Adviser to the Batelle Memorial Institute, and representing the steel industry, made the prognostication at the 1936 annual meeting of the A. I. M. E. that the next era in structural steel would be one of low carbon 1.5% copper alloy, a hidden tonnage that may run over 350,000 tons of copper content annually, the equivalent of the entire U. S. domestic output of copper for all purposes in 1934.

The basic materials producers will have further to conduct coöperative research to provide ever more advance MATERIALS SERVICE in advantageous alloyed forms and in *progressively enriching metals containing small quantities of economically unextractable alloys*. Ford has now substituted 1-3% copper alloyed cast steel for forged steel in crank and cam shafts and many other parts, improving his product and simplying his process. The tonnage of copper may run to 100,000 tons annually in these low percentage uses, but is economically non-extractable from the subsequent scrap, ∴ a scientific later-day service of distribution of the enriching scrap and its vanishing minority metals must of necessity develop.

The inevitable trend involved includes not only the elimination of all economic waste and attendant cost in non-scientifically liquidated product, but also recognition of the fact that any industry, the product of which returns regularly to the market, is an industry of SERVICE THROUGH MECHANICALLY WORKED AND REWORKED MOBILE PROPERTY and is not an industry of STATIC DISSIPATION and IRRESPONSIBLE LIQUIDATION.

Scrap—Coup d'Etat of the Random Element

Once an industry has become one of ABSTRACTED SERV-ICE instead of *physical sale*, it must recognize further that its service is based on the efficiency of RENTAL rather than on the *sale* of *property*.

When the basic materials producers have come fully to realize the expediency of this new industrial cycle and its continuity efficiency, they will eventually and inevitably adopt the new principle of RENTAL OF MATERIALS, as practiced for instance by the renters of radium. This may be a long time off, but I think not. Under the cartel-sanctioning effect of the N. R. A. Copper Code, the producers intuitively provided that they should have *priority* options on the repurchase of the ultimate scrap of their respective specific sales, in effect a rental proposition.

When copper, for instance, in alloyed form, is rented to industrial manufacturers for periods of time consistent with the specific longevities of products in the respective manufacturing industries (eight years in automobiles, twenty years in ships, etc.) the copper refining and materials alloying service industry will be able to accelerate the re-employment of their ever-improving product through their ability, contained in the terms of their leases, to withdraw inferior products to be replaced by more expedient alloys, and by surcharges for overlong use of material. Then FREQUENCY IN RENDITION OF FABRICATION SERVICE will replace TURNOVER AND LIQUIDATION OF NEW PRODUCT as the economic incentive. When this new coöperative, durable materials service has been developed the course of rapid industrial growth will be truly renewed.

Herein lies the key to the new world economics; for through it ACCELERATION, rather than *retardation*, of design improvement in scientific satisfaction of ever-improving standards will PAY. There will then be no question of inflation or deflation of dollars, for the dollar values will be in the terms of the ENERGY INVOLVEMENT in ABSTRACT SERVICE, and FREQUENCY rather than in the terms of the INTRIN-

SICS of RAW MATTER. While the automobile industry suffers from lack of such a service to a vast extent, the mass-production building industry is practically prevented from inception by its non-integrated existence.

Scrap is the economic "straw" that is breaking the back of Fincap, to wit: SCRAP is changing Fincap willy-nilly into a good boy, painlessly, as man-evolved, man-prosecuted reform might never do. Fincap Jr. must become a bright-eyed "yes man" to science to save his breeches.

The economics of "scrap" as connoting inanimate materials, selectively synthesized by scientific mind, ever more temporarily "on the shelf" in obsolete-to-current-efficient-use-form, progressively enriching in minor percentage alloy constituents and consequently ever improving in weight-strength factor, versatility and non-corrosiveness, and constituting a mobile above-grade mine of high concentrate representing a net efficiency of use availability now in most cases superior to that of raws, makes this resource a floating "international" resource rather than "national," which below-grade resources must be. Wherefore *Science*, the central factor that is obsoleting the connotation of SCRAP as meaning "FIGHT," is forwarding the unromantic *inanimate* dump heap Scrap to the Sir Galahad rôle as saviour of man from the sacrificial *animate* dump heaps of predatorily engendered war. Hail! Humble scavengers and mongers—circle closers of the Industrial Cycle of continuity—Knights of the Random Element!

38

Old Woman Who Lives in a Shoe

Eventually the government, after surveying the enormous cost of the non-integrated inefficiency of maintaining a population in hovels, will be forced, through ever persistent economy, into the transfer of unemployed city multitudes from such habitations to those of the highly modernized, efficient skyscrapers with which the government, willy-nilly, has been saddled by mortgage moratorium, *et cetera*.

The largest number of dwelling units ever built in the U. S. in one year by the combined building industries at peak load was 280,000, in 1925, and we are currently shy (this is admitted by the most conservative authorities) six million minimal-standard adequacy dwellings. Such seemingly pro-social legislation as the Wagner Housing Act, which at best might develop 20,000 new and, most questionably "low" cost homes in New York City *per annum* where 700,000 unemployed families or bachelors now "exist" without ability to pay rent, must be utterly futile. Such legislation is promoted, in reality, by the most selfish of the "conservative" finance interests to avoid even public mention of the one obvious method of wholesale relief of the housing problem, i.e., migration from the tenements to such buildings as the modernly equipped, relatively empty Empire State Building.

From a future viewpoint, there is rationality both in the sky-scraper building of the city and in the mass production dwelling for the urban and suburban community. They do not follow contradictory forces. The two forces involved are: (1) decentralization for physical activity, work or play, and (2) centralization for mental activity, work or play. The latter is primarily transient and the former primarily of long duration.

Skyscraper construction companies (George A. Fuller, Inc. and Hegeman-Harris, Inc.) have recently been contracting the building of the speculative homes in N. Y. C. suburbia, throwing all the efficiency learned in the erection of the Chrysler Building in thirty-six weeks into the building of many little houses theretofore handled by relatively poorly equipped contractors and builders. Louis J. Horowitz, president of Thompson, Starrett Company, recently observed: "The near future of the building business is not in skyscrapers and not in the multiplication of the structures of government. It is in housing—housing to take the place of city slums and the lonely discomfort of unimproved farm dwellings."

If an Empire State Building can be erected in 300 working days, or 2400 working hours, the operation being threaded piecemeal through the tumultuous center of New York City, and if it is the equivalent in volume and materials standard of 2400 "high-class," fire-proof SING-FAM-DWELLS, then under the same degree of design and method organization that was applied to the Empire State, these senior builders ought in the open fields to be able to put up one house an hour. The builders are waking up to this argument at last, now that they have nothing else to do—no "chips" anywhere else. However, they are still far from the solution mark, as will be pointed out a few chapters later, in "Scientific Dwelling Service."

It is not our contention that all skyscrapers should be utilized for the slum dwellers' rescue. There are logically highly rented business structures such as those in Radio City which have been cleverly designed around the interests of the new radio industry and its attendant high communication, publicity, advertising and news potentials, and logically placed relative to amusement and other requirements of a city's populace, albeit their building was originally conceived as an emergency gesture. It would not be surprising if the new city of New York growing out of the nucleus of Radio City might not in time become so dominant as to bring about the natural substitution of "RADIO CITY" for "*New York City*," a meaningless title today.

Old Woman Who Lives in a Shoe

Mr. Rockefeller's agents in certifying the occupancy of Radio City forced, through interlocking directorate activities, literally hundreds of big business operations to transfer their headquarters to Radio City. Small fry contiguous businesses were forced to move in by the hundreds. The writer received the following in a letter in January, 1938, which, though practically impossible of "authentication" nevertheless "explains the process":

Anent the Rockefeller camouflage of putting up three new skyscrapers to give men employment, as announced in today's papers, one of them had already been rented out entirely to two firms: the National Cash Register Co. and the Associated Press, before the work-making *quasi*-pro-social announcement. The Rockefeller interests are "taking over" the National Cash Register Co.'s 16 years-to-run-lease in its present quarters at $50,000 a year. They are doing similarly with the unexpired term of the Associated Press's lease and, moreover, are paying all cost of that company's moving, installation of wires, 'phones, and so on. They have even agreed to name the building the Associated Press Building. How the A.P. came into the picture is interesting: One of the firm (I can give you his name) was having a cocktail at a fashionable hotel bar, idly conversing with a real estate company's employee at the same bar.

Said the A.P. executive, casually, "We'd rather like to move because we need more space."

"Where would you like to go?" asked the real estater. "Any particular section?"

"Oh, we don't know. Most anywhere. Probably in the vicinity of Radio City."

Soon after this conversation the real estater sauntered over to the Rockefeller interests' office. One word was all he needed to say. He was told to "drop the whole thing," not even to go near the Associated Press. "We will do it all," they promised, and did.

The real estater is receiving a $60,000 commission and the Associated Press has a building named after it.

Standard Brands, now a tenant of the Fuller Building, has likewise been approached. They were offered a taking-over of their unexpired leasehold and a new rental price of $1 per ft. for five years if they would move into the second of the three new buildings recently announced as *planned* "to give employment." Standard Brands did not accept the offer. They did use it, however, to force cancellation of their present lease and the substitution of a new 10 years' lease at a substantial reduction in the rent. American Tobacco Co., also, has been offered a lease in one of the new Radio City buildings for five years at $1 a year plus the take-over of their current lease.

These and similarly organized rental shifts have increased the undertenancy of multitudes of older buildings, which would be highly suitable for the housing shift to the modern skyscraper.

In one of the ever increasing-in-frequency panic "emergencies," it is inevitable that the sparse business tenancy of these many skyscrapers will have to be shifted to an efficient industrial management tenancy of the most logically situated skyscrapers, completely evacuating enough modern buildings to provide ample space for our wholesale migration of the work-disenfranchised populace from the slums.

There are many other ramifications of this re-orientation of building and land occupancy in the mammoth cities which are only supposedly beyond proper revamping. A general prognostication includes the eventual tearing down of a majority of the buildings in New York City—for instance, virtually all buildings under ten stories in height, which height has been proven to be the minimum that may be efficiently serviced by central steam plants—and the conversion of the ground area of the razed buildings into all-important parking zones for the automobiles which mammoth buildings have called into the city. Our prognostication indicates, moreover, that within a few years the building code will call for the provision not only by new skyscrapers, but also by old ones, of parking space within the first ten stories above the street floor sufficient to house every automobile involved in the occupancy of that skyscraper. This means that "ten stories and under" must be converted to 100% garages or torn down.

If, for the purpose of clarification of this problem, we imagine every automobile removed from the streets of mid-Manhattan except those involved in the occupancy of Radio City, it would become readily apparent that the proprietors of Radio City have certainly built way over their "lot line" in all directions and for many blocks, for, be it remembered, automobiles (as developed in the phantom captain concept) are actually extension parts of people as much as are their shoes and shirts, and so a Radio City office worker's or playgoer's car, parked five blocks away, is a part of that office worker's or paying visitor's occupancy of Radio City. Actually, therefore, the Rockefellers are illegally collecting rental for the ground occupied by the worker's car, since the streets are not their property, not their "legal" property at any rate.

Considering another phase of the problem, we find that the wholesale migration of the populace into skyscrapers would result in a reduction in populace-maintenance cost, through the elimination of filthy environment, articulated in hospitalization and penalization savings that would be staggering. The street cleaning bill of New York City runs into an annual figure of approximately 70 million dollars. This cost of picking up the burnt or rotting refuse of the slums, now indirectly underwritten by the central government, would be almost completely eliminated by the transfer of the populace to efficient skyscrapers and the substitution of parks for slums.

Furthermore, there would be a stupendous basic energy saving, through the central steam plant's ability to furnish heat to skyscrapers with a relatively low heat loss *vs.* the inefficiency, shrinkage and high heat loss in the distribution of coal in trucks from docks to a multitude of yards, whence they are recarted to the cellar of "Tony," the coal-and-ice man, for sale in paper bags for use in heat-losing, squalid hovels, also necessarily entailing constant energy loss in the starting and burning out of little fires.

But Fincap, through his unrelenting though dwindling political hold on government, is doing everything in his power to avoid this efficiency. His efforts are greatly abetted, unfortunately, by the short-sighted ignorance of the people themselves who, as laborers banded together in workers' unions, are still dominated by representatives of the at-one-time-most-important building trades. Even on the eve of the on-rushing total industrialization of shelter they continue to fight for the resuscitation of old-time building activity suitable to the limited handicrafts of the dead-as-a-door-nail building trades. It is to be noted that the crafts unions, now that the lines are being finely drawn between themselves and the industrial unions, are confined primarily to the building trades. These federated crafts unions constitute so strong a political body that Fincap finds in them an invaluable ally in the maintenance of the intrinsic worth of his one-time-important city land monopoly.

No one group has had a greater retarding effect on government's official recognition of the industrially prefabricated shelter as the ultimate solution of housing than the American Federation of Labor. At its 1935 epoch-introducing annual convention in Atlantic City, when Lewis, head of the United Mine Workers, came to actual blows with Hutchinson, head of the carpenters' union, the issue was pertinent to the major thesis of this book. Hutchinson represented the old faction, crafts unions; Lewis, the new faction, industrial unions. (This book was first being written at the time of that occurrence. Since then, the significance of industrial *vs.* craft organizations has come into universal consideration.)

Political interests have obscured the fact that no "housing" unit has developed in the C. I. O., which at one fell swoop would include every worker engaged in housing production, no matter whether an assembler in the field or a machine tender in a factory, thus eliminating the skull-busting, housing-improvement prohibiting, jurisdictional disputes within craft-labor's ranks. Such a general "Housing Workers Union," when evolved, will almost overnight put the American Federation of Labor, which has practically all of its eggs in one building basket, out of business, and will bring industrially reproduced scientific shelter to the fore. This has not happened as yet because popular (government) attention has been focused, by long-faced "sociologists" and egotistical reformers, on the scientifically untenable, out-moded methods of building construction that now only thinly keep alive the crafts with which Fincap is perforce friendly.

In November, 1937, the A. F. of L. and the C. I. O. considered a tentative division of the labor field to facilitate a truce in their three year old dispute. The experimental formula for the division of jurisdiction, as worked out at a joint conference of peace committees, involved suspending the causes of dispute rather than first establishing a truce, as follows:

1. The Federation to grant full jurisdiction to the C. I. O. in the rubber, newspaper, maritime, furrier, steel, coal and certain other industries.

2. The C. I. O. to grant complete jurisdiction to the A. F. of L. in the building trades, engraving and particularized craft industries.

3. Compromises in fields where each group has strong unions.

Naturally no agreement was arrived at. *No true one ever will be*. Scientifically spined industry can never agree that the unscientific, consciously inefficient course is tenable or even condonable. The forces at play are far bigger than the mental activity of the current labor dictators can encompass. It may be counted on that the "random element" will dance his war dance around any "parleys" of these diametrically subscribed labor divisions.

The death of the old building "business," which was primarily a handicraft affair, favoring the allocation of industrial workers to categories of no longer existing crafts in industry, and the general rise of the industrial principle in all other categories but "housing" has weakened the craft-workers' strike power. So long as automobile workers are craft-unionized under threat, they will be impeded from going on strike by virtue of the fact that they represent an agglomeration of impertinently titled unions, that is, "unions" of carpenters, metal workers, *et cetera*. The unwillingness of heads of these crafts to subscribe to the strike as an industrial unit whole has prevented workers from attaining the obvious equity adjustments which they seek in minimum wages and total hours. The C. I. O. United Auto Workers have currently dramatized this issue, wherefore Fincap has thrown his full political weight behind the A. F. of L. in Detroit.

Another aid to "conservative" Fincap's fear-born opposition to efficiency (which he would abet if there were any integrity in his newsprint clamor for governmental operating-cost reduction) is the federated resistance of a possibly less ignorant class of humans, the at-least-academically-educated "professionals": architects, engineers, and lawyers who congregate ceaselessly in "society" conventions to work out plans for a return to the old ways of doing in the hope that the "diploma" may regain its profitable status. Expectantly, they delegate potent representatives, who are gladly heralded by the controlled press, to hound government officials with an infinity of plans for resuscitation of the once exploitable, now defunct tailored-building business, or to prove profoundly that a "power yardstick" is "impossible"—page Mr. Einstein! He never thought of the application of his work to a "power yardstick," but he has the precise formula needed.

A meager success in the press-supported efforts of the "professionals" amalgamated with Fincap is demonstrated by the appropriation of government funds for the high-priced condemnation of slum areas, bringing about a transient rehabilitation of the old property-ite and the substitution of penny-pinching, inefficient five story walk-ups for former tenements. The necessary asking rental of the new structures—despite a minimum inclusion of scientific facilities—is 50% higher than 90% of the population can afford to pay under the present retrogression of wage distribution.

This truth about "professional" self-recovery, cost and revenue applies equally to the Greenbelt communistically-to-be-run communities built under the aegis of the Tugwell régime at "no one knows how much" (literally) cost. From a dollars and cents standpoint, to which both communists and capitalists stick, housing cannot be solved by reform. On the other hand, it must certainly be admitted that the most significant effect of the attempts cited has been the pulling down of old buildings and the establishment of highways and parks through and around slum-glutted areas. The *house-cleaning* is now popularly accredited through dramatic reality, but it is the random element's indirect result of a fallacious housing argument.

The Federal Housing activity with its offering of building

and reconditioning loans at the lowest rates in America's history seemed a good temporary "out" for the property-title group (primarily banks and the custodians or investors of fourth and fifth generation trust funds) but they have not proved an "out" for the beleaguered professional classes for whose benefit, upon the surface, the legislation was designed. Moreover, they have not provided even a living wage for laborers, whose wage scales have precipitously dropped from an at-peak-level-by-union-strength-pegged figure to approximately 20% of the peak original.

By trial and error the professional and worker classes will ultimately learn that the current slum clearance project is a mirage and that the chief beneficiaries are the finance-capitalists. This is mildly to be witnessed again by indirection of volition in Housing Administrator Strauss's policy, i.e., not to rebuild the old slum areas but to decentralize new mass housing to undeveloped marginal acres of cities. Once the technicians have mastered this fact, there will be an eventually-to-be-heard popular mandate for DOING the EFFICIENT thing. The C. I. O. unit, "The Federation of Architects, Engineers, Chemists and Technicians," so rapidly gaining strength in revolt against professional stupidity, is a manifest of this approaching mandate.

When the city populace has moved into the skyscraper towers, they will blow up their slums wholesale with probably the most thrilling popular fiestas of all times and convert the land into vast parks. There will emerge from the present contradictory scene a clean, beautiful and orderly settlement of towers and gardens, with retention or restoration of all historically important tracery elements, knowledge of the latter having popularly developed through inadvertence of made-work writers and artists engaged in W.P.A. projects.

From these tower and garden cities the populace may progressively and efficiently be deployed to activity, in the for-years-to-come high manual effort employing industrial reproduction of scientifically evolved shelters and contiguous industries.

The swarms of oddly-clad tenement dwellers will be incongruous when first transferred to their new environment of svelte skyscraper lobbies and elevators, but just as a transition in the stenographer's appearance from sloppiness or dowdiness to that of a "deb" occurred when she found herself in a skyscraper office, so slum dwellers will quickly avail themselves of first-class plumbing facilities, adequate warmth and fresh air, and will transform their outward appearance to conform to environment. There will be many a laugh, but that's what we are looking for: laughter and happiness.

It would not be efficient, however, simply to let slum exiles camp about the floors of Empire State buildings, along with their pots and pans, little cookstoves and filthy clothing, using the windows for general refrigeration.

No! The efficient course will be to reclothe them completely and, in consideration of the fact that the skyscrapers are to be temporary hostelries until the slum exiles can be deployed to industrial service over the land, near or far, furnish them with food as would the hotel and with medical attention as would the hospital, giving as thoughtful care to the menu or diet in relation to intestinal habits as would be accorded hotel or hospital guests. Such efficient, nourishing feeding would be no more difficult than is the solution of the dietary problem of any great city hospital. It would be efficient, also, to furnish them with the best of education and amusement. All this would, of course, save more than the whole tax bill of N. Y. C. today wherein the "debt" service alone calls for $175,000,000 in the current year.

It is interesting that, whereas the professional planners of the would-be resuscitated housing industry look to and even go to Europe for precedent in the matter of emergency housing, there is in reality no compatibility between the housing problem of Europe and that of America. The comparative figures of population per room in Europe with 25% of the world's population and in North America with 7% of the world's population show that in Europe there is, throughout compound housing centers, even today a high room shortage. In Europe the figure is in the vicinity of 2.6 persons per decently-dwellable room currently extant. In America on the other hand the average is only .9 persons per now-"available" dwelling room, not including potential skyscraper hotels. It is the decentralization-mobilization shift and rising "standard" progression that provokes "shortage" in America.

Relative only to the currently endured standard of housing, there is, so far as four walls and a roof go, actually no housing shortage in America. The need is for an efficient re-deal of shelter, and rapid satisfaction of advancing standards of adequacy production, and service method. The true 100% housing shortage in America and worldwise is of entirely new, highly mobile, scientific shelters that may be constantly and conveniently shifted from one to another currently important industrial or play sites. Relatively permanent shelters will be required, also, for the more scientific re-housing of the agricultural populace who, in the chemico-mechanical industrialization of farming, will progressively become the mechanical supervisors of agricultural production rather than agricultural labor-slaves.

Scientific, mobile shelters will be utilized, also, for the constantly moving placement or deployment of city-bogged, non-employed people to play lands of the world where it would be possible for them to develop in health, strength and intellectual ability. This might never completely rehabilitate the "lost" older generation, but would nurture its offspring into harmonious synchronization with and responsible continuance of the emergent age.

The trailer has already appeared as a gesture by small man for his need in this direction, but how sadly short of the goal it falls! The trailer, however, has its random element significance; it is forcing the automobile industry which is SCIENTIFIC INDUSTRY itself, into efficient mobile housing design considerations and to the re-design of its interior mechanisms, an important baby. But more of this in the next chapter.

Not long ago a suggestion was made in a newspaper that all relief, popular and private, be immediately terminated; that all public schools be closed; that free hospitalization cease and that

America be thrown on her "own" to prove her rugged manliness. If the suggester's impossible scheme were to be carried out, it is probable that he himself would be among the first to be eaten by the wolves. He probably was playing for a big role with Fincap as a "practical man." No! dear fellow, we are going to be truly practical and we are on the way. The way is scientific, and heavenly. Inherent in Disney's and his army of co-artists' "Snow White and the Seven Dwarfs" is the beauty and justification of the highly-mechanized industrial age,—just beginning.

39

Scientific Dwelling Service

THERE are four overlapping applications and conflicting inter-pretations of the phrase, MASS PRODUCTION HOUSE:

1) Building on the site a number of houses after any one tradi-tion-evolved master pattern, perhaps with inconsequent varia-tions, such as in Queens Village, N. Y., or in Edison's poured concrete houses. This scheme has obvious economies over build-ing one house, but it is limited to technics, units, materials, power means, and tools consistent with craft building in the open fields.

2) The "knock-down" mail-order houses, consisting of fac-tory reproduced sectional assemblies of a variety of tradition-evolved designs with essential compromise skimpings inherent in transportation, assembly, and price considerations.

3) The currently displayed models of would-be mass-produc-tion houses, such as the "Motohome," sponsored by the large basic materials and equipment corporations, or groups of the latter, in which a style "moderne," an unadorned simplification of the traditional box house, is rendered in new, more expensive, seemingly more lasting materials, and substitutes in its developer's scheme for the earlier "knock-down" mail-order wooden house of Category 2. The scheme of development of both 2. & 3. is predicated on a sliding-scale price from one to a hundred houses and is self-supporting in small quantities, though hopeful of profit through larger numbers. Its overhead on shop investment is small and cannot include and is not predicated on a moving line production. The *moving line* production in the automobile indus-try is limited to a profitable low of 125,000 cars *per annum*.

4) A competitive shelter service industry, similar to the hotel industry, and of the mechanical standard, scope, and integration

of the automobile industry, engaged in furnishing on a RENTAL basis complete scientifically-evolved individual-family dwelling machines, whose design, economy, standard of adequacy, equipment, production, erection, land rent, service, maintenance, moving and removal, improvement and replacement rate are THE ENTIRE RESPONSIBILITY OF THE INDUSTRY'S CENTRAL COMPETITIVE CORPORATIONS, and are all included in one monthly rental charge.

Common to the first three of the four categories "Mass Production House" meanings outlined above, are the following elements:

They are designed to be dependent primarily upon arterial hook-ups with politically or privately monopolized power, light, water, sewage, and communication lines, and are, therefore, limited to placement within the environs of urban developments, and therefore subject to superimposition of high realty costs and town assessments upon the original quotations.

They are compromisingly designed as DOWN adjustments to any and all impositions of finance, politics, labor, and ignorance, rather than being designed to eliminate such impositions.

They are designed and erected on the theory of their being permanently affixed to the specific spot at which they are mounted upon their permanent foundations, thus legally constituting, in most states, indivisible permanent improvements of the underlying land property.

Counter to economic trend, they are designed and financed to be SOLD, despite the current admission of the president of the National Association of Real Estate Boards, that only 3% of all dwellings in the U. S. are now owned outright by their occupants.

As soon as they are "sold," even though it be only on a second mortgage contract, responsibility of the builder, manufacturers, or the former "real" property owner ceases completely, and there is no guarantee of satisfaction backed by an industrial reputation to be sustained.

They have no turn-in value against a new model to replace them on the site.

None of them is designed with a predetermined longevity, but, conversely, they are expected to last for indefinite generations, good, bad, or indifferent, community and posterity be damned.

The best of them weighs twenty times as much per useful interior cubic foot as does the useful cabin space of PAA's "China Clipper" relative to the weight of the enclosing hull, despite the luxurious comfort of the Clipper's cabin, and the fact that it has climatic and sound proofing and stress requirements far in excess of the house.

They start with an arbitrarily predetermined aesthetic of design, rather than counting upon the inevitable design beauty that develops with pure economy in a plane, boat, or flower, in which not an ounce of excess warpage for predetermined "looks" occurs.

Being but superficial rearrangements of bed, living, dining and bath rooms with the same old standing lamps, sofas, stoves, chairs, windows, *et cetera*, they may be stated as being the most dangerous places in the world. Five out of ten million disabling accidents to humans recorded in 1936 in the U. S. occurred in homes (in contradistinction to automobile, occupational accidents, *et cetera*), and a number of *fatalities* equal to those caused by automobile accidents occurred within homes through falling, cutting, burning, electrocution, *et cetera*.

It is admitted that "The Houses of the Future" (Category No. 3) have added novelties such as air-conditioning, dishwashing machines, and so on, but these added conveniences without economy gains elsewhere, despite publicity to the contrary, place them in a price class almost double that of the individually built old handicraft house with standard equipment. The three "Motohomes," sponsored by General Electric through its subsidiary, "American Houses, Inc.," that were erected in Westchester County, N. Y. (1936), cost $41,000, or $13,666 each, a cost 1000% above the mass consumer's ability to pay.

Inasmuch as the individual parts of these "Houses of the Future" were products of mass production and inasmuch as they all took better than a month to assemble on the site, even with special field equipment, it cannot be said that IF these houses were put into production they would cost less than the old fashioned single-built house.

Vast crowds have inspected these houses, which have received wide publicity due to fictitious price rumors, mechanical novelties and the constant universal appeal of possibilities of better ways of living. For instance, in one month alone 125,000 people inspected the "New American" home placed at Marblehead, Mass., a rather inaccessible spot. This was but one of 315 "New American" homes put up by General Electric in nine months in 1935, as part of a program to "spot" one to every 100,000 of population in the U. S. More people inspected these 315 houses in the nine months than attended college football throughout the U. S. during the entire season of 1935. The 315 had an average price of $10,000 each, i.e., a house requiring a $5,600 annual income.

These *quasi*-novelty "Houses of the Future" have been employed primarily as vehicles of display and proposed outlets for the particular products of profit of their backers, which products have usually been highly inappropriate as applied.

Such popular-credit-exploiting and damaging shows as the "Motohome" have proven in every case to be failures as mass producible units. They are "damaging" because the failures by prominent backers tend to discredit the whole theory of mass production as applied to housing in the minds of other industrialists and of essential capital.

For instance, these houses when sold unfurnished, the furnishings in the model house being but camouflage to the shell and decoys of the local electrical, furniture and other stores having exclusive local sales rights from the basic equipment manufacturers, are like automobiles without seats, lights, carpets, self-starters, *et cetera*.

All of these houses have been many times in excess of the

weight of a product feasible in sustained mass production. All industrial products are calculated on a weight and number of parts basis, and on the energy and time efficiencies involved in handling such weights and parts. The average automobile weighs 3000 lbs. and has 5000 parts. The "House of the Future" attempts at would-be mass production have all incorporated the same old 300 lb. bathtub and 21 avoidable connections, despite the fact that a scientific factory-reproduced house may readily have a bathtub stamped integrally with the wall and floor panel and conduit manifold (if old accessory design notions and sources are abandoned) of not more than 50 lbs., or a 14 lb. chrome-nickel-copper toilet seat, in place of the 54 lb. porcelain receptacle, the former being of far more attractive and useful design and vastly safer than these prime causes of all fatal home accidents have been.

The Briggs Auto Body Manufacturing Company is now producing fixtures somewhat along these lines, but the latter require the identical costly plumbing connections of the old fixtures, for they are still luxury "accessories" of the 5000 year old shelter shells, not part and parcel of a scientifically interdependent design such as is represented by the spokes, axle, and rim of a wheel. The designing and fabricating evolution of the latter now makes possible their integral stamping. The function of self-cleaning *might* be carried out *in an entirely new manner* as with the "fog gun" of the Dymaxion House, doing away with all heavy plumbing inlets, drains, and water waste; for a pint of water would thereby suffice for a far more effective 15 minute bath and massage, whilst the water, being atomized, would pass off into the air circulation requiring no drain.

Dwelling Machines of the Scientific Industry of Shelter Service

Without centralization of responsibility true scientific economy of design, not only of the house, but also of the PRODUCTION, SERVICE and REPLACEMENT MEANS and METHOD, will never occur in housing.

This shelter service industry must first conduct conclusive research tests on master models of dwelling machines, even though these cost millions of dollars. They must be evolved WITH DETAILED AND RIGID REQUIREMENTS OF WHAT THEY MUST DO, and without the slightest preconception of what they are to look like, or whether people are going to like them or not. (See "Universal Requirements of Shelter," Chapter 5.)

The dwelling machines as briefly described in the fourth category must be so light, simple, integrally complete, independent of arterial hook-ups (though equipped for coupling when advantageous arterial service is available, as ocean ships are equipped for dock facilities hook-up), and so rapid in site-assembly as to be efficiently subject to constant shifting, as are army tents, in adjustment to seasonal, industrial, vocational and vacational migration of the populace, but WITHOUT ANY COMPROMISE IN HIGH STANDARD LIVING CUSTOMARILY ASSOCIATED WITH THOUGHTS OF MOBILITY AND TRANSIENCY. In other respects, the infant trailer industry fulfills embryonically the "Universal Requirements" of the true Mass Production House.

A successful solution within these terms and those of the "Universal Requirements" will certify to industrial-capital a potentially high-use occupancy: provided, further, that the dwelling machines are so complete and efficient in their mechanical satisfaction of man's highest standard of needs as to be OPERABLE on an over-all cost (including heat, light, power, etc., and rent representative of 10 year amortization, and general industrial operating cost) of *less* than 25% of the average popular income. Currently this would mean a total operation rent of $25 to $30 per month.

All this must be accomplished with greater comfort, safety and drudge-free growth for the occupants than has heretofor been available even in the most preposterously expensive homes (the same comparison as between the comfort and ability of a new Ford and that of Louis the XIV's draughty, bouncing, shaking coach of state).

Scientific Dwelling Service

All this obviously calls for COMPLETELY NEW, SCIEN-TIFIC, MECHANICAL, AND STRUCTURAL SOLU-TIONS OF THE REQUIREMENTS. Well-checked research indicates that this may be done. When this industry has succeeded in developing a satisfactory master model and industrial tool-up plan, which if set in operation with an initially produced equipment of x00,000 dwelling machines, could be rented for $x, provided that they were in use occupancy 10 months out of the year, and the rent figure of x allows of decent living at a lower over-all year round cost than in any other way, THEN INDUS-TRY MAY SAFELY ASSUME THAT NOT ONLY WILL IT BE ABLE TO RENT EVERY LAST UNIT FULL TIME, BUT ALSO THAT IT WILL BE UNABLE TO MANU-FACTURE ADDITIONAL UNITS FAST ENOUGH TO KEEP UP WITH THE DEMAND FOR A CENTURY TO COME.

The fact that the new dwelling machines may look utterly different from anything man has ever thought of living in before will be inconsequential SO LONG AS MAN IS NOT ASKED TO BUY THEM. He will be no fussier about looks than he would be over the novelties in rigging on the *Normandie* if given a chance to make a round trip to Europe in her, first class, for $50, or the novelty in design of a telephone instrument *which he has need of using*, and *can* use for five cents.

To establish mass production of housing in this way, the only way *true* mass production of housing will ever be established, will need all of the courage and foresight that inspired Mr. Ford to undertake the mass production of automobiles. It will also require vastly more initial capital, due to the automobile industry's having advanced the industrial mechanism to its present intricate state. (Ford's initial capital was $20,000; his tool-up cost for his model "A" was $45,000,000.) Furthermore, although mobile to a degree, the dwellings can never be as inherently mobile as automobiles, which may be driven away from the production line. Wherefore, dwellings will require vastly more transport equipment investment.

As this dwelling-machine-service industry calls for an "assumption of consumption," a full year's production and operation without rent income must be written, plus additional capital to tool-up anew at the end of the year for improved models designed to correct the faults apparent from the experience of the first year.

At least $100,000,000 will be required to commence, but within a decade of its inception the mass production housing industry will be doing a worldwide $100,000,000,000 gross annual business, owing to rapid competitive improvement. (This represents on a monthly rent basis of $25,—a service to only 33 million of the 400 million families of the world.)

Housing production has been, and always will be, man's most sizeable activity, but man has been too close to his house to gain perspective and develop it effectively. He started crawling about on its floors, *et cetera*. Man had dynamic perspective in viewing his transportation which moved in front of him at varying distances. Because of the vast enterprise involved in bringing dwelling production up to date (too large to have been hitherto conceived in the maze of the myriad of small problems caused by the very inadequacy of housing itself), this industry is still 5000 years behind the efficiency of the motor industry, the current leader in science benefacted coöperative labor.

Ninety per cent of the populace (granted the price in their pocket) would "walk out" of any "modern" hotel that would dare to book them in quarters characterized by design, equipment and service conditions on a par with the average private living quarters of people in even the top 20% income group, let alone on a par with the average private quarters of the whole populace.

So long as the individual is unscientifically "used" by the building world as the ultimate liquidation point of natural resources and is compelled to saddle himself apparently for a lifetime with the irresponsibility tonnaged-up-for-profit outpourings of basic material monopolies, unscientifically agglomerated under the romantic title of "individualistic homes"; with an utter inability to move his "home" (representing the investment of a lifetime's savings) .geographically in adjustment to the employment requirements of an ever more rapidly shifting, decentralizing physical industry,—just so long will individual man adhere habitually to hodge-podge, whimsy-and-notion designed houses, which represent, in reality, industrially obsolete solutions of his every requirement. The average U. S. citizen today covers annually 34 times as much environment territory as he did at the turn of the century at which turning point his area of annual coverage was approximately the same as in the stone age.

The smug propaganda of revenue-property proprietors that "own your own home" victims make the best citizenry is true only if "best citizen" means a punch-drunk moron who will buy "things" *ad infinitum* that MAY, but never DO, make life a little sweeter: who, moreover, has to foot non-dodgeable taxes (to refund public borrowing from factually obsolete private credit):* and, who, in order to maintain social standing in his irrevocable lifetime community, howls at ANYTHING he is told to howl at, WHENEVER told. No wonder only statesmen and politicians, not engineers, handle the populace. If all U. S. families were forced, despite mobilized industrial requirements, into static home owning, it would necessitate a neurologic genius as President and a Congress of Psychiatrists to manage them.

The telephone industry would be an amusement park novelty if its growth had been dependent upon the subscribers pro-rated PURCHASE not only of the contact instruments at non-transferable FIXED locations (with individual aesthetic design choices that might have developed Venuses atop Doric columns holding conch-shell mouth pieces, and horn-of-plenty receivers) but, also, of the equipment of the inter-communicating web. It is

---

* If today the U. S. Government, on the one hand, and the amalgamated bankers of the U. S., on the other, went into the world wide securities market to see which could obtain the larger loan, on the longest terms, at the lowest interest rate, on uncollateralized debenture, it is probable that the U. S. Government would obtain 100% more favorable terms than the bankers. Wherefore, "Supply and Demand" (Fincap's Hamiltonian *coup d'etat* of perversion of constitutional dogma at the time when he was administrative trustee of an infant and bona fide democracy) would "come home to roost."

impossible to imagine the howl that would have gone up from Boston's coterie of "Cape Cod style" telephone station owners if assessed a million dollars for a long distance line between Chicago and Kankakee, or in protest against millions appropriated for "preposterous" research.

The happily accepted standardization of general principles and resultant liquidity of investment in automobiles, their mobility, rapid amortization, specific longevity, annual design advance, universal flat-rate service, and parts replacement, *et cetera*, while admittedly having much room for improvement, is responsible for Americans having more cars than individual dwellings at the beginning of 1938, investing $15 in automobile purchase for every $1 in dwelling purchase, undaunted by the fact that cars are outmoded in two years and wear out in eight years. In most instances, they would not have put even the one dollar into dwelling purchase if the money had not been loaned to them on attractive government nursed terms. They "smoked away" 2½ times this amount of dollars in cigarettes. The truth is that Americans, although not voicing it very audibly even to themselves, have no use for "old world" houses, let alone for BUYING them. Despite the proffer by private and government lenders of tribillion dollars for the financing of homes in 1936 the U. S. populace bought more trailers (mobile dwellings) than fixed dwellings. 1936 is selected for comparison because that was the first year of semi-trailer production when the purchase of trailers was virtually without benefit of finance. It is of no use for industrialists to say, "We'll leave it to the government, the realty boys and the building material manufacturers to work out this housing problem." The latter cannot; they are licked.

Sing-fam-dwells

Ninety per cent of American families live in single family dwellings, despite the visual impressiveness of the cities' multiple dwellings. Therefore, it cannot be said that the sing-fam-dwell is unpopular or not in demand. A concensus of estimates of all authorities (private and governmental) on housing economics invariably indicates a current demand of from one and one half to six million units, whether old or new fashioned, merely to adjust for obsolescence and population increase due to the million marriages a year, and not adjusting for the demand for better dwellings by thirteen million families now existing in sub-decency houses.

It is unquestionably true that the 1929 break in industrial expansion, which was led off by dwelling which reached its fabrication peak in 1925 and sales peak in 1927 of the speculatively completed houses (1927's peak having been a non-demand, speculative miscarriage inasmuch as seven years were required to sell the houses built that year ultimately at one half their $ cost), was caused by the paradoxical fact that the most important production item of all, from a volume, cost and necessity viewpoint, the sing-fam-dwell, unlike every other item of man's requirement, had not yet been industrialized.

A comprehensive picture of the reason why the old business of building tailoring is impotent, if not dead, is to be seen in a comparison between the automobile business, a true industry, and the building business, a 99% non-industrialized, illiterate mess, to-wit: In 1935 three highly integrated, scientifically mechanized automobile companies produced more than 4,000,000 cars, an average of 1⅓ million each, whereas more than 200,000 non-integrated, general housing contractors in the U. S. produced only 55,000 houses or one house to four producers; science *vs.* hodge podge, industry *vs.* tailoring. (The annual payments for the house and the car—the former amortizing in 19 years, the latter in 2—are approximately identical.)

Permanent recovery in industrial expansion must wait until this new and last item of industrial importance has been maneuvered into practical design and process status, at which moment industry will march forward again to an unquestionably prosperous world conquest. The trailer may well be the beginning of this march.

HOUSING was the PRIME CAUSE of the DEPRESSION.

It did not merely take a mysterious beating along with other industries.

INDUSTRIALIZE HOUSING, and the TELESCOPING SERIES OF DEPRESSIONS WLL BE OVER. Procrastinate, and the depression agonies will be prolonged at an ever increasing cost. Nothing is to be gained by complaint about governmental spending. "Depressions" are the responsibility of all business and industry. They are no one man's job. Their ramifications include every establishment of industry and business.

Mining followed housing in the "break," and metals manufacturing took the next worst beating. Therefore, for any basic metal producer to contend (as some do) that dwelling industrialization is a fanciful possibility and inconsequential is to admit not knowing the controlling economics of his business.

Dollars are relative to satisfaction and performance efficiency. The very heart of industrial economics is centered on dollarability satisfaction. Compare a $100 second-hand Ford with $100 worth of the horse and buggy of our ancestors and you will have a comparison of transportation dollarability between an industrialized and a non-industrialized product. What do we receive today in efficiency in new houses, when we can afford them, compared to what our ancestors received? Practically the "same old thing." A bare house costs us more than it cost our ancestors and we can do no more with it than they could. The vehicle for travel costs very much less and will do a thousand-fold more. The distance and speed ability of a current 5¢ air mail stamp is 1000:1 that of the 1900 5¢ stamp. Houses of 1638: houses of 1938 ∴ 00:00.

On the whole, however, the IDEA of true mass production of dwellings has developed rapidly, considering its vastness. It has received a strong impetus from such current events as the Chicago World's Fair, the report of the National Resources Board which predicted housing as one of the six largest industrial developments of the next decade, and the present social and economic

338

revolution. The New York and the San Francisco World's Fairs of 1939 will possibly advance it still further.

Opposed to the stimuli, there have been political, economic, psychological and exploitation vicissitudes, the most important of which in order of occurrence and eradication have been as follows:

First, architects as a whole (with notable exceptions) tried hard to kill off the idea of industrialization. The once well organized traditional architectural profession, well funded by their retainers in the 1919-1929 decade of four-to-seven-billion-dollar annual productions, and secure in their stronghold of aesthetic nonsense, under the protection of the tonnage material sellers who controlled the large building projects, fought against their own ultimate salvation through industrial adoption and validation. Architects trained in beaux-arty-rococo, and proud of their lack of "commercial characteristics," controlled the spending of 50 billion dollars from 1920 to 1928. Business, which then beamingly patronized them, now protests over the government's spending four billion in attempts to patch the wreckage of this absurdity.

As the death of the old building racket has become more and more evident, since 1929, architects have espoused, one by one, the mass production idea, often surreptitiously and without the slightest conception of mechanical art and, in consequence, have developed a myriad of ineffectual end designs completely devoid of industrial process considerations (only 40% of Ford's world-wide army of workers serve in direct assemblage of the final automobile). Simultaneously, building contractors and members of the materials producing fraternity have taken over command of the abandoned architectural organization, deeming it a dignified lobbying cloak.

In 1927 the author offered the American Institute of Architects permanent custodianship of the basic patents of his mass production house (known as the Dymaxion House) with the dual intention of:

First, preventing a subsequent shelving monopoly of the development by interests that might deem it injurious, and

Second, provoking an intelligent coöperative development of the new industry by the architectural profession so that it might be emancipated from the uneconomic and constantly plaguing demands of the erratic whimsy patronage inherent in the tailoring of custom buildings.

The offer was flatly turned down. So the author allowed his basic patent applications to lapse, never taking "issue" and thus preventing publication, in order to prevent their being exploited by any selfish interest when the idea should have obtained significance. This was well, for subsequently many patents in the art have been issued to "fast workers" which in suit would be invalidated by the "prior art" disclosed by the earlier applications.

The Dymaxion House was simply an attitude and interpretive principle,—a principle of doing the most with the least in consideration of a mobilizing, integrating society necessitous of breaking its exploitable bondage through science. That the principles could be mechanically interpreted and that this was done for preëmptive patent purposes did not infer that its research arrangements and mechanical and structural interpretations required by patent law as "typical" were frozen against time evolving reinterpretation and adaptation. What the architects always missed, due to their fixation on end product, was that even the industrial manufacturing process is subservient to a distribution-and-maintenance service, which by its very nature must be world wide in design and scope, involving, if ever to succeed, the broadest of scientific attack.

The *second* vast obstacle to the new shelter industry was the 21 billion dollar mortgage debt structure and the "realty" investors' hope of value inflation, fostered by value increases in the scarcity days prior to industrial mobilization. Evolution, through bankruptcy of this mortgage structure in a decentralizing and mobilizing industrial expansion and potential abundance, which overnight depleted the intrinsic value of land in the old centers, has debilitated this obstacle. It is being finally removed by the mortgage underwriting of dwellings by the people through their government. Fortified as proprietors of the final basic tax lien, these government agencies are fast taking over the equity, having already absorbed approximately 33% authority which, in view of a 50% "obsolete" appraisal of all U. S. dwellings, means that the U. S. is now basic underwriter of two-thirds of the still adequate dwellings of the nation.

The *third*, and one of the most tenacious obstacles to a scientific housing service, has been the dominance by the building crafts of the politically all-powerful American Federation of Labor, whose units have bitterly opposed the mass production idea. The A. F. of L., together with realtors, architects and material manufacturers, has prevented recognition by the government during the last ten years of constant world wide discussion of the housing problem, as well as any official discussion by the government of the potentials of industrialized housing during a period when billions of dollars were spent to resuscitate the beyond-resuscitation tailored building business that crafts organizers themselves were highly responsible for maneuvering into a growth-proof strait-jacket.

At the beginning of 1937, after four years of marked industrial recovery, with twelve important industries establishing all-time highs, the dwelling business was still at the diminished proportion of 15% of the volume of its average for 1920-1930. It would have been almost completely obliterated had it not been for the pulmotoring activity of the government in underwriting "reconditioning," "slum clearance," "public works" grants and long-time dwelling mortgages unprecedentedly based on combined value of land and structure, offering a 10% or even no-cash-down build-your-own proposition.

The labor obstacle to the establishment of mass production dwelling has been potentially disposed of through the Lewis-sponsored breakaway of the industrial unions from the crafts unions of the A. F. of L. The latter's ranks have been severely if not fatally crippled through the desertion of members to industrial employment, loss through death and old age, and the lack of apprentice training to fill the ranks anew owing to building inactivity. The industrial unions obviously favor the mass production house, and as they become supreme they will accelerate the new shelter service industry by creating a Housing Workers Union that will not distinguish between types of work performed, in factory or field.

The three obstacles enumerated, namely, architects, the mortgage debt structure, and labor, have had to do with reactionary forces. The fourth obstacle in the INDUSTRIAL LAG is one less of reactionary nature than one of confusion, misunderstanding, fear, size-born inertia and lack of imagination concerning the solution of the problem. It has had four phases representing attitudes on the part of:

Basic materials producers and primary form fabricators such as the U. S. Steel, Aluminum Co., copper companies, and others;

Mechanical use-form fabricators and assemblers such as General Electric, Westinghouse, Ford, and others;

Final use-form assemblers and marketers (wholesale and retail); and

Industrial policy coördinators of the superficially divided interests of the first three groups who may be classified as follows:

1. *Bankers*, whose credit of the new industry was essential to the financing of its vast tool-up;

2. *The government*, by subsidy in lieu of private bankers' underwriting of the new industry; and

3. *The advertising and "public relations" industry*, which, after the War, took over the function of determining industrial production and marketing policy for banking interests due to the latter's inability to comprehend post-War technological intricacies of industry. Without a coördinating production and marketing plan, evolved by the advertising industry, the myriad establishments of the basic materials producers, mechanical use-form fabricators, and final use-form assemblers, could not be co-

ordinated or financed in a new form or item of industrial attack. Wherefore old Fincap has probably "missed the boat," and first, governmental, then later, industrial credit will be employed to underwrite this scientific dwelling service.

The attitude of the producers of basic materials such as steel, copper, lumber, *et cetera,* has been one of tolerant interest toward mass production housing, but it has been characterized by a stupid attempt either to substitute their products for other traditional products in the structural members of traditional design, i.e., steel frames for wood frames, designed after the manner of nailed lumber houses, or, equally stupid, to evolve a master plan house for mass production which would utilize their product in every possible structural and mechanical solution regardless of functional inadaptability. (The all-steel, all-copper, or all-asbestos house analogous in fallacy to an all-rubber automobile.)

The fallacy of economic philosophy most detrimental to the intelligent participation by this group in mass production housing is contained in the formerly workable, but now increasingly less tenable, notion that basic materials producers are concerned only with source possession, extraction and primary form fabrication of their basic materials, and not with those materials after the first sale. This attitude has made it impossible to take into consideration the ultimate liquidation and recirculation of their highly valuable product. Houses of yore were not only the largest consumer of their product but were supposedly built for eternity. Therefore, housing imposed no consideration of the re-circulation of materials. Six and one half million tons of copper, or one fifth of all the copper ever produced and equivalent to the ore body reserve of Canada (the world's fourth largest ore body), are latently disposed in the world's buildings.

In consideration of the recirculation phenomena, as outlined in the chapter "Scrap," the basic materials producers will have to organize coöperatively to satisfy economically the demands of industrial liquidation, or else industry will take over the function of basic materials recirculation, as Ford, the telephone and railroad companies have done already to a certain extent.

The mechanical USE-FORM fabricators have contributed thoughtlessly to the "industrial lag" in launching a mass production housing program as a result of two factors: first, a lack of coördination of their activity by advertising agencies, bankers and government, and, secondly, the automobile manufacturers, the General Electric and related companies have suffered least in the economic revolution. In fact, they have been banner carriers in highly-industrialized scientific development and have, therefore, been too "busy" to be greatly impressed by the need of a mass production house.

Nevertheless, they have been unconsciously paving the way for a scientific shelter industry by evolving a parts production out of which mass production houses eventually will be assembled. Their activity has been analogous to that of the producers of motors and other mechanical parts of the automobile. While the latter were determining the forms of progressive automobile production, the now almost extinct buggy makers continued vainly to try to dominate the young auto industry simply because they were the temporary custodians of the vehicle market. No matter how sumptuous and clever their buggy designs were, they did not evolve internal combustion engines and differentials. Unable to think beyond a horse, the buggy boys could little envision one man's developing an annual production of 2,000,000 horseless vehicles, safe and comfortable at 70 miles an hour, and the production within his life time of a total number equal to that of the total of families in the U. S. Their demise was inevitable, as must be that of the producers and designers of externally superficial, structural shells of houses who fail to see and move with the inside-outward trend.

Almost every major use-form fabricator and assembler has been making some attempt at researching and promotion of "pre-fab" housing, thoroughly profiting thereby (due to free publicity implicit in the development) by sales of current products interwoven with experimental development.

Scientific Dwelling Service

Quite unwittingly, electrical and mechanical parts fabricators, serving first the automobile industry and now evolving vital mechanical parts of the new mass production house, have been reducing the period of longevity of houses. At the beginning of the century, the average longevity of a house was about 140 years. One thousand years ago, buildings (some requiring 300 years to erect) were intended to last for ever. The longevity of houses built during the 1920's was estimated as 42 years, the limitation being due largely to the inclusion of mechanical constituents unknown before the 20th century and which become obsolete with wearing out.

Prior to the War, the mechanical accessories of housing represented 15% of the total cost. By 1929 the average was 25%, and today it is 30%. Some, indeed, have already reached 50%. In the new mass production house, devolving directly from mechanical constituents, the figure will be 75%.

Due to technological acceleration, mechanical equipment becomes of ever less efficient longevity. By the time the mass production house has been evolved as an enclosing protective complement to dwelling mechanisms, the specific longevity of housing will have decreased from the 42 years of 1920 to a 10 year span. The undeniable trend in diminution of longevity of buildings is toward complete deflation of the equities of the 21 billion dollar mortgage debt structure which is as sound as an 18 year 50% mortgage on a 1908 Locomobile.

The populace, intuitively aware of the collapse of the debt structure inherent in the accelerating cycles of mechanization, discounted this collapse between 1928 and 1932, and the bankruptcy was taken over by the government to be written off as painlessly as possible, indicating a national debt rapidly increasing to 60 billion. With this write-off, the whole of collateral in intrinsic equities is doomed. Concurrently, economic interest will be freed to concentrate on the SERVICE employment of property rather than on its sale. Fincap will exert ever less pressure upon industrial management from the property tonnage dumping angle, as represented by raw materials and land mo-

345

nopolies. Conversely, the pressure will be toward efficiency of turn-over and profit through mechanical ingenuity of alloying and instrument investment.

The contribution of final use-form assemblers and marketers to the industrial lag has been willful. Companies like the American Radiator Company, selling their products through the plumbing crafts, have been reluctant to incur the opposition of their customers (95% of the craft plumbing trade) through admitted participation in a mass production housing industry. In spite of their reluctance, however, some companies have surreptitiously participated in developments through obscure connections with subsidiary research organizations, patenting and pigeonholing as rapidly as possible any developments discovered by them in the trend. Their grudging and subversive coöperation may prove to be their own undoing. The Briggs Auto Body Company's new stamped bathroom fixtures and the airconditioning industries' copper-finned radiators have made relatively obsolete the American Radiator Company's standardsanitary cast iron vitreous enameled tubs and cast iron radiators, *et cetera*. Integrated bathrooms threaten them still further.

For many years inventors have urged American Radiator Company to back these and similar developments, and the Company has conducted experiments for patent shelving purposes. It was, however, "too smart" for such "theory" as to undertake a marketing venture. Wherefore, the auto parts and electric manufacturing industries have stolen the march. The present status of this company to the new housing industry is similar to the relationship that existed between the old horse coach crowd (Brewster Body, Locomobile and others) and the automobile manufacturers, because the former blindly adhered to the economics of vanity and stability based on sheer weight and size.

The advertising industry and capital credit group, although well aware of the potentialities of a mass production housing industry, have withheld support under the impression that its promotion was inimical to the interests of their *best* accounts.

Scientific Dwelling Service

It is only because the currently apparent beneficial inter-relationship between the service and products of their clients and the development of the mass production house reveals that their interests will be best served by promotion of the completely newly designed mass production house that they are about-facing and are now timidly supporting the development. In illustration, we cite the fact that advertising firms handling the U. S. Steel and General Electric accounts have definitely taken note of the very satisfactory profits being developed from air-conditioning equipment, kitchen cabinets, *et cetera*, implying the evolution through competition (which involves ever greater efficiency of operation) of a complete new design so that buildings will be scientifically suitable for such improvements.

There are ramifications of this evolving scientific dwelling service that would and already have filled volumes. The particular items and factors herein stressed represent those upon which attention should be currently focussed and dramatized by as much clarifying discussion and understanding as it is possible to conjure up.

There is distinctly discernible the dawning of that era for which science and true art have struggled throughout the ages.

Deftly cited, specific contradictions to the over-all trend herein outlined will always turn out, upon investigation, to be the inevitable and inconsequential back eddies of the major stream flow. If the back eddies were not discoverable, then the existence of a major river of trend might be questioned.

40

The Nine "Chains"

IN FULL consideration of the working of teleology as recited in Chapter 6, wherein it was seen that a cursory knowledge of a house or man which the house shelters is all that the average person sustains of these extraordinary mechanisms abstractly controlled by the phantom captain; and

In consideration of our observation of earth's tiny position in the sensorial universe and of man's tiny physical position on the earth's crust; and

In consideration of the fact that the amplification of the MAN phenomenon is not only directly resultant from star energy, but that the variegation of species is due to the cosmic ray "hits" (Hit me with a cosmic ray, darling); and

Considering that all physical phenomena are now becoming reducible to a specific radiation study, and

Whereas the scientific study of radiation is apparently unlocking the door at least to the secret of physical life, if not in due course to that of universal mind as well; and

Whereas radiation studies make possible accurate event prediction just as one may scientifically predict, on throwing a stone into the water, the exact time and general characteristics of impact-and-degree-of-agitation of a floating cork caused by the radiant waves in turn caused by the plunging stone; and

In consideration of the contribution to the study of radiation and the degree of its scientific authority by the currently most eminent mathematician, Mr. Einstein, and his thoughtful nomination of LONGING and FEAR as the two primary motivating forces of human activity in the bi-polar world; and

In consideration of our tracery of the effects of longing and fear, the longing into a general inspiriting of the creative and talented types of artist, the abstractionists, the scientists, and teleologic philosophers in general, and fear into the contracting and "conserving" of the materially minded, either driver or driven; and

In consideration of our tracery of these motivating forces and their results through the history of their patronage:

Firstly by a SINGULAR GOD OF DEATH.

Secondly by a PLURALITY OF GODS OF DEATH.

Thirdly by a SINGLE BUT SELFISH IDIOSYNCRATIC PATRONAGE OF LIFE.

Fourthly by LIFE, but by a SOPHISTICATED MYSTI-CAL ACADEMIC LIFE PLURALITY, in the midst of the illusion and confusion of the religious racket which had retrogressed to the point of gangstering inquisition, in counterpart of which American gangdom's shootings and "rides" have been a nursery game.

Fifthly by INDUSTRIAL MANAGERS who POPU-LARLY reproduced the artist-scientist's original creation, which service (the artist's) to the people was intercepted and exploited by the old feudalist, which might be called patronage by the PETIT BOURGEOIS.

Sixthly by the INDUSTRIAL-AGRARIAN TRANSCEN-DENTALISTS following the escape of longing to the newly discovered continent of America

Seventhly by SOCIALIZED EDUCATION, inaugurated in the new continent and fortunately overlooked when the high productivity of the longing extraction to the new continent called forth the hounds of feudalism on the scent of profit, wherefore, during this era, the patron of the arts was not only popular but specifically POPULAR IN THE REALM OF YOUTH.

Eighthly by POPULAR LIFE, which has finally attained the dawning of its greatest age (the diametric pole from the original single selfish death), that is, PATRONAGE BY POPULAR *NEW* LIFE ITSELF: AND BY ANTICIPATED POPULAR LIFE.

Ninthly, science and art have come to realize the necessity of serving not only the NEW life from birth, but that new life PRENATALLY, because the future of mankind is wrapped up in attention to the phenomenon of first entry.

NOW, THEREFORE, the house designed as an utterly prosaic scientific mechanical agglomeration for the protection, maintainance and abetment of life (as is the human machine in relation to mind, the house being an extension of the human mechanism) is typical architecture of the *ninth era* of the patronage of art and science, the ninth "chain" to the moon, in view of which no tailored house, no matter how superficially modernistic it may appear to be, may be said to belong to the ninth era of science and art.

In further consideration of the findings of a study of the ABSTRACT monopolies and of the sovereignty hoax, speculation, credit, measurements, standards and patents; and

In consideration of the current balance sheet of people in a DEBT ACCOUNTING SYSTEM providing the most startling paradoxes of all times at the dawn of the ninth era; and

In consideration of the esoteric ineffectiveness of the Yogi ruminant cults, the Yogi representing the high point of mental attainment of all time, confined, however, within a selfish esthetic cult, the potential popular usefulness of which was conceived by Christ and longingly demonstrated by Him but in so personally mystical a manner as to allow a mystical and therefore by-the-priesthood-bullying religious establishment directly defeating the original conception; and

In consideration of the MIND-OVER-MATTER-CONCEPTION as being carried out in a CONTINUOUS EVOLUTION behind the scenes by the undramatic philosophers who rationalized into a mathematical means all the miracles of the mysteries that they might be scientifically employed and non-mystically discussed by the industrious until 9-hour flights across the United States at altitudes of 5 miles above the earth have resulted as a direct objective. MIND-OVER-MATTER RA-

TIONALIZATION EVOLUTION ATTAINMENT which, although the thought source is identical, makes Yogi levitation demonstrations picayune and stupid; and

Realizing that Yogi is limited to realization in the measurements and discourse of the PERSONAL SENSORIAL world, whereas the ninth era of science and art is wedded to dimensional realization in ALL the spheres of non-sensorial energy radiation; and

Subscribing to the teleologic principle of attack, that is, of saying (after first AWARENESS of a problem), "I don't know much of anything about this awareness, but what DO I know? I know only ABSTRACT PRINCIPLES, one of which is that I must be inclusive of all the experience and thought to which I have been exposed, if I wish teleologically to produce a result satisfactory to my ideal of DOING THE MOST WITH THE LEAST"; and

Having set down, so far, as inclusive a general recital as possible (within the space and time available, consistent with doing the most with the least) of the *dominant physical characteristics of the radiating universe* and of the *behavior pattern of man* (the machine captained by the phantom universal mind) in conquest of its environment in the physical universe; and

Having found a "NOW" trial balance to reveal a current paradox between possibility and statistics.

It is nonetheless apparent that we have not yet penetrated deeply or included widely enough, in our recital, to make crystal-clear not only the trends involved, but, also, the OBJECTIVE MECHANICS and MENTAL PROCESS MEANS INHERENT IN THE TRENDS which the teleologic designer may, through his own THOUGHTFUL conjecture, ascertain to be the most important subjects of his every day, and all day, working consideration. Until the teleologists' successful completion and synchronization, in a *timely way*, with *people's doing and rationalizing*, shall make these *objectivized mechanisms, processes* and *power harnessing* the *means* of a *continuity of harmonial integrity in life*, the ninth era of science and art will not blossom,

THEREFORE to abet the conception of our end objective, a dramatic episode will be recited, involving Mr. Jones (Mr. and Mrs. Murphy's nephew), an amateur hyper-short wave radio expert, *and* a lovely young lady from XK-planet.

41

Jones and the X-ian

See second paragraph,
last page of "An Outline."

(*Note:* Although the occurrences of this drama are partially suppositional, the mechanics and measurements represent the latest and most accurate observations. The episode begins in *factual* happenings.)

EARLY in the 1914-18 World War a wealthy hobbiest, named Colonel Fabian, became piqued by War strategy problems. He imported military technicians from the Allied Armies to his multi-acred property in Geneva, Illinois, U. S. A. These military experts dug-and-built every manner of trench employed in the War zones of Europe, and this trench laboratory became tactically useful to U. S. War professionals when the U. S. A. subscribed to the War notion.

Colonel Fabian had other hobbies, such as the scientific analyses of the characteristics of sound, for which he built the "Sabin" Laboratory, the first of its kind in the U. S. A.

Another hobby was a study of the Baconian cipher. This cipher, as postulated and demonstrated by its exponents, when applied to Shakespearean verses apparently proves that Lord Bacon was the author of the works ascribed to "W. S.". Bacon, says his supporters, motivated by modesty, or humor, and being peculiarly astute, was wont again and again to indicate by cipher, as with delicate water marking in paper, that Shakespeare was only his stooge.

With the entry of the U. S. into the War, there developed a necessity among U. S. militarists for the deciphering of enemy messages unfathomable to regular staff men engaged in such work. Now, Colonel Fabian, as a cipher hobbiest, had been in correspondence with many of the amateur Baconian cipher fanatics. So, aware also of the deciphering problem through his trench-tactician contacts, Colonel Fabian, at his own suggestion, was commissioned by the government to convene a deciphering corps at his Geneva, Illinois, hobbylab home. The Bacon detectives proved themselves ingenious in deciphering intercepted enemy communications. In off hours they were allowed to study other laboratory hobbies of the Colonel.

Among the post-War demobilized, Bacon-or-the-enemy decipherists was a man named Alfred Jones. Following the War and while working for accountants and more recently for no one, Alfred Jones developed in his increasing spare time, a warborn hobby of his own, to-wit—HYPER SHORT WAVE RADIO.

On the evening of June 27, 1937 Jones was testing on his latest one tube set, which he had designed for use in the infinitesmally short waves above the visible light wave octave. (The current short and long wave radio utilizes octaves below visible, and heat wave lengths.)

Suddenly Jones tuned in on signals of novel characteristic. Immediately he hooked in his self-invented, aural-to-visual *via* sound and light sensitive cells, recording device, with inverse spectroscopic analyzer. This was an instrument with both ciphering and deciphering functions which he had designed for War communication.

Simultaneously with throwing-to the switch, there occurred a static screech-roar of deafening proportions, lasting for only the space of a flash. It was like the sound of an explosion. The recorder ceased recording, and, too quick for Jones to see how it had happened, there stood—leaning against the bench-edge in front of the recorder—a girl, strangely clothed, smiling,— "BEAUTIFUL."

Jones's heart dropped into his toes, zoomed to his throat, looped the loop. His lips moved as in motion of speech, but were speechless. The stranger grinned, likewise moved her lips in the manner of speaking and also gave forth no audible words.

Jones heard distinctly, however, as with the unuttered words of one's own thought, "Yes, I am alive and here, and though to you miraculously materialized, to me, by virtue of experience, the incident is no more wonderful than the infinity of phenomena to which we become carelessly accustomed through recurrent association. Relax, Jonesie! Have you a cigarette?—I haven't had a smoke for 150 million of your years."

The stranger went on to explain that the wave length of her speech was sub-audible and directly reactive upon the brain.

"Who ARE you?" thought Jones, scheming to test if this method were two way and, therefore, possible without his own lip motion.

"I'm from Planet 80 XK 23 in trapezoidal segment 727831 of the star layer of the expanding universe. Eighty XK 23 is one of 100 planets of one of 40 billion star-groups in our spiral nebula, which is one of the plus billions of what you term the EXTRA-galactic nebulae. You are so conceited a bunch here in your piker nebula, and puny solar system, and on your infinitely tiny planet 'CHIZLA,' that you always characterize your external fringe observations by names strong with the inference of the subordinate quality of an 'outsider.' EXTRA-galactic, indeed! Like speaking of a Chicagoan as a non-Bostonian."

"Our planet is NOT called 'CHIZLA,' it is called 'EARTH,'" said Jones.

"Oh!" smiled the stranger, "How amusing! We had nicknamed it by the most oft-repeated thought emanating from it. . . . 'EARTH?' What a funny name for a planet which is, for the brief moment, but a ball of fiery gaseous elements externally crusted with rock, ¾ water surfaced and with but 10% of its land surface dusted ever so thinly with an admixture of eroded rock, vegetable and animal compost, and star dust. . . . Earth? Ha ha! A romantic name, like your 'HOME, sweet complexity home,' evolved, I suppose, by one of your early superstition-chiselers as another illusion means of mesmerizing the 'flock' into a moral betrapped exploitation."

"Devastatingly sarcastic intruder, how did you get here, and why?" mentally queried Jones, emphasizing this time with lip motion.

"I am a reporter for the *Interstellar Gas Inquirer* and the *Nebulae News*. I also conduct a column entitled *Parallax and Paradox* by radio correspondence in *The Milky Way Times* and *The Expanding Universe Chronicle*.

"Planet 80 XK 23 is 100 earth diameters in size, and has a day, or axial rotation, equivalent in duration to 24 thousand DAYS and ten thousand days to its year, or orbital passage around its star center. Wherefore:

> 1 XK hour equals 1,000 EARTH days
> 1 XK hour equals approximately 3 EARTH years
> 1 XK day equals 24,000 EARTH days
> 1 XK day equals approximately 66 EARTH years
> 1 XK month equals 158,400 EARTH years (10 to a year)
> 1 XK year equals 1,584,000 EARTH years

"Due to the thermal index of our star, our seasonal and yearly changes are approximately identical to yours so that relative only to our specific planets my experience has been somewhat similar to your—if you don't mind, PLEASE—'CHIZLA' experience. The main difference is that on XK we have but one continent and our human species developed from a single source and spread out slowly in a land of plenty, as the single mammalian species. Being vegetarian, we have escaped the predatory, hoarding and property proclivities. X-ians speak but one tongue and, therefore, accredit one another with facility and fearlessness by virtue of non-exploited understanding. The successive and constantly accelerating rationalizations of biodynamic phenomena become readily clear to them through their understanding of the SEGREGATION of animate and inanimate, finite and infinite. . . . I am 35 years (XK) old, which interpolated into earth years is 55½ million."

"One would never guess it," said Jones, sincerely incredulous "You look just sixteen."

"Sixteen which?" asked Miss X-ian, and, smilingly appreciative of Jones's frank admiration, added, "We do not wither on XK as you do on CHIZLA; we bud and bloom and hold full bloom until exit.

"I left XK planet a year ago (XK time), approximately 1½ million years ago 'Earth' time, searching for interstellar news and paradoxical material for my column. From my studies of 'CHIZLA' for its last 6 thousand years, I don't believe I could have found better material on any other planet. The managing editor of '*The Nebulae News*' says: 'When food eats the man, that's news.'

"The way we travel from XK is as follows:

"The prospective interstellar traveler stands in the reflection center of an energy radiation beam-focuser, which latter is aimed, by careful calculation, at the center of some planet of thermal equivalence to XK, in such a manner that if means is not found for transmutation, upon contact with the objective planet, the traveler rebounds with accuracy to XK."

"What if the shot is bad?" asked Jones.

"Just too bad," she laughed, and continued:

"The orbital courses of all interstellar bodies, potential of interception of the passage, must be accurately taken into calculation, including the subsequent position of XK for the return contact. When all is ready, the traveler is subjected, by ionization-analysis-tuning-synchronization, to an energy wave-and-frequency index, determined by the traveler's specific elemental energy-dominant.

"The electron-proton course-and-speed location-predicter is then tuned in with the elemental index, and, at the calculated moment, a splayed photon shot is fired in such manner as to close the inter-electron-proton space, thus depolarizing the dominant elemental structure and uniting, in infinite energy, the corpuscular structure of the traveler, who is reflected forth on his course in the form of beamed cosmic rays—a very simple and neat process. He, or she, then travels with the speed of light. I have been traveling at an earth-measure time-and-space rate of 16 billion 86 million earth miles a day, for a million and one half earth years, or 5871 billion 536 million miles a year, a distance known to earth astronomers as a light year. Since my departure from XK, I have traveled a distance of nine hundred billion billion earth miles (900,000,000,000,000,000,000,000). I passed the sun 8½ minutes before cracking into your set, when I was retransmuted to original form through your tuning coincidence to my index."

"Wait a minute . . . WHOA!" exclaimed Jones. "You are going so fast I can't follow. If you have half a second, your XK time, how about telling me something regarding the XK philosophical development so that I can set myself straight on how you think. Don't be too detailed, you know—just give me a condensed idea that I may note down for future reference."

"Gladly," said the X-ian. "First, we evolved a completely ABSTRACTED, DEPERSONALIZED, UN-SELFED BIBLE, which is a rationalized account of the GAME OF LIFE, segregating its *unity of totality* into *chaotic multiplicity* and subsequently *rationally recomposing* it to *unity*, *to symmetry* of *unity* and to *completeness* through *synchronization*, which is the *checkmating* of *time*, against which the game is played by the totality TRUE COMPREHENSION." Laughingly, the X-ian explained, their Bible always gave X-ians a great kick because it was really great fun.

This attitude caused Jones to realize with astonishment that his earth Bible, through its mysteriously confused insistence upon explaining the reality of truth in terms of grossly imperfect interpretation of the tangible man mechanism, constantly provokes inability to explain the logically superman realities of totality; with the result that, in terms of the imperfect self mechanism, understanding of the realities has to be unreasonably recognized by a SURRENDERING BELIEF IN MIRACLES, these miracles in turn evoking an awe-ful, fear-ful, wide-eyed, secretive, cultish herding around SECRET THEORIES OF EXPLANATION OF REALITY in the TERMS OF UNREALITY, which, thought Jones, is certainly no fun.

42

Resolved to Resolve

After our scientists had completed the bible as a rational abstract, 'THE GAME OF LIFE,'* in explanation of *duality delusion*, we evolved our *resolution*," continued the X-ian, "which represented a *mutually agreeable method* and *process*, for *eliminating* the fabric of *delusion* from our populace.

"This fabric had been traditionally woven in the days of self-and-others kidding through mutual intercourse guided solely by the SURFACES of things and events. Easy perversions, through misinterpretation, of surface clues for the purpose of deceiving others-and-self into following down blind alleys intent on rape, occurred because HAPPY-CHANCE-INTERCOURSE in the scheme of surface deceits, was so rare as to necessitate such rapine."

"That is interesting," said Jones. "RESOLUTION, I now see, is a withtime synchronous word and is to be contrasted to our static word 'CONSTITUTION,' which is a statement of how we stand supposedly STILL together. CONSTITUTION is apparently a fear-born word connoting a DEFENSE FORMATION, the hollow square."

"That's right," said the X-ian. "You ARE catching on readily."

"Do you think," asked Jones, "that you could outline your resolution in the fewest words possible?"

"Certainly," said the X-ian. "Not only can I outline it, but I can *recite* it to you *precisely*, for it is *so logical* that it's *recitation, rather than a learned-by-rote formula*, is a naturally *specific description of a scientifically effective process*."

"Shoot," said Jones.

THE X-IAN RESOLUTION

RESOLVED to solve age-long problems NOW in terms of self instead of egotistically blaming primary cause on some *other thing or being*, simply saying to ourselves:

"SELF! YOU CAN ONLY BE HURT IF, WHERE, and WHEN YOU ARE VULNERABLE.

"The only lie is to yourself. ARBITRARY NON-INCLU-SION, WARPAGE, ASSUMPTION, or NON-FOLLOW-THROUGH within self of that which the universal mind sees fit to reveal or expose to, or in you is recognizable by others, if articulated to them, not as a lie, but only as intuitively to be disregarded tactically unreliable noise, reductive of your popular credit potential and, consequently your usefulness to others.

"For you can think consciously only in terms of experience; wherefore, somewhere in your experience if you do not lie, MAY BE FOUND not only the VULNERABILITY OF SELF, but the VULNERABILITY of ALL OTHERS in rela-tion to the SPECIFIC HURT INVOLVED, with a key to the locking of the particular fatal port against further hurt, not only of self, but of ALL SELVES, FOREVER.

"In this connection there is a fascinating thought correlation between the words 'blessed' and 'blessee.' There is in the last analysis NO PRIVILEGE SO GREAT AS THAT AF-FORDED BY HURT, IF we are only able to unself ourselves (*quae nocent docent*—that which injures instructs)."

How unself self,—granting that IF unselfed thought alone would remain as potentially all-effective?

There is no formula. It has been found by re-search, how-ever, that the initiation of thought solutions, or moment of first traceable awareness of any specific thought-enabling solution of a problem long attempted, was coincident with the thorough and spontaneous concentrated attention of the self mechanism to the problems of another "personality" mechanism. When completely preoccupied by the problems of the OTHER personality, the SELF personality AUTOMATICALLY, unselfed self,—that is, THOUGHT of the universal mind, which is UNDERstanding, separated from the SELF MECHANISM.

While so preoccupied it counsels the attended personality, in the matter of solution of the attended personality's problem, and probably WELL, by virtue of its greater DESELFED and therefore UNIVERSAL perspective.

It has been found to have HAPPENED that the attending personality has quite unconsciously voiced the solution of problems, not only for the attended personality, but ALSO for the self personality hitherto long and ineffectually attacked. In the nature of HAPPENINGS, the attending personality, being preoccupied with another self, is serenely UNAWARE that it HAS VOICED the SOLUTION of its OWN PROBLEM.

Subsequently, the attending personality becomes aware of the fact that it HAS already taken a hurdle in DEED; that is, it has actually written, fabricated or articulated, in some manner or other, that which it had, at an earlier period, found impossible to do.

It is only with the most persistent research that it is possible to trace the IN-VENTION of solution to the moment of deselfing attention to another self.

Why is this not a fomula?

Because one cannot arbitrarily seek others in trouble, and arbitrarily occupy oneself with the other in trouble purposely to gain a solution of one's own problem. No, the gist is that this represents a SUBSEQUENT observation of the course of events. This is the WAY in which it HAPPENS, but, mind you, it HAPPENS. (*Qui docet discit*—he who instructs learns.)

It has also been found by experience that those who are not dominated by self-concern, that is, by fear of interruption of an habitually reliable pattern of self survival, and willingly expose, or give away, the fruit of their think-ing, have no sooner completely separated themselves from the fruit of their thought, by such gift or exposure, than the vacuum in self thereby developed

causes the inrush of two or more abler thoughts. The characteristic of unfettered in-vention is a geometrical progression.

WHEREFORE, be it RESOLVED: To resolve every uni-
versally-considerate wish-evoking critical-concept into a reason-
ably-efficacious resistance-eliminating inanimate-device of
time-saving-calculability and contiguous-service time-synchroni-
zation, that may be factorable from "possibility" to "probability," thus intent to streamline man's competitive-volition,
unbeknowns to him, INto a scientifically designed direction-of-
least-resistance, upon the OCCASION of his each and every
INITIAL-DISLODGEMENT from HABIT-INERTIA; the
dislodgement being THE unit-chance-contact-factor of the in-
finite-unknown of the uni-verse; which, in its PROGRESSIVE
relativistic-cognition, adjusts to the intellect through illusion-
vanishment's comparative-vacuums.

RESOLVED by such ABSTRACT purposiveness to enable
the unselfconscious and otherwise stubbornly opposed ESTAB-
LISHMENT of an harmonious social-rationale by man; and,
thereby, a resultant unified-popular-credit-direction by the
emergency-enactment-route.

The emergency-enactment in-turn WILL, through inadver-
tent-admission of the QUESTION to popular-consideration,
make it the COMMON SENSE of preponderantly-intelligent
man, that:—

The RIGHT-TO-LIVE and, MOREOVER, to LIVE-
GROWTHFULLY, within the WIDENING limits of the
highest-common-potential-standards, is not only MANDA-
TORY upon a social progression, BUT is ECONOMICALLY
the course of OBVIOUS MINIMUM OPERATING "OVER-
HEAD," friction eliminating, and, therefore, the ONLY TEN-
ABLE COURSE of a SCIENTIFICALLY-BENEFACTED
society, evolutionarily-consequent to a "sapiens" characterized
specie "homo."

Emergent, the COMPETITIVE-URGE must COMPOUND its credit out of the "NEW," rather than by EXTRACTION from the "OLD," and therefore through UNEXPERIENCED, or UNSELFCALCULATIVE, expedition of universal-inter-service.

This will establish a "you-and-me" infinity-of-survival-and-growth, rather than an exception-discredited, statistically-predicated, self-devastating, credit-destructive, and contemporarily-demonstrated INADEQUACY of the "you-or-me" dogma of the—"survival-of-the-fittest"—religion, of the now-dying fear-motivated social-finity.

RESOLVED to practice energy-conservation for PUR-POSIVE and HARMONIC articulation of philosophies' growth.

RESOLVED that: EVOLUTION is the high-frequency alternating process, ABSTRACTLY, animately and inanimately, of INCLUSION and REFINEMENT.

EVOLUTION may be ABSTRACTLY ANTICIPATED and SYNCHRONIZINGLY CAPTURED by the animate-artificer's PROGRESS-BY-CREATION; or, the abstractly-anticipatable-evolution may PROCRASTINATINGLY BE SURRENDERED TO inanimate-dynamics' PROGRESS-BY-DESTRUCTION (EROSION and CATACLYSM).

By one, or the other, of these two courses, "We run it" or "It runs us," in a time-motion world, as demonstrated by the laws of entropy, random-element-increase, and expansive-universe, MUST we WILLY NILLY, PROGRESS.

The mind-over-matter battle is WILL vs. TIME or M-I-nd *vs.* W-I-nd, i.e. COMPOSITION-BY-SELECTION *vs.* DIS-SIPATION-BY-EROSION.

These inevitable-growth alternates are the *direction-in* or *direction-out* coincidents of GRAVITATION and RADIA-TION:—pull and push, tension and compression, suction and pressure, flexible and inflexible, female and male, attraction and propulsion, minus and plus, new and old, innate-harmony and artificial-glamour, knowledge and vanity;

BUT, as with the radii of a sphere, although ALL are COINCIDENTAL theoretically (in that they lie along the shortest course from center to outside) NONE is IDENTICAL and no formula or law may be devised which is continuously adequate.

LAWS and FORMULAS are bi-polar equations; that is, BEGINNING-and-ENDING limitations, IMPERFECTIONS.

GRAVITATION is but an abstract RELATIVE-ASSUMPTION, being the infinite unit ability of the mind-ONLY to concentrate, penetrate, include and HOLD TOGETHER as the ever present referee of rationality and balance.

RADIATION, the REALITY, is progressively-rationalizable, and FACTORABLE, through the mathematician's calculus, the essential-language of TIME, into PROBABILITIES, out of POSSIBILITIES. Thus are we:

RESOLVED to accomplish the final bridging from PURE PHILOSOPHY to BREAD-and-BUTTER-GROWTH-HAPPINESS through the expediency of the successive steps of the language of the tri-gonometrician, the geo-metrician, the bi-o-logician, and thence by mechanics to the man continuity.

"Having completed our RESOLUTION in this scientific manner," the X-ian continued, "we made a few actual tests of its efficacy by exposing ADVANCED, COMMUNALLY SCALED INSTRUMENTS to the populace and by leaving these instruments in unattended evidence.

"We then accelerated inevitable EMERGENCIES and found that the populace immediately seized on the AVAILABLE NEW INSTRUMENTS in the emergency, due to such instruments' superior survival efficiency to that of any they had had before.

"Before the emergency their snobbery of the instruments had

been excruciatingly amusing. We thus proved that our principle of social motivation into self-cleansing, through scientific-devices simply-exposed, was correct.

"Having done so, it was then scientifically expedient to survey our history that we might determine at what point the populace had developed its current haywire illusion,—that is, where did they go off the main road into their present by-way?

"We found that it was when half-baked science was wantonly overprodded or prematurely snatched from the oven by greed, vanity, over-zealousness, and most often by uncontrolled aimless sensation-seeking curiosity.

"The rationalization of science itself was all right in general attitude, but its academicians and disciples made the mistake of 'showing fools half finished work'; that is, instead of keeping their mouths shut and evolving objectifications of the philosophy in the form of instruments and processes, they just TALKED about it.

"The proposition was so exciting that the people believed in mechanically opened-up new horizons, but talked about the ideas as 'miraculous' and eventually evolved the great confusion of a never REAL true-POTENTIAL." This debilitation of scientific growth was astutely recognized by the forces of exploitation, which practiced wholesale invention-abortion by premature publicity-broadcast. Concurrently they propagandized the populace with the 'rugged' misapprehension that diseases, accidents, *et cetera*, were strengthening *via* 'immunization' adaptability.

"ADAPTABILITY of nature's STRUCTURES, MECHANISMS, and PROCESSES occurs through sustenance-source-changes NECESSITATING LONG PERIODS OF YEARS and many GENERATIONS. For instance, the evolutionary lengthening of the bill of a bird to reach RECEDING water in wells; or the frog abandoning its aquatic-cycle, the tadpole-polywog-state, through recession of waters, causing him to hatch frogs in the mature state directly from eggs: both took aeons of years, in the course of which the majority population of the species was forced to die off for thousands of generations.

"Conversely, SUDDEN ACCIDENTAL IMPAIRMENT of self mechanisms is equivalent to punching holes in a ship's side by impact on rocks. The fracture can be repaired, but the current ship is never as strong as its unimpaired original structure.

"So with the human, despite the fact that there is a potential reserve for accident repair, the repaired unit (if reparable) is never quite as able as the original. And further, the energy source so diverted for repair would, if not so diverted, have articulated itself in greater strength of structure and muscle, providing evolutionarily ever more adequate mechanical solutions of survival.

"Those who took up the propaganda and voiced this untenable and inefficient theory of immunization-through-impairment on XK were those who, through non-necessity, ostriched in a desert of moth balls and were, therefore, least subjected to such impairment. The voicers of such theory, because couched in favorable environment, and able to think only in the terms of experience as are all people, were unable to apprehend the truth. Paradoxically the voicers were currently the sole proprietors of the liquid credit essential to the realization of mechanisms which might have obviated the majority of occasions of accidental impairment of the human mechanism.

"On the other hand, those who by bitter and mortal experience had become apprised of the inefficiency of such a theory and had recognized in its stead the necessity of prevention solutions, by scientific inanimate mechanical self extension, and who, thereby inspired, had become the source of invention of such preventatives, were UTTERLY INEFFECTUAL in COMMUNICATING THE ESSENTIALITY OF THE SOLUTIONS to those otherwise POSSIBLY quite WILLING, yet unempowered-to-understand, CUSTODIANS OF THE CREDIT required. The custodians considered the individual inventions as fascinating novelties only, soon forgotten as the scheming exploiters publicized a newer, half baked invention.

"Because of these tactics of the stupid or shrewd few, it was evident," said the X-ian, "that we had silently to ARTICU-LATE the RESOLUTION in all manner of mechanisms, in-struments and processes in an assumptive stage of advance beyond the imaginative realm of the exploiters, so complete in scope as to enclose anticipatingly the then current-sphere of conscious-activity, which expanded slowly and hesitantly, pri-marily by chance, in the humpty-dumpty-world of surface-make-believe.

"This was a cinch to do, so meager a sphere of realization did the make-be-lieve world then represent.

"The *only precaution* that we had to take was to *time* the *articulation* of the *resolution* in its *determination* of the *specific state of advance* of the *mechanisms and processes*, in such a man-ner that the radiant-measure-of-time, between the surface of the humpty-dumptily-expanding-sphere and that of the-sphere-of-inclusion, which *we* were fabricating, should be a *greater time-interval* than our careful determination had revealed to-be-re-quired for the actual performance-of-fabrication of the *complete* and harmoniously-inter-related-sphere-of-mechanisms which we had for this stated purpose resolved to design."

"What a wow of an idea," said Jones. "Of course, the en-closed sphere, inevitably expanding through chance, had even-tually to expand like the bladder of a basketball into closely adherent control by your scientifically evolved 'realities' sphere, which latter, however, representing a MECHANISM and PROCESS was quite unlike that of the expansively limited in-animate basketball pigskin enclosure (that is, inanimate after the skin had been segregated from the pig mechanism, as a part of which it had been an expansive mechanism and process itself); thus your enclosing sphere, within which error and chance were captively enclosed, could be set in operation by you at the will of your abstract selective mind, at an objectively determined moment and at a decreed rate of expansion, until finally the original confusion bladder, stretched to its elastic limit, disinte-grated by failure. However, in the meantime your people, riding outward in all directions upon the interior illusion bladder's surface, were so adhesively impressed by its expansion contact pressure against your designed and controllable inanimate mechanism enclosure that willy nilly they were grafted onto the latter and carried outward in its scientifically synchronized expansion, quite happily divested of their exploded former bladder of illusion."

"Boy, oh boy," said the X-ian, "you certainly do follow me. That's just what happened. You may be interested to hear a typical exclamatory remark of the illusion-divested people."

"Do you know," said Jones, with an eagerness of interruption that the lovely lady from XK smilingly accepted, "I am so thrilled myself at realization of all that you have communicated to me that, if I were to make a thoughtful statement of my own to you, as spontaneously provoked at this very minute, I rather think that it would not be dissimilar to the exclamatory remarks of your X-ians as their heads were emerging through the surface to the universe of reality, extruded, as it were, through the mesh-of-rationalization by the time radiant pressure of their own sphere of illusion."

"All right, let's hear it," said the X-ian.

43

Anthem

I HAVE experienced the exquisite unity of refinement of the finity within, and completeness of inclusion of the in-finity without,—conversely viewed, as to finity and infinity, by male and female, and the conversal coincidence identity I have checked through your understanding, the latter born of your innate unspoiled unselfishness, in complement of-and-to my regained unselfishness, OUR universal heritage of all unselfishness, attained, and de-self articulated before us—and time was-is-wiswist not, therefore I KNOW—as I knew I would know, when I was told that if I would comprehend (courageously, unquestioningly) TIME,—rationalize, mathematize, geometrize, and synchronize IT and un-selfishly radiate the knowledge of it—to the objectivized state of a from-self-divorced-instrument, word or tool, or vehicle, or means, that the knowledge revealed to me, i.e., that, despite vanity—and illusion glamour of the self-satisfaction urge—infinity could not be comprehended or enunciated in the language of finity (non-ending perfection described in terms of ending-imperfection-error) (sanity described in terms of unsanity)—BUT that finity COULD, by its essential language—mathematics, be discovered and its limits ramified in the terms of itself, RELATIVITY (of imperfection) as a time-calculus POSTULATE, and PROBABILITY reduction to POSSIBILITY and thereby REAL-I-ZATION thereafter to become STATISTICS of "IT HAS HAPPENED; and its (Time's) (Finity's) ERROR, and, therefore, its "ALL" (for all Time is—is an error illusion) eliminated by its successful pronouncement, thus inevitably isolating infinity, by elimination of all error—by the comprehension of the latter. Infinity, isolated, evolves its own awareness—perfectly. I KNOW because I have effected that which I was empowered to effect, the check of which is your understanding and our witnesses' understanding that we DO understand.

I know I have been, and may at will be, synchronized, and I know, not only that I may accelerate my sphere of comprehension ahead of the mean expansive rate—or delve within to all ages of the past, but, also, that I may be utterly aware timelessly of infinity, as necessarily demanded for cleansing of error of fixation concept —

WHEREFORE, if, and whenever, I am un-selfish, for outward necessity through longing-for-understanding, not inward necessity of fear-of-misunderstanding, and over and beyond the state of unselfishness, OBJECTIVELY HARMONIOUS, radiantly-synchronizing the articulation, I may factually prove for man's experience "conceived" knowledge, my ability to control the course and rate of the time expansion veins of realization (not its checking or warping) by the intuitively accredited SELECTION BY INTELLECT instead of procrastinatingly submitting to inevitable non-rationalized destructive natural erosion expansion-entropy.

Thereby I may constantly, and harmoniously, be of service to mankind—as its "runner"—and I am you—and you and I are WE—and WE are life's "runners"—its radiating sphere dwellers of outer and inner expansion contact—kiss. This I could not say unless I—WE—KNOW!

"Right-O, Jones, old kid. You're pretty happy, aren't you?"

"And how!" exclaimed Jones. "By the way, could you describe some general characteristics of the X-ian mechanisms?"

"Certainly," said the X-ian. "We first determined to provide a PRIMARY INDIVIDUAL-USE-MECHANISM that should serve BOTH as a receiving apparatus for the individual, tunable to all the sources of scientifically provided means of sustenance and growth; AND as a broadcasting apparatus of complete ability to put-on-the-air every growthfully-provoked articulation of the individual whose every articulation so broadcast would find a receiver or receivers in a like manner individually instrumented, to whom the first individual's articulation represented a reciprocal part in the combination of the infinity of parts thus constantly broadcast into a totality of synchronized mechanism evolutionarily replacing the worn-out or, in time inadequate,—that is, obsolete parts.

"This receiving and sending apparatus of the individual had also to represent a SCIENTIFICALLY ADEQUATE SHELTER of the individual, or groups of individuals, against our now-all-known harnessable forces which pre-known were chaotically disintegrating.

"Having determined at the outset on such an individual shelter and environment control with complete receiving and broadcasting ability, we designed the shelter mechanism in such a manner that the individual parts could be interchanged in location at will, due to the fact that all fitting of parts was accomplished through angular wedging of a determined angular-degree-modular-division of the whole.

"We were thus able to keep children out of epidemics via radio education. But a vastly greater attainment was the INTELLECTUAL ADVANTAGE of the progressive and spontaneous choice by our children of our EXQUISITELY-SIMPLY THINKING scientists on XK (similar to your Mr. Einstein), as their leaders, instead of forcing the children into mass attendance upon the educational wholesale menus of Miss Non-Einstein-Understanding-But-Has-to-Work-for-a-Living-BROWN.

"These scientific dwelling machines available to all through mass production industry were doubtingly and fearfully circumvented by the majority on XK at frightful but habitual costs and were finally accredited only through the emergency of a civil war released necessity,—that is, through mortal threat to the whole human XK family, being gas and shock, though not shell proof. Due to their individual-deployment-ability over the land they were recognized to be relatively a safer survival mechanism for the populace, when so deployed, than in concentration habitats of cities. Thus they were seized upon with the notion that they were but temporary expedients.

"The war threat to XK civilization over, dissipated by the wide deployment of the populace, the latter never returned to their humpty dumpty vanity tailored habitats of pre-War days. They had found INCIDENTAL to the emergency occupation of the scientific dwelling machines that a new and thrillingly immunized LIFE was unfolding in fulfillment of age old dreams of freedom and growth.

"In answer to the inevitable query of those of your harmonious and mystery-loving earthian souls who are ever wary of the potentially prosaic, I may state that our houses on XK, of strictly scientific structure and mechanism, are not dissimilar in principle to the mortal portion of the human, or to depersonalize the picture they are like pianos, or other musical instruments, that is, completely-abstracted-MEANS by which music may mutably be played in satisfaction of all senses, but ONLY when PLAYED by the specific individual concerned, by the phantom captain of the mechanisms sensorial.

"You might think, Jonesie, if it weren't for this simile of the individually articulated shelter mechanisms with the piano, that our dwelling mechanisms would promise a devastatingly limited prosaicness of existence, because you are so accustomed, despite your adeptness in understanding what I say, to a surface-be-all-ness and end-all-ness, and to a tattoo-limited harmonic and to a tiresome obviosity, in your earthian confusion, identical to our X-ian confusion before we scientifically segregated the animate completely from the inanimate."

Jones was thoughtful for awhile, and then said, suddenly, "I've been thinking about that point of yours regarding an obvious prosaicness in these machine shelters; and have been thinking of what you said about their being like pianos—that is, instruments out of which music may mutably flow, music for all the senses, but only when played by life, the phantom captain.

"It is quite remarkable that, on earth, we have already developed an abstracting mechanism for sound to a far greater extent than in relation to our instruments for articulation of sight, touch or smell-taste harmonies.

"Long, long ago on earth man's only means of aural harmonic articulation was his voice or the beating with his hand, or a stick, upon a resonant surface.

"However, man observed in nature a multitude of sounds which he could not imitate with his own voice and which, IF imitable he felt he would love to compose in symphonic arrangement. Sometimes, also, he heard harmonic arrangements not audible in nature.

"Slowly man evolved many musical instruments, all of which, from a structural viewpoint, were highly demonstrative of the full family of mechanical functions, and extraordinarily representative of understanding of the field of science now most provocative to us, RADIATION.

"Every conceivable type of sound, and the full octave limits of sound, became represented by man's musical instruments.

"What was the result? Bach, hearing the music of the universe, was enabled to record somewhat of the beauty that he heard, for OTHERS not only to hear, but also to PLAY.

"TIME had been completely conquered by the musical world, both in the actual continuity of the music, and in the LATENCY OF TIME BETWEEN ARTICULATIONS.

"That is, musical notations made by Bach, on paper, could later be printed, and, by another, orchestrated. Orchestrations for the full family of musical instruments could be printed by the abstract printing machine on synthetic product-paper made by other machines, and these musical notations could be laid upon the shelf for an hundred years or more. THEN, three or more generations having INTERVENED, a group of men, able to play the family of musical instruments, could be led into an orchestral articulation of that music heard by Bach.

"Still further—over the microphone STEPPED-UP electrically this music enters a super-or-sub-sensorial wave-length frequency that makes it broadcastable, apparently BACK INTO THE UNIVERSE AGAIN, the full LATENT broadcast of which men on ships at sea, an aviator in the air, or Julia Murphy in a city hovel, or the farmer's wife, can tune in upon, without any personal-equation dissonance by unwanted diverting human beings in their presence, and so hear the music of the universe that Bach heard years ago.

"Here *is* IMMORTALITY!"

"Darling,"—that radiant flash of infinite understanding had flashed between Jonesie and the X-ian—"I can understand those houses all right."

AD INFINITUM